UNDERSTANDING JEWISH MYSTICISM

Volume II

THE LIBRARY OF JUDAIC LEARNING
VOLUME IV

EDITED BY
JACOB NEUSNER

University Professor
Professor of Religious Studies
The Ungerleider Distinguished Scholar of Judaic Studies

BROWN UNIVERSITY

UNDERSTANDING JEWISH MYSTICISM

A Source Reader

Volume II

The Philosophic-Mystical Tradition
and
The Hasidic Tradition

by

DAVID R. BLUMENTHAL

The Jay and Leslie Cohen Professor of Judaic Studies
Emory University

KTAV PUBLISHING HOUSE, INC.
New York, 1982

Library of Congress Cataloging in Publication Data (Revised)
Main entry under title:

Understanding Jewish mysticism.

(The Library of Judaic learning ; v. 2, 4)
Bibliography: p.
Includes indexes.
Contents: v. 1. The Merkabah tradition and the
Zoharic tradition—v. 2. The philosophic-mystical
tradition and the Hasidic tradition.
1. Cabala—Collected works—Translations into
English. 2. Mysticism—Judaism—Collected works—
Translations into English. 3. Philosophy, Jewish—
Collected works—Translations into English.
4. Hasidism—Collected works—Translations into
English. I. Blumenthal, David R. II. Series:
Library of Judaic learning ; v. 2, etc.
BM526.U5   296.1'6   78-6544
ISBN 0-87068-334-9 (v. 1)   AACR2
ISBN 0-87068-205-9 (v. 2)
ISBN 0-87068-225-3 (v. 2 pbk.)

Manufactured in the United States of America

CONTENTS

UNIT I THE PHILOSOPHIC-MYSTICAL TRADITION

UNIT II   THE HASIDIC TRADITION

For Opi

. . . for he received me and opened the door of his house to me, so that I was as a son with him . . .

Exodus Rabbah 4:2

ACKNOWLEDGMENTS

The editor gratefully acknowledges permission to reprint excerpts from various books as follows:

Maimonides' *Guide of the Perplexed,* Part III, Chapter 51, translated by S. Pines, © 1963 by the University of Chicago;

Seletion from *The Earth Is the Lord's* by A. J. Heschel, © 1950 by Abelard-Schuman and Harper & Row;

Selections from *Souls on Fire,* by E. Wiesel, © 1972 by E. Wiesel;

Selections from *Levi Yitzhak of Berditchev* by S. Dresner, © 1974 by Hartmore House;

Selections from *Sparks of Glory* by M. Prager, © 1974 by M. Prager;

Selections from *Hasidic Prayer* by L. Jacobs, © 1972 by L. Jacobs;

Selections from *Your Word Is Fire* by A. Green and B. Holtz, © 1977 by A. Green and B. Holtz;

Selections from *9 1/2 Mystics* by H. Weiner, © 1969 by H. Weiner.

The cover design is by Florence Slomowitz of Providence, Rhode Island.

PREFACE

The study of religion is a field filled to the brim with profound and sparkling problems. It is an area of human endeavor that reaches into the depths of human awareness and to the farthest reaches of human consciousness. The texts and problems assembled here come from one such tradition, the Jewish mystical tradition, and each text together with its problems contains a world unto itself.

Why should one undertake pondering over such problems? Why should one immerse oneself in the obscurities and difficulties of mystical texts? Why reach out to the limits of man's consciousness, to the point where language fails? Perhaps Freud and Marx are correct: Man's interest in the transcendent is nothing but a distraction from rather unpleasant social and psychological worlds. Perhaps, however, man's concern with the transcendent is a function of a capacity for spirituality, a sense for the holy in its manifold forms, present in each human person. Studying mysticism, then, is a "natural" activity. It is part of just being what we are. This was the answer of the medieval thinker Judah Ha-Levi, as well as of the twentieth-century theologian Abraham Joshua Heschel. Perhaps it is because the transcendent will not let *us* alone. It pursues *us,* as it pursued Jonah. Or, at least, it haunts us, giving us only brief respite from the power of its reality. Whatever the reason, the texts stand as they are, reflecting something of the dimension of the sacred in the lives of those who wrote, and ultimately evoking an echo in our own lives.

This book, which is a sequel to *Understanding Jewish Mysticism,* Volume I, continues the task of of presenting original texts in translation from the Jewish mystical tradition. Unit I presents texts from the philosophic mystical tradition and deals with such questions as: Where did philosophy and religious experience meet and overlap in medieval Judaism? What was the motivating force, the heartbeat, of Jewish philosophy? And, what is the relationship between the mind and the holy? Unit II presents texts from the Hasidic tradition and deals with such questions as: What is the relationship between mystical ecstasy and the folk-story? What are the various types of mystical ecstasy within Hasidism? And, how did the holy embody itself in a mass movement, in

xi

the Hasidic community? With the setting-forth of these two traditions, the presentation of the sources for the study of Jewish mysticism is, to my mind, complete.

The texts presented here are, as in Volume I, not easy. They include instructions from a mystical manual, reports on ecstasy, strange hierarchies, and so on. Some have argued that I ought not present such selections since scholars do not agree on the simple literal meaning of many of these texts. I acknowledge this and caution the student-reader, again, that there is very much that we do not understand about these texts. Nonetheless, I feel strongly that, with the help of the explicatory commentary and patience, the student-scholar *will* be able to elicit the core of their teachings. I feel strongly, too, that we—student-scholars all—must expose ourselves to these texts, as best we can and with all due scholarly reserve, for there is something in them that rings a bell in us. As I wrote in Volume I: "The techniques and ideas may be strange to the twentieth century, but some shadow of the experience should not be too far from our awareness" (p. xii). One suggestion: Do not feel compelled to read the material in this book, or in its predecessor, in the order in which it is presented. Different bodies of literature appeal to different readers. Choose a section and begin; skip if necessary and choose again. The echo will eventually be heard.

In bringing this project to its conclusion, I wish to acknowledge my gratitude to the many people who have helped to make this book possible. I am grateful to my wife, Ursula, who urged me to continue my work when it seemed to slip from me, and who patiently typed the numerous drafts. I am also grateful to my students, some of whose work appears here as it did in Volume I, for their questions and their participation in the formation of this book. I owe a particular debt of gratitude to my distinguished colleague, Jacob Neusner, whose insistence on high standards of clarity has forced me to explain that which seemed so self-evident yet was not. And, finally, no dedication can express my love for the person to whom this book is dedicated.

FOREWORD

Every book must address a problem or configuration of problems. This book addresses itself to two major problems: the relationship of intellect to worship, and the relationship of ecstasy to the everyday life of the masses. Each problem is dealt with in a separate unit.

In Unit I, the problem is the relationship between mind and religious experience. What is, according to the Jewish mystical tradition, the relationship between intellect and worship? Between philosophy, or theology, and mysticism? What is the religious experience that undergirds philosophical theology? To resolve that problem, the reader must enter the strange world of medieval astrophysics and metaphysics. The reader must learn about Intelligences, hypostases, spheres, flows of energy and light, etc. At the same time the reader must realize that in the Middle Ages, truth was a body of eternal verities that were "out there" waiting to be "known." But what did one do with "truth" when one had "acquired" it? And what did that have to do with metaphysics and astrophysics? And how did these parts fit into a religious whole? How did all this relate to religious experience?

The basic answers to these questions were given by Maimonides, the greatest of medieval Jewish thinkers. He is the paradigm for the resolution of these problems. Accordingly, after the questions are set forth in Chapter 1, Chapter 2 is devoted to an explication of the elements and structure of Maimonides' thought on these subjects. After Maimonides, the path was clearly marked, and all who wrote on these subjects were, in some way, his disciples. Accordingly, Chapters 3 and 4 are devoted to two (of the many) types of followers of Maimonides, one from the East (Yemen) and one from the Mediterranean (Spain-Italy-Israel). In these chapters, the thought structure of these two men will be presented and analyzed for the differences and similarities to the Maimonidean paradigm.

Another major problem dealt with in Unit I is: How does one induce a mystical trance? Readers of books on mysticism know that there are many ways to ecstasy. But what was the Jewish Way, or more accurately, what was the Jewish Way as reflected in the most detailed "cookbook" on the subject? To resolve this problem, I publish here for the first time sections from a true mystic manual. What techniques were used? Hebrew letters are crucial in Jewish mysticism; how were they used? Were there special "staging effects"? Were there special body movements? Breathing techniques? All this will be spelled out. Then we will have to ask: Were these techniques as learned as the rest of the Jewish mystical tradition? What is the relationship of these texts to Maimonides? And, why have these texts never been published before? Chapter 5 summarizes the unit and makes some concluding observations.

In Unit II, the problem is a constellation of phenomena known as "Hasidism." This is the best known of the Jewish mystical traditions. Why? It is the latest of the Jewish mystical traditions. What does that mean? What are the continuities and discontinuities with the past? Hasidism is also the only one of the Jewish mystical traditions to survive into the modern period. Is there, then, something essentially "modern" about it? Is Hasidism more than something quaint, exotic, and picturesque? Will it survive the twentieth century? How and why?

To help the reader resolve these problems, I have divided the mass of data into three parts: Hasidic stories, the Hasidic prayer-life, and the Zaddik-community relationship. Chapter 6 introduces the unit. Chapter 7 is a study of the Hasidic story, the short instructive type that has become so popular. In this chapter, classical Hasidic stories are cited and explained. Even a story from the world of the Holocaust is quoted. In the concluding section, the essence of the Hasidic story is analyzed and instructions are given on how to write such stories. It can be done; just follow the instructions. Chapter 8 is a study of the prayer-life of the Hasid. First, the religious and psychological dynamics of usual, or normal, rabbinic prayer are presented. Then, various types of Hasidic prayer are shown and explained, including the classical mystical types as well as the newer mystical types (meditative ecstasy, tumultuous ecstasy, intimate presence). Did these forms of prayer have bodily movements? How does one manage the flow of human consciousness in prayer? How does one just "talk" to God? All these issues are discussed. Chapter 9 is a study of the relationship between the Zaddik and his community. Like the Hasidic stories, this information is easier to grasp. But it, too, involves some strange phenomena: the enormous variety of styles in Hasidic leadership, the "split-level" spirituality of the system, and the absolute loyalty on both sides of the relationship. Chapter 10 summarizes the unit and offers four answers to the question: What makes Hasidism modern?

As each book must address a problem or configuration of problems, so must each set of books address a problem or configuration of problems. With the presentation of the philosophical and Hasidic mystical systems, the presentation of the basic texts of the Jewish mystical tradition is, to my mind, complete. There are, of course, other texts. But they do not seem to me to be so qualitatively different from those included here and in Volume I. Accordingly, Chapter 11 deals with the overall evaluation of the Jewish mystical tradition based upon the texts contained in both volumes. The questions addressed there are: (1) What have we studied? What are the salient characteristics of each system? (2) How does the new data affect the general definition of mysticism, the five-fold characterization of Jewish mysticism, and the conclusions about the relationship between Jewish mysticism and rabbinic tradition made in Volume I? (3) Are any new conclusions warranted? Finally, no prolonged study of the Jewish mystical tradition, especially one which has dealt with the contemporary forms of Hasidic mysticism, could be considered complete without some speculations about the future of Jewish mysticism. Accordingly, the closing section of Chapter 11 suggests several types of Jewish mysticism for the end of the twentieth century and states my own preference.

The book concludes with suggestions for further reading and teaching.

No one can say what the best way into Jewish mysticism is. The two volumes of *Understanding Jewish Mysticism* have presented texts with explicatory commentary. They have also presented questions at various levels of generalization. The reader-student should feel free to begin anywhere. There are many many doors to the palace, and each must choose his or her own.

Unit One

The Philosophic-Mystical Tradition

1

GENERAL INTRODUCTION

What is the relationship between mind and experience? What is the relationship between the systems which the human intellect articulates to explain reality and the profound stirrings of the soul and of consciousness that comprise the raw data of religious experience? Scholars in the fields of the history-of-religions and philosophy have argued long and hard about these issues. Some have maintained that intellectual structure is only an afterthought. Others have maintained that it is an indispensable preparatory stage. Still others have maintained that thought is of the essence, and experience only an appendage. This issue, to be sure, cannot be resolved in these pages. But the evidence from one very important stream within the broad river of the Jewish mystical tradition can be adduced as evidence in the general debate.

In considering the relationship between mind and experience, perhaps we ought to ask (and immediately answer) the more general question: Why, given the intellectual richness of the philosophic and theological traditions, should we seek a mystical or experiential dimension? The answer to this lies in the fact that mysticism is the aspect of religious culture that enables the practicing believer to learn the paths to, and to actually traverse the Way to, the transcendent reality which is the core of religious culture. There are, to be sure, many paths and many perceptions of transcendent reality, but mysticism is the gnosis and the praxis for attaining an awareness of that dimension of religious life. Without this numinous dimension, philosophic theology is at best an algebra of religious concepts, and at worst it is a superficial harmonization of conflicting traditions of thought. Without the mystical dimension of religious life, philosophical theology is casuistry and systematic dogmatics is work fit for a computer, not for a human mind. Searching for the experiential component of religious philosophy is, therefore, essential. Furthermore, the evidence itself suggests that while some medieval thinkers were logicians of the holy, for the overwhelming number of them, philosophical theology was but a step, the penultimate step, in an awareness of the holy. For most religious philosophers of the Middle Ages, systematic thinking

3

was a preparation for religious experience. For the student of religion, then, the questions of Unit I will be: What are the various cosmological and metaphysical world-views of the Jewish philosophic mystical tradition? And, how did these intellectual systems relate to religious experience? What kind of religious experiences did such a tradition presuppose?

Students of philosophy, by contrast, generally deal with a different set of issues. They seek definitions and contradictions, dealing with such issues as God's omnipotence and man's free will, the nature of perfection in man and God, the relation between God's true action and such traditional descriptions of God's action as "creation" and "redemption," the relationship between metaphor and true language about God (the doctrine of attributes), the conflict between the laws of nature and a God Who can work miracles, etc. For students of philosophy, then, the questions raised by this material are quite different. Ours are: What was the religious heartbeat of these world-views? What profound religious experience informed and motivated the complex articulations contained in these philosophic systems? The question for students of philosophy in connection with the material presented here is not: How was theology the handmaiden of philosophy? but: How was philosophy the handmaiden of theology, and theology the handmaiden of religious experience?

It is to the consideration of these issues that we now turn. First, we will study Maimonides' synthesis (Chap. 2), and then we will study two variants of it (Chaps. 3 and 4). In the General Conclusion (Chap. 5), I will suggest some answers and speculate about the present and future of this tradition which fuses mind and heart.

2

THE MAIMONIDEAN PARADIGM

Medieval Astrophysics and Metaphysics

The words "astrophysics" and "metaphysics" would hardly be used in one sentence in the twentieth century. Yet in the Middle Ages, these two "sciences" were closely related. People assumed that the study of the mechanical principles which govern the heavens ("astrophysics") was intimately connected with the study of the governance of the cosmos ("metaphysics"). It is one such system, as embodied in the works of the greatest of the medieval Jewish thinkers—Moses Maimonides—that we will study now. Our questions will be: What is Maimonides' view of the universe? And then, how was this view related to his view of true religious experience? To answer these questions, we must first know something about Maimonides and the sources with which he was in dialogue.

Maimonides was a fascinating figure. He grew up in Spain but had to flee with his family from the Almohade persecutions. Before reaching the age of twenty-three, Maimonides had written in Arabic a six-volume *Commentary on the Mishna*. Later in life, he wrote the first major *Code of Jewish Law,* which was so authoritative that it is still cited today. Toward the end of his life, he wrote his philosophical treatise, the *Guide of the Perplexed*. In between, he wrote books on logic, on sex, on medicine, on law, etc. He was a court physician and a leader of his local Jewish community (Fayyoum, Egypt). So prestigious was Maimonides' authority that centuries after his death, he was referred to simply as "Our Rabbi, may his memory be a blessing." So central was his work that no one, even today, can enter the field of medieval studies without mastering at least some part of Maimonides.

With whom was Maimonides in dialogue? When a medieval Jewish (or, for that matter, Islamic) philosopher cited Aristotle, that thinker was not citing Aristotle directly. Medieval philosophers did not read Greek; they read Arabic (or Hebrew). Consequently, Maimonides, when he cited Plato or Aristotle, was relying on the Arabic translations made in the early years of the Islamic empire. These translations included most of the works of these two philosophers. However, through one of those quirks of history, the corpus of Aristotle included, for Maimonides and his contemporaries, a book called the *Theology of Aristotle*. This work was actually written by a third-century pagan named Plotinus, but it was thought to be part of Aristotle's writings and was treated accordingly. This seemingly trivial fact had, however, enormous consequences, for while Aristotle was prepared to talk of God in certain highly abstract terms as the ultimate cause of motion, he was not, judging from his original works, ready to talk of God as active in any way. Nor was he ready to speak of God as the religious reality that stood behind this world. Plotinus, on the other hand, clearly understood the numinous element in the divine and clearly comprehended that there is some ongoing connection between this Source of Being and the world as we know it. In this respect, Plotinus was closer to Plato than to Aristotle. The interested reader may wish to follow this matter further. For our purposes, it is enough to point out that Maimonides was in dialogue with an Aristotle who was very strange to modern scholars, for it was Aristotle, Plato, and Plotinus all rolled into one. In fact, one of the crucial works known throughout this period was al-Farabi's *The Conciliation of Plato and Aristotle*. We shall call this synthesis "neo-aristotelianism."

What was the neo-aristotelian system of astrophysics and metaphysics? The neo-aristotelian world-view, common to Jewish and Islamic philosophers of this period, contained two chains of being: a material hierarchy and a spiritual hierarchy. The material hierarchy comprised the physical universe, as it was known then. It was a geocentric universe, and it was a world in which there was no empty space. (This latter is very hard for moderns to understand. The world, to the ancients and medievals, was like an onion with each layer actually touching the one above it and below it. There was no space.) At the center was our Earth with its inhabitants and atmospheric air. Above and completely encircling the Earth were four spheres, each of which touched the one above and below, and all of which were transparent. They were the spheres of elemental earth, elemental water, elemental air, and elemental fire. From these elements, their real counterparts were made, and from the counterparts, all of physical reality was compounded. Above and completely encircling the spheres of the four elements were nine more spheres. Each touched the one above and below; all were transparent. The material substance of these spheres could not be made up of the elements, for the elements were below these spheres in the hierarchy. Rather, the material substance of the nine spheres was made up of a fifth substance, called the "quintessence." Each of these spheres contained something. Medievals differed on the sequence but they did agree on the following: The lowest sphere contained the moon. (This is very difficult for moderns to understand because we think of the moon as a body moving in space. But there was no space in the Middle Ages. So the moon was set in a solid, transparent sphere which revolved around the Earth.) The other spheres contained the planets: Mercury, Venus, Mars, Jupiter, and Saturn. (The remaining planets are modern discoveries.) The sphere in the middle of the hierarchy contained the sun. The next-to-the-highest sphere contained all the other stars (because they all appear to move in unison). The outermost, or ninth, sphere was the one that rotated once every twenty-four hours. It was called the "diurnal sphere." This, then, was medieval physics and astrophysics. Some, like Maimonides, questioned certain aspects of it, but this system was the best they had, and it explained for them the material chain of being, the material hierarchy.

The spiritual chain of being began, of course, in God. But God, in this understanding of Him, was not the talking, walking, feeling, anthropomorphic, anthropopathic God of the Biblical and rabbinic traditions. Rather, He was the abstract God; the God removed from all change, motion, feeling, and action. He had been purified, perfected into a beatitude. He had been made so sublime that He did nothing. At most, He contemplated Himself. God, in this understanding of Him, was thought thinking itself. He was knower, known, and knowing—all rolled up in one. As a result of this pure contemplation, being overflowed from God. The medievals called this process of the overflow of being "emanation," and they used two fine metaphors for it: God's being overflows as the fountain continuously and effortlessly flows forth, or as the sun, without conscious will or effort, radiates light. This overflow from God did not spill indiscriminately through reality but formed into a nonmaterial being which was made up only of that which it had received. This first being was called the "First Intelligence." It, too, like God could think. It was, then, the first "mind" outside of God. Because of this, however, it could contemplate both God and itself. The First Intelligence thus contained duality and, hence, was no longer God Himself. When the First Intelligence contemplated God, the overflow emanated from it further into reality, generating the "Second Intelligence." When the First Intelligence contemplated itself (a lesser degree of reality than God), the overflow emanated the outermost, or diurnal, sphere. We have, then, the beginning of the generation of the material hierarchy and the continuation of the spiritual hierarchy. From here, things were simple: The Second Intelligence contemplated the being above it, the First Intelligence, and emanated the Third Intelligence. It also contemplated itself and emanated the eighth sphere. The Third Intelligence contemplated the Second Intelligence and generated the Fourth Intelligence. It also contemplated itself and generated the seventh sphere. Things proceeded to the Ninth Intelligence, which contemplated the Eighth and emanated the Tenth Intelligence. It also contemplated itself and generated the sphere of the moon, together with the spheres of the elements.

The role of the Tenth Intelligence (sometimes called the "Agent Intelligence" or the "Active Intellect") was very special in medieval neo-aristotelian thought. When the Tenth Intelligence contemplated the Ninth Intelligence, it generated the human intellect. The human intellect, then, stood in the direct line of the spiritual hierarchy. It was a "chip off the old block," so to speak. (The Tenth Intelligence also generated, by this same process, the Platonic idea behind each species.) When, however, the Tenth Intelligence contemplated itself, it generated all the Platonic ideas needed to form the specific objects of this world. (Plato believed that the ideas of tableness, of humanness, of beauty, etc., actually existed somewhere. Philo, followed by Plotinus, followed by the neo-aristotelians, believed that the location of these Platonic ideas was the mind of God—i.e., the lowest of the Intelligences, the Tenth Intelligence.) The Tenth Intelligence, then, contained the Platonic ideas and, through self-contemplation, emanated them to reality as necessary.

This, then, is the philosophic world-view which Maimonides had to somehow harmonize with the Biblical-rabbinic tradition to which he was also heir:

1. There was a spiritual hierarchy which began with God and descended through spiritual beings down to the human intellect and the Platonic ideas.
2. The spiritual hierarchy functioned by contemplation of one's superior and of oneself. Furthermore, this contemplation was actually generative. Being flowed from thought.
3. There was also a material hierarchy, clearly defined by the physics and astrophysics of the time, which was shaped and given form by the parallel spiritual hierarchy. (This universe of thought is depicted in Fig. 1.)

The philosophic world-view, as Maimonides understood it, was essentially a downward flow of being. But was there no upward movement? Was there no "climbing of the ladder of being"? There was such an upward movement, and we can see it in the neo-aristotelian theory of perception and knowledge. According to this world-view, every phenomenon in the universe contained in itself a Platonic idea. Every table participated in tableness; every work of art participated in beauty; every good act in goodness. The purpose of man was to identify and to accumulate these ideas as follows: The senses perceived phenomena. The lower parts of the mind (the imagination and the rational soul) enabled men to form mental images of the phenomena and to abstract the Platonic

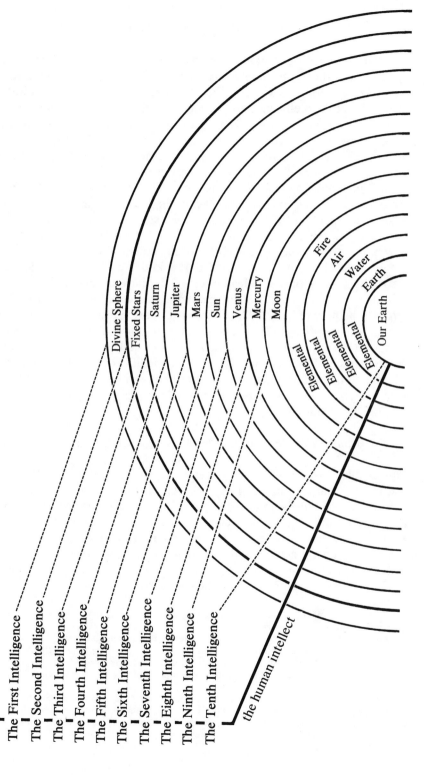

God
The First Intelligence
The Second Intelligence
The Third Intelligence
The Fourth Intelligence
The Fifth Intelligence
The Sixth Intelligence
The Seventh Intelligence
The Eighth Intelligence
The Ninth Intelligence
The Tenth Intelligence
the human intellect

Divine Sphere
Fixed Stars
Saturn
Jupiter
Mars
Sun
Venus
Mercury
Moon
Elemental Fire
Elemental Air
Elemental Water
Elemental Earth
Our Earth

Fig. 1. THE NEO-ARISTOTELIAN HIERARCHY

9

ideas therefrom. The upper part of the mind (the intellect which comes directly from the Tenth Intelligence) then compared the abstracted sense data to an absolute standard of Platonic ideas which it received directly from the Tenth Intelligence. If the data and the standard corresponded, "truth" had been generated. These "truths" were then stored, becoming what the medievals called the "acquired intellect." The greater the quantity of verified Platonic ideas one acquired, the more one was like the Tenth Intelligence—i.e., like God. Everything now fits together: God is mind. God's mind contains Platonic ideas. The human mind is a "chip off the old block," so it too contains a set of these ideas. The purpose of man is to use his faculties to identify, verify, and store the Platonic ideas he has discovered in reality. In this, man is like God. We have, thus, an upward flow of the chain of being, a climbing of the ladder of reality.

But what does one do with the Platonic ideas one identifies and recovers? Is man only an idea-collector? Is there no distinctly religious stage that man can reach, beyond gathering that which has been dispersed through the flow of being? The answers to these questions are the key to philosophic mysticism. Its nature cannot be understood without understanding the astrophysics and metaphysics in which it exists, but one must not lose track of the religious core of this medieval world-view either. It is, then, to the philosophic mysticism of Maimonides that we now turn. It is to search for the religious heartbeat of the philosopher *par excellence* that we direct our attention.

Maimonides Guide of the Perplexed, *Part III, Chapter 51*[1]

This chapter that we bring now does not include additional matter over and above what is comprised in the other chapters of this Treatise. It is only a kind of conclusion, at the same time explaining the worship as practiced by one who has apprehended the true realities peculiar only to Him after he has obtained an apprehension of what He is; and it also guides him toward achieving this worship, which is the end of man, and makes known to him how providence watches over him in this habitation until he is brought over to the "bundle of life."[2]

---

[1]The translation is that of S. Pines (University of Chicago Press, 1963), pp. 618–28. I have changed a word here and there to conform more closely with the original Arabic text and have deleted the italics for Hebrew words. There are three main questions which will lead the reader to an appreciation of what Maimonides is saying here: (1) What is the difference between "love" and "passion"? (2) What is the "link" between man and God? And (3) what language does Maimonides use to describe those aspects of true worship which are beyond rational processes?

[2]The "bundle of life" is the World-to-Come, and the phrase is drawn from I Samuel 25:29. Maimonides now begins with a parable. He is, unfortunately, not very precise in his interpretation of it. The reader should try to identify: Who are those closest to the ruler? furthest from the ruler? It is always interesting to compare these groups with those in one's own religious community.

I shall begin the discourse in this chapter with a parable that I shall compose for you. I say then: The ruler is in his palace, and all his subjects are partly within the city and partly outside the city. Of those who are within the city, some have turned their backs upon the ruler's habitation, their faces being turned another way. Others seek to reach the ruler's habitation, turn toward it, and desire to enter it and to stand before him, but up to now they have not yet seen the wall of the habitation. Some of those who seek to reach it have come up to the habitation and walk around it searching for its gate. Some of them have entered the gate and walk about in the antechambers. Some of them have entered the inner court of the habitation and have come to be with the king, in one and the same place with him, namely, in the ruler's habitation. But their having come into the inner part of the habitation does not mean that they see the ruler or speak to him. For after their coming into the inner part of the habitation, it is indispensable that they should make another effort; then they will be in the presence of the ruler, see him from afar or from nearby, or hear the ruler's speech or speak to him.

Now I shall interpret to you this parable that I have invented. I say then: Those who are outside the city are all human individuals who have no doctrinal belief, neither one based on speculation nor one that accepts the authority of tradition: such individuals as the furthermost Turks found in the remote North, the Negroes found in the remote South, and those who resemble them from among them that are with us in these climes. The status of those is like that of irrational animals. To my mind they do not have the rank of men, but have among the beings a rank lower than the rank of man but higher than the rank of the apes. For they have the external shape and lineaments of a man and a faculty of discernment that is superior to that of the apes.

Those who are within the city, but have turned their backs upon the ruler's habitation, are people who have opinions and are engaged in speculation, but who have adopted incorrect opinions either because of some great error that befell them in the course of their speculation or because of their following the traditional authority of one who had fallen into error. Accordingly because of these opinions, the more these people walk, the greater is their distance from the ruler's habitation. And they are far worse than the first. They are those concerning whom necessity at certain times impels killing them and blotting out the traces of their opinions lest they should lead astray the ways of others.

Those who seek to reach the ruler's habitation and to enter it, but never see the ruler's habitation, are the multitude of the adherents of the Law, I refer to the ignoramuses who observe the commandments.

Those who have come up to the habitation and walk around it are the jurists who believe true opinions on the basis of traditional authority and study the law concerning the practices of divine service, but do not engage in speculation concerning the fundamental principles of religion and make no inquiry whatever regarding the rectification of belief.

Those who have plunged into speculation concerning the fundamental principles of religion, have entered the antechambers. People there indubitably have different ranks. He, however, who has achieved demonstration, to the extent that that is possible, of everything that may be demonstrated; and who has ascertained in divine matters, to the extent that that is possible, everything that may be ascertained; and who has come close to certainty in those matters in which one can only come close to it—has come to be with the ruler in the inner part of the habitation.

Know, my son, that as long as you are engaged in studying the mathematical sciences and the art of logic, you are one of those who walk around the house searching for its gate, as [the Sages], may their memory be blessed, have said resorting to a parable: Ben Zoma is still outside.[3] If, however, you have understood the natural things, you have entered the habitation and are walking in the antechambers. If, however, you have achieved perfection in the natural things and have understood divine science, you have entered in the ruler's place into the inner court and are with him in one habitation. This is the rank of the men of science; they, however, are of different grades of perfection.

There are those who set their thought to work after[4] having attained perfection in the divine science, turn wholly toward God, may He be cherished and held sublime, renounce what is other than He, and direct all the acts of their intellect toward an examination of the beings with a view to drawing from them proof with regard to Him, so as to know His governance of them in whatever way it is possible. These people are those who are present in the ruler's council. This is the rank of the prophets. Among them there is he who because of the greatness of his apprehension and his renouncing everything that is other than God, may He be exalted, has attained such a degree that it is said of him, *And he was there with the Lord* [Exod. 34:28], putting questions and receiving answers, speaking and being spoken to, in that holy place. And because of his great joy in that which he apprehended, *he did neither eat bread nor drink water* [ibid.]. For his intellect attained such strength that all the gross faculties in the body ceased to function. I refer to the various kinds of the sense of

---

[3]Drawn from Talmud, *Ḥagiga* 15a. There are several things worthy of note here: heretics in belief are more dangerous than ignoramuses, observant ignoramuses are very low on the scale of true worshippers, and students of philosophy are only at the beginning stages of worship.

[4]This paragraph adumbrates the core of Maimonides' teaching. His problem is: What comes *after* philosophical understanding? Note the use of "after," as well as the use of such phrases as "set their thought to work after," "turn wholly toward God," "renounce what is other than He," "joy," and "being with Him." Note, too, the description of some sort of ecstatic state. Maimonides here refers to prophets only. Later, he will include others.

touch. Some prophets could only see, some of them from close by and some from afar, as [a prophet] says: *From afar the Lord appeared unto me* [Jer. 31:3]. The various degrees of prophecy have already been discussed by us. Let us now return to the subject of this chapter, which is to confirm men in the intention to set their thought to work on God alone after they have achieved knowledge of Him, as we have explained. This is the worship peculiar to those who have apprehended the true realities; the more they think of Him and of being with Him, the more their worship increases.

As for someone who thinks and frequently mentions God, without knowledge, following a mere imagining or following a belief adopted because of his reliance on the authority of somebody else,[5] he is to my mind outside the habitation and far away from it and does not in true reality mention or think about God. For that thing which is in his imagination and which he mentions in his speech does not correspond to any being at all and has merely been invented by his imagination, as we have explained in our discourse concerning the attributes. This kind of worship ought only to be engaged in after intellectual conception has been achieved. If, however, you have apprehended God and His acts in accordance with what is required by the intellect, you should afterwards engage in totally devoting yourself to Him, endeavor to come closer to Him, and strengthen the bond between you and Him—that is, the intellect. Thus it says:[6] *Unto thee it was shown, that thou mightest know that the Lord* [Deut. 4:35] and so on; and it says: *Know this day, and lay it to thy heart,* [Deut. 4:39] and so on; and it says: *Know ye that the Lord He is God* [Ps. 100:3]. The Torah has made it clear that this last worship to which we have drawn attention in this chapter can only be engaged in after apprehension has been achieved. It also says:[7] *To love the Lord your God, and to serve Him with all your heart and with all your soul* [Deut. 11:13]. Now we have made it clear several times that love is proportionate to apprehension. After love comes this worship to which attention has also been drawn by [the Sages], may their memory be blessed, who said:

---

[5] Maimonides is referring to the well-known mystical technique of repeating a formula over and over again until one falls into a trance state. In Islam, the technique was called *dhikr*. It was also known to the fathers of the Greek Orthodox and Russian Orthodox churches. Maimonides rejects this type of mysticism as anti-intellectual, and in this he is correct. Note again, however, the terms Maimonides uses for post-philosophical religious activity: "totally devote yourself to Him," "come close to Him," and "strengthen the bond between you and Him."

[6] Having indicated that true worship is intellectual plus something else, Maimonides now interprets his sources to prove (scripturally) that he is correct. This first set of verses establishes that (philosophic, i.e., true) knowledge is a commandment.

[7] Here, Maimonides makes two of his most important points: (1) that "love" of God is a function of (philosophic) knowledge of God, and (2) that after love comes "worship" (or "service"; Heb., *ʿavodah,* Arab., *ʿibada*). He very beautifully intertwines statement with verse-citation.

This is the worship in the heart [Talmud, *Ta'anit* 2a]. In my opinion it consists in setting thought to work on the first intelligible and in devoting oneself exclusively to this as far as this is within one's capacity. Therefore you will find that David exhorted Solomon and fortified him in these two things, I mean his endeavor to apprehend Him and his endeavor to worship Him after apprehension has been achieved. He said: *And thou, Solomon my son, know thou the God of thy father and serve Him,* and so on. *If thou seek Him, He will be found of thee* [I Chron. 28:9], and so on. The exhortation always refers to intellectual apprehensions, not to imagination: for thought concerning imaginings is not called "knowledge" but *that which cometh into your mind* [Ezek. 20:32]. Thus it is clear that after apprehension, total devotion to Him and the employment of intellectual thought in passion for Him should be aimed at.[8] Mostly this is achieved in solitude and isolation. Hence every excellent man stays frequently in solitude and does not meet anyone unless it is necessary.

A call to attention. We have already made it clear to you that that intellect which overflowed from Him, may He be exalted, toward us is the bond between us and Him. You have the choice: if you wish to strengthen and to fortify this bond, you can do so; if, however, you wish gradually to make it weaker and feebler until you cut it, you can also do that. You can only strengthen this bond by employing it in loving Him and in progressing toward this, just as we have explained. And it is made weaker and feebler if you busy your thought with what is other than He. Know that even if you were the man who knew most the true reality of the divine science, you would cut that bond existing between you and God if you would empty your thought of God and busy yourself totally in eating the necessary or in occupying yourselves with the necessary. You would not be with Him then, nor He with you. For that relation between you and Him is actually broken off at that time. It is for this reason that excellent men begrudge the time in which they are turned away from Him by other occupations and warn against this, saying: *Do not let God be absent from your thought* [Talmud, *Shabbat* 149a]. And David says: *I have set the Lord always before me; because He is at my right hand, I shall not bend down* [Ps. 16:8]; he means to say: I do not empty my thought of Him, and it is as if He were my right hand from which, because of the rapidity of its motion, my attention is not distracted even for an instant, and therefore I do not bend down—that is, I do not fall.[9]

---

[8]The stage beyond "love" is "passion." In other terms, the stage beyond "knowledge" is "total devotion." Note that this latter stage is achieved "in solitude and isolation," while the former stage is clearly labeled "intellectual apprehensions." Finally, be sure to note that Maimonides is no longer speaking of prophets but of "excellent men." Whom does he mean?

[9]Again, Maimonides rejects a well-known mystical technique: completely emptying one's mind. Mysticism, for Maimonides, is intellectualist. Our author now proceeds to give

Know that all the practices of the worship, such as reading the Torah, prayer, and the performance of the other commandments, have only the end of training you to occupy yourself with His commandments, may He be exalted, rather than with matters pertaining to this world; you should act as if you were occupied with Him, may He be exalted, and not with that which is other than He. If, however, you pray merely by moving your lips while facing a wall, and at the same time think about your buying and selling; or if you read the Torah with your tongue while your heart is set upon the building of your habitation and does not consider what you read; and similarly in all cases in which you perform a commandment merely with your limbs—as if you were digging a hole in the ground or hewing wood in the forest—without reflecting either upon the meaning of that action or upon Him from whom the commandment proceeds or upon the end of the action, you should not think that you have achieved the end. Rather you will then be similar to those of whom it is said: *Thou art near in their mouth, and far from their reins* [Jer. 12:2].

From here on I will begin to give you guidance with regard to the form of this training so that you should achieve this great end. The first thing that you should cause your soul to hold fast onto is that, while reciting the *Shemaʿ* prayer, you should empty your mind of everything and pray thus. You should not content yourself with being intent while reciting the first verse of *Shemaʿ* and saying the first benediction. When this has been carried out correctly and has been practiced consistently for years, cause your soul, whenever you read or listen to the Torah, to be constantly directed—the whole of you and your thought—toward reflection on what you are listening to or reading. When this too has been practiced consistently for a certain time, cause your soul to be in such a way that your thought is always quite free of distraction and gives heed to all that you are reading of the other discourses of the prophets and even when you read all the benedictions, so that you aim at meditating on what you are uttering and at considering its meaning. If, however, while performing these acts of worship, you are free from distraction and not engaged in thinking upon any of the things pertaining to this world, cause your soul—after this has been achieved—to occupy your thought with things necessary for you or superfluous in your life, and in general with worldly things, while you eat or drink or bathe or talk with your wife and your small children, or while you talk with the common run of people. Thus I have provided you with many and long stretches of time in which you can think all that needs thinking regarding property, the governance of the household, and the welfare of the body. On the other hand, while

concrete advice on how to live a ritually complete Jewish life and, at the same time, to train oneself to "direct one's attention" toward the special meditation on God which is true worship.

performing the actions imposed by the Law, you should occupy your thought only with what you are doing, just as we have explained. When, however, you are alone with yourself and no one else is there and while you lie awake upon your bed, you should take great care during these precious times not to set your thought to work on anything other than that intellectual worship consisting in nearness to God and being in His presence in that true reality that I have made known to you and not by way of affections of the imagination. In my opinion this end can be achieved by those of the men of knowledge who have rendered their souls worthy of it by training of this kind.

And there is a human individual who, through his apprehension of the true realities and his joy in what he has apprehended, achieves a state in which he talks with people and is occupied with his bodily necessities while his intellect is wholly turned toward Him, may He be exalted, so that in his heart he is always in His presence, may He be exalted, while outwardly he is with people, in the sort of way described by the poetical parables that have been invented for these notions: *I sleep, but my heart waketh; it is the voice of my beloved that knocketh* [Song of Songs 5:2] and so on.[10] I do not say that this rank is that of all the prophets; but I do say that this is the rank of Moses our Master, of whom it is said: *And Moses alone shall come near unto the Lord; but they shall not come near* [Exod. 24:2]; and of whom it is said: *And he was there with the Lord* [Exod. 34:28]; and to whom it was said: *But as for thee, stand thou here by Me* [Deut. 5:28]. All this according to what we have explained regarding the meaning of these verses. This was also the rank of the Patriarchs, the result of whose nearness to Him, may He be exalted, was that His name became known to the world through them: *The God of Abraham, the God of Isaac, and the God of Jacob . . .; this is My name for ever* [Exod. 3:15]. Because of the union of their intellects through apprehension of Him, it came about that He made a lasting covenant with each of them: *Then I will remember My covenant with Jacob* [Lev. 26:42], and so on. For in those four, I mean the Patriarchs and Moses our Master, union with God—I mean apprehension of Him and love of Him—became manifest, as the texts testify. Also the providence of God watching over them and over their posterity was great. Withal they were occupied with governing people, increasing their fortune, and endeavoring to acquire property. Now this is to my mind a proof that they performed these actions with their limbs only, while their intellects were constantly in His

----

[10]Maimonides' instructions include, then, the possibility of a person being able to sustain a meditative state even while going about his normal business. This state is called, later in this paragraph, "union of their intellects through apprehension of Him"—a clearly mystical, yet intellectualist, state. It also entails a greater degree of Providence. Who merits such a continuous meditative state?

presence, may He be exalted. It also seems to me that the fact that these four were in a permanent state of extreme perfection in the eyes of God, and that His providence watched over them continually even while they were engaged in increasing their fortune—I mean while they tended their cattle, did agricultural work, and governed their household. [This] was necessarily brought about by the circumstance that in all these actions their end was to come near to Him, may He be exalted; and how near! For the end of their efforts during their life was to bring into being a religious community that would know and worship God. *For I have known him, to the end that he may command* [Gen. 18:19], and so on. Thus it has become clear to you that the end of all their efforts was to spread the doctrine of the unity of the Name in the world and to guide people to love Him, may He be exalted. Therefore this rank befitted them, for these actions were great, absolute worship. This rank is not a rank that, with a view to the attainment of which, someone like myself may aspire for guidance. But one may aspire to attain that rank which was mentioned before this one through the training that we described.[11] One must beseech God that He remove the obstructions that separate us from Him, even though most of them come from us, as we have explained in certain chapters of this Treatise: *Your iniquities have separated between you and your God* [Isa. 59:2].

A most extraordinary speculation has occurred to me just now through which doubts may be dispelled and divine secrets revealed. We have already explained in the chapters concerning providence that providence watches over everyone endowed with intellect proportionately to the measure of his intellect. Thus providence always watches over an individual endowed with perfect apprehension, whose intellect never ceases from being occupied with God. On the other hand, an individual endowed with perfect apprehension, whose thought sometimes for a certain time is emptied of God, is watched over by providence only during the time when he thinks of God; providence withdraws from him during the time when he is occupied with something else. However, its withdrawal then is not like its withdrawal from those who have never had intellectual cognition. But in his case that providence merely decreases because that man of perfect apprehension has, while being occupied, no intellect in actu; but

---

[11]Maimonides seems to be saying that achieving a *continuous* sense of being in God's presence even while going about one's business is beyond the powers of all but the most exalted of the prophets (Moses and the Patriarchs). However, lesser prophets *as well as non-prophets* (like himself) can aspire to a sense of being in God's presence which is *intermittent,* or limited. This would be one of the highest states achievable by man. Maimonides follows up this insight in the next paragraph with an interpretation of Providence as being directly proportional to the degree of intellectual-mystical awareness achieved by man. Note the fine metaphors for intermittent religious consciousness, as well as Maimonides' theory of why the pious (prophets or "excellent men") suffer.

that perfect man is at such times only apprehending potentially, though close to actuality. At such times he is like a skillful scribe at the time when he is not writing. On the other hand, he who has no intellectual cognition at all of God is like one who is in darkness and has never seen light, just as we have explained with regard to its dictum: *The wicked shall be put to silence in darkness* [I Sam. 2:9]. He who apprehends and advances with his whole being toward the object of his apprehension, is like one who is in the pure light of the sun. He who has had apprehension, but is occupied, is while he is occupied in this state like one who has a cloudy day in which the sun does not shine because of the clouds that separate it and him. Hence it seems to me that all prophets or excellent and perfect men whom one of the evils of this world befell, had this evil happen to them during such a time of distraction, the greatness of the calamity being proportionate to the duration of the period of distraction or to the vileness of the matter with which he was occupied. If this is so, the great doubt that induced the philosophers to deny that divine providence watches over all human individuals and to assert equality between them and the individuals of the other kinds of animals is dispelled. For their proof for this opinion was the fact that excellent and good men experienced great misfortunes. Thus the secret with regard to this has been explained even according to the requirements of their opinions:[12] The providence of God, may He be exalted, is constantly watching over those who have obtained this overflow, which is permitted to everyone who makes efforts with a view to obtaining it. If a man's thought is free from distraction, if he apprehends Him, may He be exalted, in the right way and rejoices in what he apprehends, that individual can never be afflicted with evil of any kind. For he is with God and God is with him. When, however, he abandons Him, may He be exalted, and is thus veiled from God and God veiled from him, he becomes in consequence of this a target for every evil that may happen to befall him. For the thing that necessarily brings about providence and deliverance from the sea of chance consists in that intellectual overflow. Yet an impediment may prevent for some time its reaching the excellent and good man in question, or again it was not obtained at all by such and such imperfect and wicked man, and therefore the chance occurrences that befell them happened. To my mind this belief is also shown as true by a text of the Torah; He, may He be exalted, says: *And I will hide My face from them, and they shall be devoured, and many evils and troubles shall come upon them; so that they will say in that day: Are not these evils come upon us because our God is not among us* [Deut.

---

[12]This restatement is as clear and concise as can be: philosophic mysticism is the standard; even non-prophets are included; evil is the result of loss of this awareness. Note: "He is with God and God is with him."

31:17]? It is clear that we are the cause of this hiding of the face, and we are the agents who produce this separation. This is the meaning of His saying: *And I will surely hide My face in that day for all the evil which they shall have wrought* [Deut. 31:18]. There is no doubt that what is true of an individual is true of a community. Thus it has become clear to you that the reason for a human individual's being abandoned to chance so that he is permitted to be devoured like the beasts is his being veiled from God. If, however, his God is within him, no evil at all will befall him. For He, may He be exalted, says: *Fear thou not, for I am with thee; be not dismayed, for I am thy God* [Isa. 41:10] and so on. He says: *When thou passest through the waters, I will be with thee, and through the rivers, they shall not overflow thee* [Isa. 43:2] and so on. The determination that "when thou passest through the waters and I will be with thee, the rivers shall not overflow thee," is accounted for by the fact that everyone who has rendered himself so worthy that the intellect in question overflows toward him, has providence attached to him, while all evils are prevented from befalling him. It says: *The Lord is for me, I will not fear; what can man do unto me* [Ps. 118:6]? And it says, *Acquaint now thyself with Him, and be at peace* [Job 22:21], meaning to say: turn toward Him and you will be safe from all ill.

Consider the *song on mishaps* [Ps. 91]: You will find that it describes this great providence and the safeguard and the protection from all bodily ills, both the general ones and those that concern one individual rather than another, so that neither those that are consequent upon the nature of being nor those that are due to the plotting of man would occur. It says: *That He will deliver thee from the snare of the fowler, and from the noisome pestilence. He shall cover thee with His pinions, and under His wings shalt thou take refuge; His truth is a shield and a buckler. Thou shalt not be afraid of the terror by night, nor of the arrow that flieth by day; of the pestilence that walketh in darkness, nor of the destruction that wasteth at noonday.* He then goes on to describe the protection against the plotting of men, saying: If you should happen to pass on your way a widely extended field of battle and even if one thousand were killed to your left and ten thousand to your right, no evil at all would befall you. Do you not perceive and see with your eye God's judgment and retribution directed against the wicked that are killed while you are safe? These are its words: *A thousand may fall at thy side, and ten thousand at thy right hand; it shall not come nigh thee. Only with thine eyes shalt thou behold, and see the recompense of the wicked.* This is followed by what is said about divine safeguard; then it gives the reason for this great protection, saying that the reason for this great providence being effective with regard to the individual in question is this: *Because he hath set his passion upon Me, therefore I will deliver him; I will set him on high, because he hath known My Name.* We have already explained in preceding chapters that the meaning of "knowledge of the Name" is: apprehension of Him. It is as if [the psalm] said that this individual is protected because he hath known Me and then has had a passion for Me. You know the difference between the terms *one who loves* [*'oheb*] and *one who has a passion for* [*hosheq*]; an excess of love [*mahabbah*], so that no thought remains that is directed toward a thing other than the Beloved, is passion [*'ishq*].[13]

The philosophers have already explained that the bodily faculties impede in youth the attainment of most of the moral virtues, and all the more that of pure thought, which is achieved through the perfection of the intelligibles that lead to passion for Him, may He be exalted. For it is impossible that it should be achieved while the bodily humors are in effervescence. Yet in the measure in which the faculties of the body are weakened and the fire of the desires is quenched, the intellect is strengthened, its lights achieve a wider extension, its apprehension is purified, and it rejoices in what it apprehends. The result is that when a perfect man is stricken with years and approaches death, this apprehension increases very powerfully, joy over this apprehension and a passion for the object of apprehension become stronger, until the soul is separated from the body, at that moment, in this state of pleasure. Because of this the Sages have indicated with reference to the deaths of Moses, Aaron, and Miriam that the three of them died by a kiss. They said [Talmud, *Bava Batra* 17a] that the dictum [of Scripture], *And Moses the servant of the Lord died there in the land of Moab by the mouth of the Lord* [Deut. 34:5] indicates that he died by a kiss. Similarly it is said of Aaron: *By the mouth of the Lord, and died there.* [Num. 33:38]. And they said of Miriam in the same way: She also died by a kiss. But with regard to her it is not said, "by the mouth of the Lord" because she was a woman, the use of the figurative expression was not suitable with regard to her. Their purpose was to indicate that the three of them died in the pleasure of this apprehension due to the intensity of the passion. In this dictum the Sages, may their memory be blessed, followed the generally accepted poetical way of expression that calls the apprehension that is achieved in a state of intense passion for Him, may He be exalted, a "kiss," in accordance with its dictum: *Let him kiss me with the kisses of his mouth* [Song of Songs 1:2] and so on. [The Sages], may their memory be blessed, mention the occurrence of this kind of death, which in true reality is salvation from death, only with regard to Moses,

---

[13]This distinction is crucial to Maimonides. He makes it elsewhere in his works too. Maimonides uses both the Hebrew and the Arabic terms to make his point clear. "The Rabbi" now resumes his discourse on the stages a person who seeks philosophic mystical perfection can reach, and he describes the ideal death of such a person. Note, again, the mystical terminology: "lights," "purified," "joy," etc.

Aaron, and Miriam.[14] The other prophets and excellent men are beneath this degree; but it holds good for all of them that the apprehension of their intellects becomes stronger at the separation, just as it is said: *And thy righteousness shall go before thee; the glory of the Lord shall gather thee in* [Isa. 58:8]. After having reached this condition of enduring permanence, that intellect remains in one and the same state, the impediment that sometimes veiled it having been removed. And it will remain permanently in that state of intense pleasure, which does not belong to the genus of bodily pleasures, as we have explained in our compilations and as others have explained before us.[15]

Bring your soul to understand this chapter, and direct your efforts to the multiplying of those moments in which you are with God or endeavoring to approach Him, and to decreasing those times in which you are with other than He and in which you make no efforts to approach Him. This guidance is sufficient in view of the purpose of this Treatise.[16]

Conclusion

By the time Maimonides died, his authority as "the Rabbi par excellence" *and* as the "excellent man" ("the philosopher par excellence") was firmly established. His works were read in Arabic, or in Hebrew translation, throughout the Jewish world. His legacy was vast. Two aspects of it are particularly relevant to our inquiry. First, Maimonides had established the authority of the neo-aristotelian world-view. The material and spiritual hierarchies, the downward flow by emanation, the upward flow by acquisition of knowledge, the existence and definition of perfection, the relationship between nature and creation—all these ideas had been presented, discussed, and authoritatively integrated with rabbinic teaching. In short, "Jewish philosophy" had been set on its feet. No one was to write in this area without reference to Maimonides' thought.

---

[14]Again, only the most exalted of the prophets (Moses, Aaron, and Miriam) can achieve this state. Others (lesser prophets and "excellent men") experience an intensification of philosophic mystical awareness at death, though it is not as intense as a "kiss."

[15]Maimonides' theory of life-after-death is contained in these three sentences. He seems to be saying: (1) that the human intellect—which is emanated directly from the Tenth Intelligence and which is the "link" between man and God (or, the "image" of God in which man is made)—can be strengthened, by repeated philosophical reflection and mystical directedness, in its awareness of God (i.e., of the part of God that is accessible, the Tenth Intelligence); and (2) that in the moment of death, the human intellect can be in a state of such passion, or attachment, that it will remain in a state of permanent intellectual mystical bliss. This would, of course, be the ultimate that man could achieve. (There are many questions left open on this issue: the relationship of the intellect to the soul, the individuality of the intellect, etc. But that requires another book.)

[16]Note the switching from second to third person throughout this chapter. What does Maimonides mean to convey by this?

Second, Maimonides had ventured beyond philosophy into the realm of religion. He had set rational thinking within the framework of worship. In doing this, he had made four important generalizations:

1. The way to worship was through philosophy, i.e., religious experience was predicated on the neo-aristotelian chain of being, and not on a Merkabah-type universe. Maimonides thus assumed that the right type of philosophic and moral preparation was necessary for true relation between God and man.
2. Because the way to worship was through philosophy, worship itself had a distinctly intellectual, contemplative component. Worship was mind working at its own edges, the human mind touching the divine mind. In this, Maimonides rejected the magical and non-philosophic character of Merkabah mysticism. He rejected, too, the mind-emptying character and mindless techniques of the mystics of his milieu. He would have rejected the Zoharic world-view, too, as not neo-aristotelian.
3. Maimonides did make clear, however, that philosophy was only a station on the pilgrim's path, that thought was but a stage on the Way. Beyond thinking was experience, beyond "love" was "devotion." Maimonides' terminology and his description of such states in this world and in the afterlife make this quite clear.
4. Finally, in structuring the relationship between man and God in this way, Maimonides made it possible for any serious student-sage to be both intellectual and pious. He opened the door of direct mystical experience to scholars. In short, "Jewish philosophic mysticism" had been set on its feet, and no one was to write in this area without reference to Maimonides' phenomenology.

Time, however, has a way of displacing even the most comprehensive and luminous syntheses, and this happened to Maimonides. In the East, his works were diligently studied. There, they were integrated with other streams of thought. In the West, his works were studied from the new critical (averroesian) point of view. There, the discussion rapidly degenerated into philosophical casuistry and intellectual hairsplitting. For religious and mystical insight, thinkers in the West turned to the pre-Zoharic, and then the Zoharic, tradition. Yet everywhere the weight of Maimonides' authority was very great, and most scholars—philosophers and mystics alike—continued to define themselves vis-à-vis "the Rabbi." One was either a follower-disciple or one was an opponent. Certain of the mystics, whose views differed vastly from those of Maimonides, even circulated a story (which gained credence very quickly) that on his deathbed, Maimonides had renounced his philosophic bent of mind for a more avowedly mystical one. This made it even easier for almost everyone to be in the Maimonidean tradition. Through another of the twists of history, this legend was later unmasked. Maimonides was restored to his place as a philosopher, and then he was distorted in the other direction—into a philosopher only, on the model of Kant. The debate on the relative weight of philosophy and mysticism within Maimonides still rages today.

We turn now to two medievals, one from the East and one from the West, both of whom regarded themselves as disciples of Maimonides. In studying them, we must ask ourselves: In what way were they true disciples, and in what way were they not? Finally, we must pose the question: Does it really make a difference after all?

3

A YEMENITE SYNTHESIS

Introduction

Two hundred years after Maimonides' death, Yemenite Jewry underwent a renaissance of letters. Books on all subjects, mostly written in Judaeo-Arabic, flourished. Unraveling the filiation of these ideas is a complex process, yet one figure stands out as the primary formative influence on these writers: Maimonides. Everyone had to deal with "our Rabbi, may his memory be a blessing." Hoter ben Shelomo was one of the savants of this renaissance, and it is to his views that we turn. We need to know, however, one important element in Hoter's thinking that was not in Maimonides' world-view in order to understand his conception of philosophic mysticism.

The neo-aristotelian world-view (set forth in the preceding chapter) was composed of: (1) a spiritual hierarchy of ten Intelligences, the human intellect, and the Platonic ideas, and (2) a material hierarchy of supernal spheres, elements, and the physical world. Being, or energy, emanated down these chains and could be accumulated by properly trained men. Mystical contact between man and the Intelligences was also possible. There was, however, a variant of the neo-aristotelian world-view which postulated a different hierarchy of beings. In this other system—called the "neoplatonic" world-view—spiritual and material beings were in the same hierarchy, with the latter simply being lower. The hierarchy, according to the neoplatonic tradition, then, was as follows: God, the One; the First, or Universal, Intellect; the First, or Universal, Soul; Nature (the Platonic ideas); the Prime Matter (the substrate of all physical reality); Body (the Prime Matter plus the Platonic idea of body-ness); the Supernal Spheres; the Elements; and the physical world as we know it. (This is shown schematically in Fig. 2.) Hoter ben Shelomo, caught between these two traditions, the neo-aristotelian and the neoplatonic, chose to harmonize them. He did this by expanding the neoplatonic First Intellect into the neo-aristotelian ten Intelligences (see Fig. 3). This was

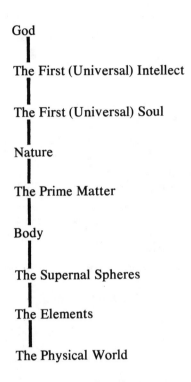

God

The First (Universal) Intellect

The First (Universal) Soul

Nature

The Prime Matter

Body

The Supernal Spheres

The Elements

The Physical World

Fig. 2. THE NEOPLATONIC HIERARCHY

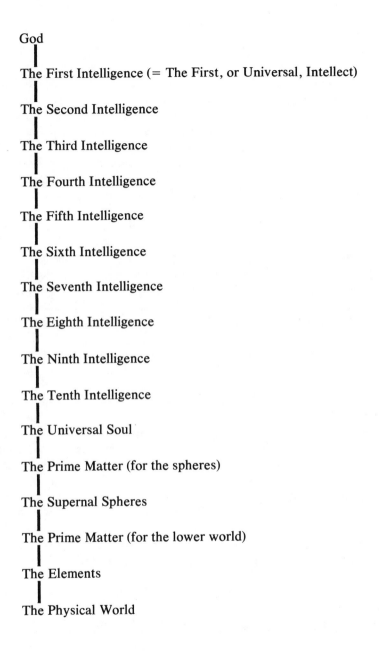

God
|
The First Intelligence (= The First, or Universal, Intellect)
|
The Second Intelligence
|
The Third Intelligence
|
The Fourth Intelligence
|
The Fifth Intelligence
|
The Sixth Intelligence
|
The Seventh Intelligence
|
The Eighth Intelligence
|
The Ninth Intelligence
|
The Tenth Intelligence
|
The Universal Soul
|
The Prime Matter (for the spheres)
|
The Supernal Spheres
|
The Prime Matter (for the lower world)
|
The Elements
|
The Physical World

Fig. 3. HOTER BEN SHELOMO'S SYNTHESIS

easy to do because in Arabic the words for "Intellect," "Intelligence," and "intellect" are the same. This new synthesis gave Hoter ben Shelomo a slightly more complex hierarchy than Maimonides. But in the Middle Ages, when man had more time, complexity was not a vice. It also enabled him to treat both the (rational) soul *and* the human intellect as "chips off the old block," i.e., as divinely given and as participating in the process of the acquisition of true knowledge.

As we turn to these passages, note the harmonized hierarchy. Note, too, that Hoter has preserved the dynamic flow of emanation-acquisition, and that it culminates in his view of life in the World-to-Come.

The Descent-Ascent of the Soul

Now the philosophers are agreed that, from the One, only one being can emanate [and that the emanated being is] its equal, each of them being perfect, according to the demonstration for the unity [of things].[1] Thus, [we can reason that] the first [thing] that God, may He be exalted, created was a perfection; that this perfection was called beyond doubt, "rationality"; that "rationality" is the "[power of] perception," as our Rabbi, may his memory be a blessing, has said in Part Two of the *Guide*. . . . Then this perfection flowed out to the existents, and it did not pass through any of the levels of the existents without being influenced by thickness and deficiency.[2] Until, finally, it came to the realm of man. And when it had become settled there, it began to seek that perfection which had formerly been its [possession]. It began to seek it by acquisition, bit by bit. Whenever it perceived one of the levels of the existents in the course of [its] ascent, it demanded back that perfection which had been taken from it when it descended. And then it concealed that which it had perceived of that which had been taken from it—nothing more—until the perfection which had been its [possession] had been completed, for it had been oppressively stolen from it.[3] This is all that I can say in answer to this question, for it is bound up with the things [which are] the secrets of the Torah. "Woe unto me if I say them, and woe unto me if I do not."[4]

---

[1] This passage is drawn from Hoter ben Shelomo's *One Hundred Philosophic Questions and Answers* (ed. and trans. by D. Blumenthal), Question 43. The author here describes the descent of the rational soul from its heavenly roots and then its slow ascent by acquisition of knowledge.

[2] This is very neoplatonic: that, as spiritual entities get further from their roots, they get "thicker" and "more deficient" in perfection. When they ascend, they get "purer" and "more subtle."

[3] Note the underlying idea that perfection was inherent to the soul but that the soul had been wrongfully deprived of it. The soul, therefore, must recover its lost perfection.

[4] Quoted from Talmud, *Bava Batra* 98b.

Prophecy as Mysticism

Was the Law bestowed upon Moses, our teacher, by means of an intermediary from the Almighty, or [was it bestowed] without intermediation?[1]

The [following] saying of the Sages, may their memory be a blessing, is already known:[2] "The Holy One, blessed be He, does nothing without reflecting upon the heavenly family." And they have also said, "He does nothing; rather He and His court [act], as it is said, 'Let us go down and confuse their tongues there' [Gen. 11:7]," which indicates a plural [subject].

Thus, when Moses' rational soul had achieved perfection, and when the link between him and the Tenth Intelligence, which our Rabbi, may his memory be a blessing, has explained in the Closing Chapter of the *Guide,* had grown strong, then Moses' soul became enmeshed with the Universal Soul, and his intellect [became enmeshed, unified] with the Tenth Intelligence, [and it] emanated to him that which was emanated of the supernal perfections and the unique, radiant lights which are called "Torah," which are perfected to the end of time.[3] They shall never cease from being with us, as He, may He be exalted, has said, "As the days that the heavens are above the earth" [Deut. 11:21], and as He, may He be exalted, has said, "The hidden things are God's but the revealed things are ours and our children's forever" [Deut. 29:28]. This perfection just referred to was bestowed upon Moses through the intermediation of the Universal Soul from the Agent Intelligence,[4] which is called "The Prince of the World," with the acquiescence of the Originator of All Who emanates to everything, may His praise be proclaimed. And this [perfection] is referred to [by the verse], "I speak with him mouth to mouth" [Num. 12:8].[5]

---

[1]This passage is also taken from Hoter ben Shelomo's *Questions and Answers,* Question 5. Here the author addresses the problem of the ultimate stage that man can reach in this world. For Hoter, as for Jewish thinkers in general, this was represented by Moses.

[2]The quotations are from the classic rabbinic sources and are used by Hoter (and before him by Maimonides) to "prove" that God did not communicate directly even with Moses but that He acted through the spiritual chain of being, i.e., through the Intelligences and the Universal Soul.

[3]Hoter's answer is that Moses' intellect received emanation from its source, the Tenth Intelligence, while Moses' soul received emanation from its source, the Universal Soul. Prophecy as an experience, then, had two aspects: one involving the intellect and one involving the soul. Maimonides envisioned the former and not the latter, as we have seen. Hoter is forced to expand Maimonides because of his own expanded hierarchy. (For those interested in exegesis, how do you think Hoter explained the "(two) horns of light" that radiated from Moses' face [Exod. 34:35]?)

[4]See Fig. 3, that the light/energy descends from God, through the Intelligences, through the Universal Soul, to man.

[5]The communication by emanation is, thus, as direct ("mouth to mouth") as communication from God can be.

The Philosophic Mystical Pilgrimage

I have seen fit to mention here the character of the ranking of men and their climbing in [their] knowledge of the existents which include four categories: compounded bodies, simple bodies, souls, and Intelligences.[1] The Sages, may their memory be a blessing, already set these four ranks over against the holidays by means of verse-interpretation, for when a man moves from rank to rank when he is studying, then that is a holiday for him. . . .

The first advancement, then, that a man [makes is] from the sensible compounded beings by ranking the knowledge of their forms, for the forms of the sensibles are the goal when one is studying, just as the fruit is the goal of real wheat.[2] Then, after this, he advances to the perception of the simple bodies, which are, beyond doubt, more perfect than the compounded bodies. Nonetheless, the intent here is also only the perception of their forms. Note that it says, "the fruits of the tree" . . .[3] After this, he advances to the perception of the realm of the souls. Look and consider what the just Tradition has said, "On the New Year, we pass before Him as in a line of counted sheep." We have already said, specifically and generally, that the goal of the human soul is the complete return to this level.[4] After this, he advances to the perception of the spiritual forms, which, [as] we have explained more than once, are the separated Intelligences. The Sages, may their memory be a blessing, have

---

[1]This passage, too, is drawn from Hoter's *Questions and Answers,* Question 78. The problem the author attacks here is that of philosophic mysticism for *every* man. He says that every man can enjoy this experience, and that the Rabbis demonstrated this by setting the stages of knowledge-acquisition over against the annual cycle of the holidays (i.e., by a philosophic mystical reinterpretation of the holiday cycle).

The four stages of knowledge-acquisition are: (1) perception of the Platonic ideas in the objects of everyday physical reality (the "compounded bodies," i.e., compounded out of the elements); (2) perception of the Platonic ideas in the supernal spheres (the "simple bodies," i.e., not compounded but comprised only of the "quintessence" and Platonic ideas); (3) perception of the universe of the souls (animal, human, of the spheres, and the Universal Soul); and (4) perception of the Intelligences (they are "separated" from matter, i.e., have no matter in them).

The four holidays are Passover, Shavuot (Pentecost), the High Holidays (Rosh ha-Shana and Yom Kippur), and Shemini Atseret (the last day of Tabernacles). The sequence and symbols are drawn from Mishna, *Rosh ha-Shana* 1:2.

[2]The first stage, then, is perception of the Platonic ideas (called, here and elsewhere in medieval Judaeo-Islamic philosophy, "forms") that are in physical matter. The "fruit of the wheat" is a reference to the grain offering of Passover.

[3]The second stage is perception of the Platonic ideas of the spheres. The "fruits of the tree" is a reference to the first-fruits offering of Shavuot.

[4]The third stage is perception of the world of the souls. The image of the "sheep" is drawn from the mishna cited above. (It was later incorporated into a liturgical poem, well-known in European Jewish circles.) Maimonides, commenting on the mishna, refers to an esoteric meaning which, however, he does not explicate. Hoter does so and interprets the "sheep" as the souls of men which are judged on the High Holidays.

said, "On the holiday, they decide about the water," and we have explained many times in this Question and in others that the term "water" refers to what one masters in the knowledge of God, may He Who is "a source of living water" [Jer. 2:13] be exalted.[5] Thus He, may He be exalted, used the holiday of Sukkot as a metaphor for all these forms in saying, "When you gather in" [Deut. 16:13]. The claim of the Torah does not urge men to understand the sensibles, for they are quick to that [on their own]. Rather, it requires an awakening to the intelligibles, in whatever situation one be. It is up to you to consider why happiness is greater on Sukkot, more than on all the other holidays.[6]

---

[5]The final stage is perception of the Intelligences. Note the multi-level exegesis of God as the source of "water" (i.e., the Intelligences) and man who must "decide about the water" (i.e., must acquire knowledge of God; actually, of the Intelligences). The "water" is a reference to the prayer for rain said on Shemini Atseret.

[6]Sukkot is called the "holiday of our rejoicing" because, according to Hoter's interpretation, on Sukkot man achieves the height of philosophic mystical meditation.

Life in the World-to-Come

This Principle does not need a commentary other than that which our Rabbi, may his memory be a blessing, has already mentioned concerning the [ultimate] happiness and misery, and the explanation of what the World-to-Come is.[1] Nonetheless, I am not excused from saying that which has occurred to me on this level—I mean, the ultimate state of existence—whether it be concerning the happiness of the righteous or the misery of the wicked.

I say, therefore, that the happiness of any being, its pleasure, and its ease are that which were created for it. Thus, the pleasure of the eye is in seeing beautiful forms. The pleasure of the ear is in hearing pleasant melodies. And the pleasure of any faculty is in that which has been created for it. Now, there is no thing which has a function more noble than God, may He be exalted. Thus, the pleasure of the heart is in the knowledge of God, may He be exalted, and for that it was created. I do not mean with the word "heart," here, that piece of flesh, made from dust, which is found in the bodies of a man, an ox, a horse, and the other animals. Rather, I mean here with the term "heart" that within man which perceives. Have you not noticed that when a man does not know something, he is sad, and that when he has learned it, he is, then, happy? Therefore, wherever, in reality, the place of an intellected object is greater, there the pleasure is greater. Take note that, when a man knows the vizier of the Sultan, he is content with that. But, if he knows the Sultan himself, then he has greater ease and greater joy.

Furthermore, there is nothing in this, our world, more noble than the human intellect nor is there anything in all of reality more noble than God, may He be exalted, since all nobility, glory, happiness, perfection, and beauty derive from Him, may He be exalted, and all the wonders of the world are from the traces of His wondrous work. Thus, there is no knowledge more glorious and more noble than the knowledge of Him, may He be exalted and glorified. And the human intellect has no pleasure except in the knowledge of God, may He be exalted.

The pleasure of the passions of this world, however, are bound up with the animal soul which is in man and which is the instrument of the rational soul.[2] This animal soul is composed and perishes at death. As for the

---

[1]This is drawn from Hoter ben Shelomo's *Commentary to Maimonides' Thirteen Principles* (ed. and trans. by D. Blumenthal [Leiden: E. J. Brill, 1974], pp. 166–170). Hoter also used this section in his commentary to the Torah (unpublished). Here Hoter again attacks the problem of philosophic mysticism for every man—this time in the context of the nature of the World-to-Come. He begins by pointing out that every organ has a purpose, that of the heart and the intellect being the acquisition of knowledge about God. (Note that Hoter appears, in good early medieval fashion, to locate the intellect in the heart and not in the brain.) He then points out that knowledge yields pleasure and joy.

[2]Here Hoter begins to expound his theory of the nature of "life" in the World-to-Come. Note the types of souls and their fates.

rational soul, if it has grown large and old in the knowledge of God, may He be exalted, and of His creatures, it does not perish at death. Rather, it will possess the World-to-Come, for it has come out of the darkness into the light, for "death is the birth of the perfected soul and the destruction of the inferior soul."[3] This destruction is the being deprived of the World-to-Come. See how greatly those who cling to the senses fear death! There are many demonstrations of this idea and the purpose of the philosophers is to acquire knowledge of these matters.

Consider the embryo in the womb of its mother:[4] Were it to be articulate and were someone to say to it, "Will you come out of this narrow, dark, vile place into the spaciousness of the world; and will you smell the air, sit in the company of men, move to the horizons of the world, be nourished with beneficial food other than this nourishment to which you have become habituated, be associated with members of your own species, be content with possessions, clothing and other oils and goods, as well as with all the forms of contentments which men enjoy," then, such an embryo—were it possible for it to have articulate speech—would say, "Deceive someone else! I shall never cease being in this place, nor shall I leave it." It would say this, beyond doubt, on the basis of the habit to which it had been become accustomed. Just so, is our state in this world: We do not willingly separate ourselves from the sensibles and the passions [to which we have become accustomed].

Would that the celebrated man could see with the eye of his heart the perfection to which he will go from this base, despised, vile, darkened, purposeless, decaying world which is in a continuous state of corruption! For the world to which he goes is, undoubtedly, a world of continuity without end, of life without cutting off, of existence without non-existence, of pleasure without pain, of joys without grief, and of ease without anxiety! Indeed, that world is in the beauty of the spiritual, sovereign, holy Presence to which the substances of the angels are bound, and it is the abode of absolute good, absolute beauty, absolute pulchritude, and absolute perfection. But this pleasure cannot be described with any attribute. Nor is there any relation between the pleasure of this world and the pleasure of that one. How could that which has no cutting off of its existence have a relationship with that which is incoherent and unenduring?! This level of existence is that which is intended by the phrase, "the World-to-Come."

"There is no eating, drinking, or familial life there. Rather, the righteous sit, with crowns on their heads, and benefit from the radiance of the

---

[3]This is a common idea in Judaeo-Islamic culture. Note very carefully the definition of "hell" in the next sentence. Hoter, following Maimonides, does not think of hell as a positive place but as a being-cut-off from bliss.

[4]This analogy, too, is common. The late Harry Emerson Fosdick is said to have used the same metaphor. Note the rhythm and style of the language in the next paragraphs.

Shechina."[5] He who merits this level of existence is he of whom it is said, "You are all gods and higher beings" [Ps. 82:6]. Whereas he who has not reflected on intellectual problems and [hence] does not know that, indeed, the world has a God except from that which he has heard from another will not cease being steeped in the vanities of the world from the time that he leaves the womb of his mother to enter the womb of his passing and until he returns to it—and there are instances of this each day. He, also, does not know what he is, or where he is from, or where his resources come from. Woe unto him! How he will be shackled and fully recompensed after his death with the punishment which he shall receive in the Afterlife, especially if his rational soul has attained to some part of the sciences! His soul will remain in great suffering and its punishment will not ever be mitigated. Perhaps, however, these persons [i.e., those whose reflection has been inadequate] will benefit from the intercession of the merciful angels, for they are innocent and have harmed no one else.

However, he whose belief is thus [i.e., who has some true knowledge] and who yet continually harms others, either by informing or by wronging them monetarily or verbally, has no part in the World-to-Come or in this world, nor can he ever hope for intercession. This is the suffering which will be meted out in full to the wicked after their death in place of the pleasures of the World-to-Come described earlier. Whereas, he whose soul has attained to no knowledge whatsoever shall enjoy an abundance of God's mercy, may He be exalted. His soul shall lack for nothing but shall become one with the souls of the animals.

Consider, therefore, you who are a thinker, what the condition of the righteous is and what the condition of the wicked is. Consider with the eye of your heart, and do not let the world deceive you with its passions, for there is no escape from the reckoning.

Conclusion

The world of Hoter ben Shelomo and his colleagues in the East was, in large measure, a continuation of the world of their master, Maimonides. In it, God was mind contemplating itself and, by that process, emanating energy or light to the spiritual and material chains of being. In it, man

---

[5]The quotation is drawn from Talmud, *Berakhot* 17a, and is used by Maimonides too. Hoter proceeds to differentiate four types of persons: (1) he who does not reflect and, hence, knows nothing—his soul joins the souls of the animals in eternal happiness; (2) he who reflects insufficiently and, hence, knows a little—his soul is punished but may benefit from the intercession of the angels of mercy because he has harmed no one; (3) he who knows the truth and still harms others—he has no salvation; and (4) the righteous. This theory of retribution is most un-Maimonidean, and therefore Hoter apologizes for it.

the world (the Platonic ideas). Through this knowledge-acquisition, man could prepare himself for ''contact'' with the divine spiritual realm, in this world and in the next. The scholars from the East had a more complex chain of being and, hence, a more complex philosophic mysticism, but the principle was the same: Religious life was steeped in philosophy and in mysticism. The Way was both intellectual and experiential.

We turn now to the followers of Maimonides in the West, and there we shall encounter not only a new chain of being but also radically new techniques for achieving philosophic mystical experience.

4

THE ABULAFIAN TRANSFORMATION

Introduction

Maimonides died in 1204, and in the West (i.e., in Spain and Provence), three important religious streams formed in the century following his death. First, there was the "Maimonidean Controversy," which was an extended argument over Maimonides' rationalism, in philosophy and in Jewish law. That cannot be dealt with here. Second, there was the creation of the *Zohar* by Moses de Leon at the end of the thirteenth century. This text, which was to become the "third Bible" of religious Jews, has been partly explicated in Volume I of *Understanding Jewish Mysticism*. Third, there were several types of Jewish mysticism which surfaced, left a mark, and then receded. For instance, in Gerona (Spain), there was an important kabbalist named Azriel who wrote a commentary on the *Sefer Yetsira*, who apparently had some contact with certain distinctly neoplatonic thinkers, and who evolved a theory of sefirot which differed from that of *Sefer Yetsira* and yet was not the same as that of the *Zohar*. Also, a strange book called *Sefer ha-Bahir* ("The Book of the Radiant One"), the text of which we still do not understand, was in active circulation during this century. And a strange man named Abraham Abulafia introduced some strange techniques into the Jewish mystical tradition, some of which we shall study in this chapter. In all, the thirteenth century was a time of deep turmoil and profound searching, of serious upset and astounding creativity.

Before turning to the Abulafian transformation of Maimonides, we might well pause to note four important historical events of the thirteenth century. First, in the year 1215, the Fourth Lateran Council met under the leadership of Pope Innocent III. This Council promulgated several decrees regarding the Jews, the most famous of which were: that Jews must dress differently from Christians (this is the beginning of the "Jewish badge"), that Jews may not appear in public during Christian holidays, that Jews may not hold public office, that converts to Christianity must cease all Jewish observances, and that Jews must remit the debts of all Crusaders. Second, in 1239–40, the Jewish calendar changed from the year 4999 to the year 5000. This provoked in the Jewish, and in the Christian, world a great deal of messianic fervor. Third, in the year 1240, there was a public disputation in Paris between a rabbi and an apostate which culminated in the burning of the Talmud. And fourth, in 1263, another disputation took place in Barcelona (Spain) between a rabbi and an apostate, from which the rabbi barely escaped with his life. Did these events "influence" the development of mysticism in southern Europe? Did they "cause" the turmoil and the searching? Or did men's understanding of God deepen by reflection and by experience? Did Jewish mysticism flourish because of exposure to new ideas and loyalty to old ones?

Abraham Abulafia

Abraham Abulafia, who called himself "Abraham, the prophet [sic], the son of Rabbi Samuel," was born in Spain sometime after the turn of the eras (1240). Orphaned early, he traveled to the Holy Land. When the Christian-Muslim conflict made a further stay there impossible, he returned to Spain via Greece and Italy. During these years, he began to study Maimonides as well as *Sefer Yetsira* and the other mystical works circulating in the southern European Jewish community. In 1271, he claimed to have had visionary experiences which he qualified as "prophetic." For this, he was attacked and had to leave Spain, again for Italy and Greece. During these second wanderings, he wrote many books, among them a long mystical *Commentary to "The Guide of the Perplexed"* (by Maimonides) and several "prophetic books." In 1280, Abraham Abulafia decided to go see Pope Nicholas III. He regarded this visit as having messianic import. The Pope seems to have agreed, for he sentenced Abulafia to death. However, the Pope died suddenly before the sentence could be carried out and Abulafia was released. After his release and until his death (1280–1291—the same years as the creation of the *Zohar!*) Abulafia wrote most of the mystical manuals for which he later became famous. What made Abraham Abulafia so strange? What justified the violent opposition to his work? He wrote down explicit techniques for inducing trances. He knew and respected Christian mystics. He claimed "prophetic" visions. He had students, and some became apostates. He saw himself as a messianic figure. And he presented himself, in this century of turmoil and searching, as authentically Maimonidean, i.e., as completely within the authoritative stream of Jewish philosophic mysticism. Even so, the questions remain. Unfortunately, very little of the original works of Abulafia has been published, though a fragment of a book by one of his disciples has been made available by Scholem (see below, "For Further Reading and Instruction"). We shall, therefore, jump two centuries and examine the life and work of one of the later men of the Abulafian school.

Rabbi Judah al-Botini and His Sullam ha-ʿAliyah

In his classical study on the history of Jewish mysticism, Scholem described the personal reticence of Jewish mystics: They did not write autobiographies, and they did not let their personalities interfere with their statements of mystical insights. Scholem also noted that Jewish mystics exercised enormous self-censorship over the materials they published. One genre of mystical literature which was suppressed was the mystic manual. Such manuals did exist (and still do), but they were, by unspoken agreement, allowed only very limited circulation. Strangely enough, even modern scholars have been reluctant to publish these manuals. Scholem himself has only published a few fragments, and of these only one in English, while Jellinek published only a few fragments in German. As recently as the new (English) edition of the *Encyclopaedia Judaica,* Scholem remarked that the restrictions on the literature of mystical technique were those which were adhered to the longest. Even these documents, however, deserve publication for two reasons. First, these texts are truly documents of the numinous, gems hidden in the vast mountain of the human spirit. And second, they reveal to us the high degree of knowledgeability and of self-discipline required of the mystic in Jewish tradition, for Jewish mysticism was (and is) no occupation for the dilettante or the ignoramus.

The text presented here is part of *Sullam ha-ʿAliyah* by Rabbi Judah al-Botini. The author came from a distinguished rabbinic family which had served the Jewish community of Lisbon, Portugal. His grandfather, Joseph ibn Ḥayyūn, had written several books, including a commentary to the Torah and another to the *Ethics of the Fathers.* The family seems to have left Portugal just before the expulsion of the Jews, which took place in 1497, and it moved to Israel, where some relatives settled in Safed, which was to become the great center for kabbalism and law in the sixteenth century, while Rabbi Judah himself settled in the Holy City of Jerusalem. There, he became the head of a Yeshiva (rabbinic academy) and, as such, took his turn as chief rabbinic judge of Jerusalem. Several documents with his approbation are known from this period. During his stay in Jerusalem, where he died in 1519, al-Botini wrote several works, most of them legal in nature. Three of his works, however, dealt with philosophy and mysticism: (1) *Mar'ot Elohim,* which he appears to have been working on when he died and of which we have no copy, dealt with the mysteries of Creation and the Merkabah; (2) *Yesod Mishne Torah,* which was also left incomplete, is a commentary to Maimonides' great

Code of Law, but it contains a series of "Introductions" which are of interest; and (3) *Sullam ha-ʿAliyah,* his mystical manual, part of which is presented here.

Sullam ha-ʿAliyah ("The Ladder of the Ascent") is composed of ten chapters, and as with many such works, its parts are scattered in different libraries. Only a part of it—Chapters Seven through Ten—has been published in Hebrew (G. Scholem, in *Kirjath Sefer* 22 [1945]: 162–171, and in *Kitvei Yad ba-Kabbala,* pp. 225–230). Chapter Seven deals with the mystical conception of prophecy. Chapter Eight deals with the mystical techniques of numerology and word-association. Chapter Nine deals with the mystical techniques of breathing and intonation. And Chapter Ten deals with the final preparations for ecstasy and magic. These last three chapters are presented here, and while the material is complex, it is not beyond the understanding of the serious student.

As we turn to the material itself, we may well ask several questions: What is "Jewish" about these techniques? Are some of them so "non-Jewish" as to be the cause of the vociferous objections made to this type of mysticism? Why were these techniques kept secret? Was Abulafia (and his followers) justified in speaking of these techniques as producing "prophetic" visions? What possessed al-Botini, the head of a Jerusalem Yeshiva and a rabbinic judge in the Holy City, to set down these techniques in writing? And, what happened to this type of mysticism?

Rabbi Judah al-Botini's Hierarchy[1]

Indeed, our holy rabbis, peace be upon them, the prophets, the sons of the prophets, the Tanaim, and the Amoraim, who had in their hands the true Tradition from Moses, our Rabbi, peace be upon him, together with the wise men of the Kabbala of recent generations and even the ancient wise men of research of the nations [of the world] who inclined toward the wisdom of the Sages of Israel in [these] matters—all agree that the worlds which encompass all created beings are three [in number]: the world of the separated Intelligences with its "ten steps" and hosts; second, the world of the spheres with its ten heavens, the stars, the constellations, and their hosts; [and] third, the world of the lower beings with its four elements, inanimate, vegetable, living, and human beings and their progeny. And the Master of all rules over all of them, as David, King of

---

[1]This text is taken from al-Botini's commentary to Maimonides' *Code of Law.* The Hebrew text was published by M. Benayahu in *Sinai* 36 (1955–56), 251–252. Al-Botini's problem is as follows: On the one hand, Maimonides taught a world composed of three levels—the ten Intelligences (called by Maimonides, "the ten steps"), the supernal world of the spheres, and the physical world as we know it. On the other hand, the *Zohar* taught (remember that al-Botini is writing after 1497, while Maimonides wrote in 1190 and the *Zohar* was written about 1290) a world composed of ten sefirot (called by the kabbalists,

Israel, peace be upon him, said, . . . But all those whose wisdom has been exalted [and who have] seen the luminescent and the non-luminescent glass[2] agree that, between the Cause of the causes, may His Name be praised, and the world of the separated Intelligences, there is an intelligent, spiritual, simple existent entity [which is] subtler than the subtlest, very much exalted above the world of the separated Intelligences, as light is exalted above darkness. This intelligent existent entity was emanated from the Ein Sof, may He be praised, from the depths of the hiddenness of the Tetragrammaton, and they called this intelligent, spiritual being "the world of the Emanation." . . . The wise men of the Kabbala, the author of *Sefer Yetsira,* which is ascribed to Abraham, our father, peace be upon him, at their head, have agreed that this intelligent existent entity is the "ten holy, spiritual steps" from which the levels of the angels and the separated Intelligences are emanated. The kabbalists (*hamekubbalīm*) call these ten holy steps "the ten sefirot" . . . indicating that they are ten [in number], holy, "sefirotic," pure, luminescent, and the subtlest of the subtle; [that] their radiance, "sefirocity," subtlety, and intelligence is greater than [that of] the "Holy Beasts" which are the highest of the ten ranks of the angels; [and that] they are immeasurably above [these] "Holy Beasts."[3]

"the world of emanation," also "the ten steps"), etc. Al-Botini's problem is how to harmonize these two hierarchies. He has two choices: (1) He can "sandwich" the one into the other, as Hoter ben Shelomo did in a different context, or (2) he can say that the Intelligences and the sefirot are identical. Which option does he choose?

[2]Compare *Understanding Jewish Mysticism,* Vol. I, pp. 133–139.

[3]Al-Botini, then, chose to insert the ten sefirot above the ten Intelligences in the chain of being. They are, thus, closer to God, the Source of all being. Interestingly, Abraham Abulafia chose the other option: he simply asserted the identity of the Intelligences and the sefirot. (Since, however, Abulafia was a contemporary of the author of the *Zohar,* we are not sure what kind of sefirot he intended.) The "angels" are identified by Maimonides as the Intelligences. The "Holy Beasts," known to us from the Merkabah tradition, are identified by Maimonides as the first (i.e., the highest) Intelligence.

Three Chapters from al-Botini's Sullam ha-ʿAliyah

THE EIGHTH CHAPTER, which deals with the Ways of "leaping" and "jumping" (*dillūg u-ḳefiṣā*) which are the goal and the end of all the Ways which preceded them in these chapters.[1]

It [i.e., the two methods together] is a very broad Way, which includes all, or most of, the Ways [mentioned] previously. It includes [the secret skills] of "gematria," of "permuting," of "transformation of letters," of their "division," their "separation," their "combination," their "balancing," their "exchange," and their "substitution." In addition to all these Ways, [there is] "leaping and jumping"—that is, the use of initial letters to form other words, or the [use of] letters from the middle or the end of words, or by combining the initial letters to the medial or the final ones. And with all these Ways [of working the letters], one "leaps and jumps" from one Way to another Way either with the help of a newly-created word or with the help of the letters which have been mixed together [during these processes] from the beginning, the end, or the middle of their [respective] words. Or [one "leaps and jumps"] by "permuting," "transforming," "dividing," "combining," "exchanging," or "substituting"—[using] one of the Ways mentioned here, as you shall see for yourself, for when you look into the matter of all these "permutations" in this chapter, you will find methods of all the above-mentioned Ways. For this reason, I say that the Way of the "leaping and jumping" is the goal of all the [other] Ways.[2] For, as the "final cause" is superior to all causes preceding it—since all the [other] causes have existence only in the process of causation and are, therefore, included in it [i.e., in the final cause]—just so all the aforementioned Ways are as prefaces and premises in studying the Ways which one must master before one can "work" and use the skill of "leaping" mentioned above.

In truth,[3] if one lacks knowledge of the [above-mentioned] Ways, he

---

[1]This chapter presents a series of numerological and alphabetological techniques for inducing a trance state. In this introductory paragraph, al-Botini simply lists them; he will illustrate each in the following pages. At this point, the reader must only know: (1) that each numerological and alphabetological technique is called a "Way," and (2) that "leaping and jumping" is used in three senses: (a) it is one of the alphabetological techniques (the one by which a permutation is formed); (b) it is the free-association technique by which one switches from one technique to another; and (c) it is the collective term for all these techniques.

[2]"Leaping and jumping," then, in its broadest sense includes all the other techniques. Note the philosophical terminology of the next sentences. By using it, al-Botini places himself squarely in the philosophic mystical tradition.

[3]Al-Botini begins here a description of what happens to the soul of one who practices this type of mysticism. Note carefully such philosophic mystical terms as "soul expands," "finds pleasure," "releases thought," "adhesion," "passion," "acquisition of knowledge," "from potency to actuality," etc. Some of these terms are taken directly from Maimonides, while some are derived from a more neoplatonic, but nonetheless philosophic mystical, vocabulary. By contrast, the "root of its origin from which it was hewn out" is Zoharic language.

will not know how to "work" or how to use this awesome technique. [However], he who is an expert in this Way and who knows it, he who is agile and quick in its perfect execution—his soul expands and finds pleasure. [Such a person] releases thought from the prison of the natural realm and raises it to the Divine realm. [Such a man's soul] expands and finds pleasure in this until it feels as if it has separated from the body and as if it no longer has supervision over the body at all because of the intensity of its adhesion to the root of its origin from which it was hewn out. How much stronger [will be the ecstasy of] the person who has an overriding, consuming passion to acquire [this] knowledge, who considers his body and its faculties as worthless in comparison to the acquisition of this knowledge. For then this passion stimulates the soul, increases its warmth, and speeds its movement, bringing it from potency to actuality.[4] The soul then adheres to the Agent Intelligence, and because of this adhesion, the soul wraps itself in the faculty of the imagination, in the form of "the image [of God]," and it [i.e., the soul] grants him [i.e., the person] the perfections of the foreseeing of the future and of the revealing of hidden things; or [the soul grants the person] whatever he requested or whatever he set his imagination and thought to know of such subjects. The soul further wraps itself up, becomes more subtle, and finds pleasure in the intellectual faculty. And it grants him the perfection of comprehending the metaphysical first principles which are hidden in the concealed places of this world and the next. It [i.e., the soul wrapped in the intellect] then comprehends something of the knowledge of the Creator, may He be praised, and of His created, simple beings according to its power of, and its preparation for, comprehension. We shall expand on this matter and we shall explain it more fully in the Tenth Chapter, which deals with the "Ways of isolating oneself" which one reaches by means of this Way of "jumping and leaping" which, in turn, includes all the Ways which preceded it, as I have already explained to you.

To enable you to see this matter with your own eyes, I shall write down and permute a little bit of it, and from this you should analogize as best as you are able. I shall begin to manipulate and permute two or three words, and I shall not give all the necessary permutations of each word, for that would be a vast undertaking. Rather, I shall present only four or five permutations of a given word, whether they are comprehensible or not, and from these [permutations], I shall "leap and jump" to other words, "leaping" from one of the aforementioned Ways to another. I shall begin

---

[4]Al-Botini here adumbrates the ultimate state that man can achieve: the union of the soul with the Tenth Intelligence (also called the "Agent Intelligence" or the "Active Intellect"). Two things happen when this "adhesion" (Heb., *devekut*) occurs: (1) the soul makes use of the imagination to acquire knowledge of the future, and (2) the soul makes use of the intellect to acquire knowledge of God and the basic structure of the universe. These are the philosophic mystical gifts.

by permuting the words *dillūg* and *ṣērūf* [i.e., the words "leaping" and "permutation" themselves] . . . And I say:

[The text here continues with several lines of permutations. In order to make these accessible to the reader, I have extracted them, arranged them in tabular form, and introduced each permutation with a note. Throughout these charts the reader will have to be familiar with the Hebrew letters, their names and transcriptions, and the number value of each letter. This is given in Fig. 4. Finally, the reader must be aware that the actual text is only a few lines long. Al-Botini's narrative resumes on p. 52.]

SFARDI NAME	SOUND	NUMERICAL FORM	HEBREW NAME	LETTER
Alef	'	1	אָלֶף	א
Bet	B	2	בֵּית	ב
Gimel	G	3	גִּמֶל	ג
Dalet	D	4	דָלֶת	ד
Hay	H	5	הֵא	ה
Vav	V/U	6	וָו	ו
Zayin	Z	7	זַיִן	ז
Het	Ḥ	8	חֵית	ח
Tet	Ṭ	9	טֵית	ט
Yod	Y	10	יוֹד	י
Kaf	X	20	כָּף	כ

SFARDI NAME	SOUND	NUMERICAL FORM	HEBREW NAME	LETTER
Lamed	L	30	לָמֶד	ל
Mem	M	40	מֵם	מ
Nun	N	50	נוּן	נ
Sameh	S	60	סָמֶךְ	ס
Ayin	''	70	עַיִן	ע
Pay	P/F	80	פֵּא	פ
Tzadee	Ṣ	90	צַדִי	צ
Kof	Q	100	קוֹף	ק
Resh	R	200	רֵישׁ	ר
Shin	Š	300	שִׁין	ש
Tav	T	400	תָו	ת

Fig. 4. THE HEBREW ALPHABET AND GEMATRIC EQUIVALENTS

1. Introductory Note

The first technique to be demonstrated is "permutation." This technique allows the mystic to rearrange all the letters in any given word, using each letter only once. For example, using the word "saw," we would get the following "permutation": saw, aws, swa, asw, was, wsa. Note that most of the terms are nonsense, though one of them is a comprehensible word. Another example: shoe, soeh, sohe, ehos, ohes, hose, esoh, . . . Here, too, only one permutated term has meaning. (A meaningful permutation is called an "anagram" in English.) The mathematical formula for the number of permutations for a four-letter word, using each letter only once, is: $4 \times 3 \times 2 \times 1$; for a three-letter word, it is: $3 \times 2 \times 1$; for a ten-letter word it is: $10 \times 9 \times 8 \times 7 \times 6 \times 5 \times 4 \times 3 \times 2 \times 1$. This is called: $n!$, "n-factorial." [The formula for multiple use of each letter would be: $(n)^n$.]

Text

1a: DLUG,* DLGU, DGLU, DGUL, GUDL, GDUL†
1b: ṢRUF, ṢURF, FURṢ, FUṢR, RṢFU, RṢUF‡
1c: 'HBH, H'HB, HH'B§

‫1א: דלוג, דלגו, דגלו, דגול, גודל, גדול‬

‫1ב: צרוף, צורף, פורץ, פוצר, רצפו, רצוף‬

‫1ג: אהבה, האהב, ההאב‬

---

*Al-Botini here permutes three words: DLUG, ṢRUF, 'HBH. To make things easier for the (Hebrew) reader, he has used, in the first two lines, only those permutations that are also words (in Hebrew). Otherwise, he would have 24 (=4!) terms per line. The meaning of the words is not significant.

†The author now "leaps," by free association, from the first term of this set to the first term of the next set. His free association is: DLUG ("leap")—ṢRUF ("permute"). Another person, or the same author at another time, would have a different association and, hence, a different second set of terms. The technique of "leaping," then, enables each mystic to express himself differently. We shall see some rather heretical "leaps" later on.

‡The author now "leaps" again by associating the last term of this set, which is read raṣúf, with Song of Songs 3:10, where it appears as: ve-tōkhō rāṣúf 'ahāvā. He then permutes 'ahāvā.

§The last term in this set is nonsensical. Al-Botini stops the meditation here and starts another. He does not tell us what his association ("leap") between meditations was.

2. Introductory Note

Al-Botini here demonstrates two additional techniques, "separating" and "gematria." In "separating," one takes the letters of a word and recombines them into two words: e.g., chairs = his arc; seats = as set; etc. One thus has a two-word term where formerly one had only a one-word term. The two-word terms are indicated here by a slight space before and after each word. There is, however, a larger space and a comma before and after each whole term.

The second technique demonstrated by al-Botini is an old technique called "gematria." It is based on three simple principles: First, every letter of the alphabet has a numerical value. Using our alphabet, the sequence would be: A = 1, B = 2, C = 3, D = 4, E = 5, . . . I = 9, and J = 10. To indicate the number eleven, we would write: JA, 12 = JB, 13 = JC, etc. The sequence would continue: 20 = K, 21 = KA . . . 30 = L, 40 = M, 50 = N, 60 = O, 70 = P . . . 90 = R, and 100 = S. Then, 200 = T, 300 = U . . . 700 = Y, 800 = Z. To form larger figures, we would have to add: ZS = 500, etc. How much is ZTMI? How much is SOD?

Second, all the letters of any word can be converted to their numerical equivalents and summed, regardless of the order of their appearance. Thus: PEN = 70 + 5 + 50 = 125; MAGIC = 40 + 1 + 7 + 9 + 3 = 60; etc. What is the gematria of your name? of the word "God"? For the enthusiasts, try "antidisestablishmentarianism."

Third, using the general principle "things equal to the same thing are equal to each other," one may substitute words of equal value for one another. Thus: LEEK (= 30 + 5 + 5 + 20) = 60 = MAGIC; KELP (= 20 + 5 + 30 + 70) = 125 = PEN; etc. What words are the gematric equivalents of your name?

Of course, al-Botini did not do any gematria with our alphabet. He knew no English, and latinic letters were not the mode of God's creative speech. Rather, al-Botini used the Hebrew letters, and a chart of those letters plus their numerical values is given in Fig. 4. This technique of gematria, once one gets used to it, is enormously flexible. One can assign value not just to words but to whole Biblical verses. One can then substitute whole words and phrases, some of them with very suggestive meanings. If one then combines gematria with "separating" and "permutation," the limit is only the skill and patience of the "worker."

Text

1a: HHXMH,* KH H'DM, MKH H'D†
1b: YHYH VHVH VHYH,‡ MGLH,§ HGLM
1c: (MLT),‖ HLM, LHM, LULBY, LYUBL, XH LB HY, "H,
        HG", G"H, 'GD"

1א: החכמה, כח האדם, מכח האד

1ב: יהיה והוה והיה, מגלה, הגלם

1ג: (מלת, וצ"ל: מלח), חלם, לחם, לולבי,
     ליובל, כח לב חי, עח, הגע, געה, אגדע

---

*Al-Botini begins with the world *ha-hoxmah,* meaning "the wisdom." Then he "separates" *ha-hoxmah* into XH HMH (read as: *koah ha-mah,* "the power of the what"). The reference is probably to the Zoharic sefira Hokhma, also called *mah* ("what-ness"). So much for the technique of "separating" *(perud).* Al-Botini now converts XH HMH into its gematria: 20 + 8 + 5 + 40 + 5 = 78. He substitutes 'DM (read: *Adam*) = 45 for MH (read: *mah,* "what") and arrives at XH H'DM (read: *koah ha-'adam,* "the power of man"). The process is now complete: HHXMH ("the wisdom") by separating yields XH HMH ("the power of what-ness," the sefira Hokhma); this term, by gematric summing and substitution, yields XH H'DM ("the power of Adam" or "of man"). The technique is elegant and the sequence of ideas very suggestive.

†This third term is derived from the second by permutation. Its suggestive meaning is "from the power of the vapor [of Creation]" (Gen. 2:6). Note how, in one line, al-Botini has "leaped" from technique to technique.

‡This is one term with three words. They mean: "He will be; He is; and He was." Together, they have the gematria of 78 and, hence, continue the gematria set in the preceding line.

§This term, too, has a gematria of 78. It means: "he who reveals." The next term, as you can see, is derived by permutation.

‖All the terms in this line have a gematria of 78. If we emend the first term to MLH (a small orthographic change), it too will equal 78. Note that some terms have more than one word. Note, too, that two pairs are also permutations. Do you see them?

3. Introductory Note

Al-Botini here demonstrates two new techniques: "jumping" and "filling-out." "Jumping" is a technique already known to us. It is the technique by which we form acronyms. For example: SALT = Strategic Arms Limitation Talks; NEH = National Endowment for the Humanities; etc. Al-Botini, however, adds three variations that we do not usually use. First, one can form an acronym by combining the terminal letters. Using the two examples above, we would get CSNS and LTS, respectively. Second, one can form an acronym by combining medial letters. Again, using the two examples above and combining the third letters of each term, we would get RMML and TDM, respectively. Third, one can combine methods of acronym-formation. Using the initial *and* final acronyms on our two examples, we would get SALTCSNS and NEHLTS, respectively. I am afraid that too many people in Washington would have loved al-Botini.

To "fill-out" a letter, one simply spells out the name of the letter. Thus, the letter *D* is called "dee," and to "fill-out" that letter is to write: DEE. The letter *M* is called "em" and is "filled-out" as EM. Again, al-Botini was not concerned with our alphabet but with the Hebrew alphabet because the Torah is in Hebrew. In Fig. 4, all the letters with their names are listed.

Text

1a:	'GD" QRNY R'MYM*
1b:	QUF RŠ,† QŠR FU, QU ŠRF
1c:	QRYM‡
1d:	HRQMH,§ HMQRH

1א: אגדע קרני ראמים

1ב: קוף רש, קשר פו, קו שרף

1ג: קרים

1ד: הרקמה, המקרה

---

*Taking the last term of the previous series, the author "leaps" to a verse. Actually, he has distorted the verse, which reads: *ve-qarney reshaᶜim 'agadeᶜa* ["I shall cut off the horns of the wicked"] (Ps. 75:11), by reading: "I shall cut off the horns of the Re'em." The horns of the Re'em, whatever animal it may be, are actually a source of blessing (e.g., Deut. 33:17, Ps. 22:22), and the author has "slipped" in his association.

†The author now "jumps" through the term *qarney re'emim* and extracts the initial letters [i.e., forms an acronym] of each word [q, r]. He then "fills them out"—i.e., writes out their names *qof, resh*. The five letters of these two terms are then permuted, each permutation having a meaning: "the knot of his mouth" and "a burning line," respectively.

‡The author returns to *qarney re'emim*, takes the initial letters (q, r) *and* the final letters (y, m) and forms a new word, *qarym*, which has a numerical value of 350.

§This is a gematria for the preceding term with a value of 350. How is the last term generated?

4. Introductory Note

Al-Botini's numerological and alphabetological techniques are very complex and there are many more of them. I have skipped the rest of them and present here a sequence whose content is astounding. To understand what happened, you must remember that the purpose of these techniques is to dissociate the mind from rational thought. Now, when one does that, one creates a good situation for free association and projective thinking. Sometimes the results, as here, are very strange.

Al-Botini began with the word for "evil impulse" and moved to "the oppressor of the Jews" (i.e., Haman). Working again from "evil impulse," he arrived at "Darius," a name with messianic significance (Dan., chap. 6; etc.). The sequence then continued: "the dwelling of Jesus," "the dwelling of the gods of the nobility of the land," "and Miriam," "he is [in] rebellion," "she is Mamre [another messianic name]," "the essence [or, bone] of the food," and "a clever profaner." "Miriam" is, of course, Mary. And "the essence of the food" is a reference to the eucharist. What a strange associative sequence for a Jewish mystic! Yet the evidence is there: several distinctly christological "leaps." To be sure, not all Jewish mystics (and scribes) were happy with these associations, either because they were explicitly christological and hence were out of place, or because one could construe these associations as derogatory ("he is [in] rebellion," "clever profaner," and "they shall prostitute [sic] themselves after the gods [sic] of the nobility of the land"). An attempt was therefore made, in parallel texts, to delete and to cover up the most explicit reference by changing one permutation from "the dwelling place of Jesus" to "there is a generation." This change destroyed the associative rhythm and, of course, deleted the most explicit of the christological references. Al-Botini's version was one of edited texts; the original appears elsewhere and is cited by Scholem in the footnotes to the published Hebrew text.

Text

1a: YṢR R", ṢRR HYHVDYM*
1b: YUD RŠ,† DRYUŠ, YŠ DUR, DR 'LHY NXR‡
1c: YUD RŠ, DRYUŠ, DR YŠU,§ DR 'LH[Y] NXR, H'RṢ
1d: UMRYM, HU MMRH, HY MMR', "ṢM HM'XL,‖ MḤLL
        FQḤ

‏1א: יצר רע,   צרר היהודים‏

‏1ב: יוד רש,   דריוש,   יש דור,   דר אלהי נכר‏

‏1ג: יוד רש,   דריוש,   דר ישו,   דר אלהי נכר,‏
‏   הארץ‏

‏1ד: ומרים,   הו ממרה,   הי ממרא,   עצם המאכל,‏
‏   מחלל פקח‏

---

*"Leaping" from *yeṣer* of the previous series (omitted here), the author comes to *yeṣer ra"* ["evil impulse"] and by gematria to "the oppressor of the Jews" [i.e., Haman, Esther 9:10]—a very nice association, in addition to being a gematria of 570.

†Al-Botini now "jumps" through *yeṣer ra*ᶜ to form an acronym of the initial letters (*y, r*). He then "fills-in" those letters (i.e., spells out the names of the letters). The next two terms are permutations. The first is read *daryavesh* and is the Hebrew for "Darius" (see above).

‡This term is derived by gematria. It equals 502 and, hence, equals the other terms in this line. The final two words of this term are *'elohey neikhar* and are derived from Deut. 31:16, "And this people will arise and will prostitute itself after the gods of the nobility of the land."

§If you examine carefully, you will note that line 1c is almost a duplicate of line 1b. Actually, it is a parallel text drawn from a different source and it contains three variants: (1) this (i.e., the third) term, (2) the missing letter Y later on in this line, and (3) the term H'RṢ added at the end. The missing letter Y is easiest to account for: The scribe of that text simply skipped it, so I have supplied it and indicated that by putting it in brackets. The additional term H'RṢ is also not hard to account for: It is the concluding word of the phrase from Deut. 31:16—*'elohey neikhar ha-'areṣ* (". . . of the land"). From the point of view of the gematria, however, H'RṢ belongs in line 1d because it, and each of the other terms in that line, has a value of 296. This (i.e., the third) term is, as you can see, a simple permutation of *daryavesh*, "Darius." It is read *dar yeshu*, "the dwelling place of Jesus," and it is the first of the christological associations. The parallel term in line 1b reads *yesh dor*, "there is a generation." It is a perfectly good permutation of *daryavesh*, "Darius." However, by using it, the author (or scribe) changed the associative sequence from: ". . . Jesus . . . of the land . . . Miriam . . .," etc., to: "there is a generation, . . . of the land . . . Miriam . . .," etc. The author (or scribe) thus interrupted the christological association and, at the same time, deleted the most explicitly Christian reference—all by a simple permutation.

‖This is read *'eṣem ha-ma'axal*, "the essence [or, bone] of the food," and it is a reference to the eucharist. The next term is read *meḥallel piqeaḥ*, "a clever profaner," and it probably refers to Jesus, in which case it is derogatory. It may, however, refer to the mystic, in which case it is laudatory.

* * * *

He[5] could have created many more words, according to the limits of the phrase, but he only wanted to show us the methods of "leaping" and "permutation" and what he could do with them.

Then, in the tenth sequence, we return to the permutation of many gematriot by the above-mentioned Ways of "dividing" and "combining" in order to complete that which is the meaning of [all] this by stating "that power comes to the intellect of man from the Shechina and that everything must be done with wisdom."[6] For if one does not do all these "permutations" and "leapings" with wisdom, understanding, knowledgeability, with delicacy of the mind, with the simplification of the intellect from the material forces, and with a strong passion for studying this science and knowledge, he will not achieve the degree of perfection which he merits. But if he gives his heart over to isolating himself, to probing deeply, and to understanding the profundity of the matter and its root using these Ways, he will certainly come to know that the nature of the letters—their "permutation" and their "transmutation"—together with their [accompanying] movements and vocalizations (which I am going to explain in the next chapter) are the very teachers of man [which instruct him] in knowledge and insight, and which reveal to him the secrets of the Torah and the mysteries of Wisdom. They [i.e., the twenty-two letters of the Hebrew alphabet] are the very angels which appeared to the prophets in prophetic visions, for from the twenty-two letters and their "permutations" and "transmutations," the angels [themselves] were created and all created beings were made. Furthermore, as it is the nature of fire to warm and of water to cool, so is it the nature of the letters themselves to do all manner of creation and request for those who "mention" them in wisdom and knowledge. In this matter, the Ari [Rabbi Isaac Luria], may his memory be a blessing, said, "Bezalel [the architect of the Tabernacle] knew how to permute letters, for by them the heavens and the earth were created." Similarly, all the other prophets and pious men in every generation were able to make miracles and do wonders, upsetting the order of Genesis, by means of the "permutation" and "transmutation" of the letters with their [accompanying] movements, as is stated in our holy Talmud that Rava created a man and sent him to R. Zera . . . [Talmud, *Sanhedrin* 65b].

I return now to complete this chapter with a summary explanation of

---

[5]This reference to a third person, plus the fact that al-Botini's text for the christological "leap" was not the original text, makes it almost certain that al-Botini was not the author of these permutations. It is most probable that he only copied and explained them. I have omitted here his lengthy explanations, substituting my own notes, although mine are, of course, based on his. The text resumes here.

[6]This sequence is not presented here. Al-Botini goes on to explain that these techniques, together with those in the next chapter, enabled prophets to prophesy and rabbis to do miracles. Note the shift back into the philosophic mystical language: "intellect," "passion," "isolating himself," "knowledge," etc.

"leaping," and I say that if you examine closely that which was newly presented in this chapter concerning "leaping and jumping," you will find that "leaping" is a category with two types. The first is the extracting of letters—as they are, i.e., initial, medial, and final letters, or as they [result from the] mixing of the initial with the medial, the medial with the final, or the final with the initial letters—in order to build out of these actual letters other names, words, permutations, and gematriot either by "necessary permutation" or by "dividing and combining," or by "exchange," "substitution," "hewing out," or "balancing." The second [type] is the extracting of one or two or more letters from a single word or from several words [followed by] the complete or partial spelling out of the names of these letters in order to build and permute from those extracted letters, to invent and to innovate other names and words, and, furthermore, [in order] to "leap" among them from one of the aforementioned Ways to another by means of a letter or a word generated by the spelling out of some or all of the letters.

Using these rules, one whom God has favored with wisdom and knowledge is able to expand his intellect, to float on the sea of wisdom, to write books endlessly by virtue of his expanded intellect, and to attain to perfection according to his capacity and effort. Even though the subject matter of this chapter on the types of "leaping" is profound, and [even though] it is difficult to practice at first thought, know for certain that if a man is alert, quick, and very practiced in using those Ways mentioned in the preceding chapters, it will be very easy for him to use the Way of "leaping" and to accustom himself to it and to the other Ways by writing them down in ink, in a book, many times. So much so that the time [will come when] they will be habits of speech, tongue, and intellect—just as a man is accustomed to recite the verses of the *Shema* which he has learned and grown accustomed to since his youth. [Then] he will not find it necessary any more to write them down in real ink, with real paper and quill. Rather, he will "permute" and "transmute" them in his thoughts as the High Priest would do when "mentioning" the Tetragrammaton together with its "permutations" and "transmutations," for he would "permute" and "transmute" in his intellect and thought while his mouth and tongue [functioned] externally, and he did not have to write it down or even read it from a book. All this is an easy matter for him who perseveres for a while in this skill, providing he has [made] the necessary preparations for this work—all or some of them—as we shall explain [in Chapter Ten] with the help of God, may He be praised.[7]

---

[7] Al-Botini ends by assuring the reader that "practice makes perfect," and that one can eventually acquire enough skill to perform these functions mentally. Note his interpretation of the Priestly Blessing—that while reciting it [Num. 6:24–26], the High Priest must be "permuting and transforming" it in his mind. (On "transforming," see below.)

THE NINTH CHAPTER, which deals with something of the Ways of the vowel-sounds, the imaging of them in the inner heart, and the method of [accompanying] movements of the head and the external limbs.[1]

From this [chapter], you will have knowledge of a wondrous matter concerning the "mentioning of the holy Names" as they were "mentioned" by the High Priest at the time of the Temple or by the saints and the pious ones who made use of the holy Names—how they would "mention" them, their vowel-sounds, and their [accompanying] movements. But, before this explanation, you must know that the vowel-sound of a letter is, so to speak, as a soul to it, and it [i.e., the sound] "moves" it [i.e., the letter]. And if you would wish to pronounce any letter without its vowel-sound, this would be impossible because of the nature of the reality of speech, for "sound, breath (spirit), and speech is the Holy Spirit." "Sound" is divisible into five units by means of the "breath," while "speech" is encompassed by both of them in the following manner.

Know[2] that the origin of all the vowel-sounds of speech as they proceed from the mouth consists of only five sounds, no more. And these are they: "O", "A", "EI", "I", "OO". The mnemonic symbol therefore is *NŌṬĀRĒĪYĪQŌŌN,* and they are also to be found in two words from the Torah: *PĪTŌŌḤĒI ḤŌTĀM* [Exod. 28:11]. You will also find that the names of each of the twenty-two letters of the alphabet are also encompassed by these five types of enunciated sounds, and they [i.e., the letters]

---

[1]Having taught in the previous chapter a set of mind-freeing techniques which were numerological and alphabetological in nature, al-Botini now sets about explaining the rules for breathing and the intonation of words. These techniques, too, will generate a mystical state. However, they are also meant to be used during the mystical trance. We shall see for what ends. To understand this technique, we will need to know some medieval grammatical theory, and this will be explained below. Note that the Way of intonation and breathing taught here is called "mentioning the holy Names." Al-Botini means that the words to be intoned are the Names of God in various permutations and transformations. The term "mentioning" (Heb., *hazkarah*) is the same term as that referred to by Maimonides (cf. above, p. 13). Maimonides, however, probably had in mind the technique of repeating the same phrase over and over, while al-Botini intends something completely different, as we shall see.

[2]The following are the relevant rules of medieval Hebrew grammar as understood by al-Botini (other grammarians had variations): (1) There are twenty-two letters in the Hebrew alphabet. Each is a consonant. Consonants alone, however, cannot be "pronounced"; one needs vowels. (If you doubt that, try to "pronounce" the following: bkth.) (2) In writing a Hebrew word, one uses supplementary signs which are written below, above, or between the consonants to indicate the appropriate vowel-sound. Theoretically, any vowel-sound could be used with any consonant-letter. (3) There are five "primary" vowel-sounds and four "secondary" vowel-sounds. (These, together with their pronunciations, names, and sigla, have been set forth in Fig. 5. The reader must know thoroughly the names, sigla, and pronunciations of the five primary vowel-sounds.

English Symbol	Hebrew Symbol	Pronounced as	Name
O	וֹ	*o* in "hole"	ḥolam
A	ָ	*a* in "father"	qameṣ
EI	ֵ	*a* in "hay"	ṣeire
I	ִ	*e* in "weed"	ḥiriq
OO	ֻ	*oo* in "food"	shuruq*
A	ַ	*o* in "pot"	pataḥ
(none)	ְ	sound of the consonant	sheva
E	ֶ	*e* in "pet"	segol
OO	וּ	*oo* in mid-Western "roof"	shuruq

*Later called, kubuṣ.

Fig. 5. THE HEBREW VOWEL-SOUNDS

55

are pronounced with them.[3] Two of the letters have the vowel ḤOLAM [in their letter-names] and are read with an ["O"]: YŌD and QŌF. [Ten of the letters have the vowel] PATAḤ [and are read with] "A", either as a QAMEṢ [i.e., long "A"] or as a PATAḤ [i.e., short "A"]: 'Ā[LEPH], DĀ[LED], VĀ[V], ZĀ[YIN], KĀ[F], LĀ[MED], SĀ[MEKH], 'Ā[YEN], ṢĀ[DEI], TĀ[F]. And seven have the vowel "EI", as a ṢEIRE [i.e., long] or as a SEGOL [i.e., short] or as a SHEVA [i.e., very short]: BĒI[T], HĒI, ḤĒI[T] ṬĒI[T], MĒI[M], PĒI, RĒI[SH]. Their origin is from one [source] as will be explained. Two [letters] have the vowel "I" as a ḤIRIQ: SHĪ[N], GĪ[MEL]. And one has the vowel "OO" as a SHURUQ and is read with an "OO": NŪ[N]. This [reading of a letter(-name) with its appropriate vowel-sound] is called "vocalization appropriate to the letter," meaning that the letter is enunciated by the mouth. Thus, speech which is according to the vowel-sound itself, as it is read,—for example, [in saying] YŌD, QŌF as they are vocalized with an "O"—is called "vocalization appropriate to the letter." But when they [i.e., the letters] are vocalized with one of the other four vowel-sounds, it is not called "vocalization appropriate to the pronunciation of the letter."[4] After one has realized that [all] the origins of speech are encompassed by these five vowels and [their] sounds, know too that there are [actually] nine vowel-sounds. In all the letters of the Torah: the five original [i.e., primary] vowel sounds which we have already mentioned: ḤOLAM, QAMEṢ, ṢEIRE, ḤIRIQ, SHURUQ (when written with three dots). The other four, which are encompassed by the original enunciation of the five aforementioned [sounds] are: PATAḤ, SHEVA, SEGOL, SHURUQ (when written as a dot in the letter [VAV]). This SHURUQ is also called "the mouthful."[5]

After this, know that the matter of the "movement"[6] of the letter by the vowel in the inner heart and in the external limb is as follows: Note that when the High Priest, or the other prophets, or the righteous men[7] who

---

[3]Since every letter has a name (see Fig. 4) and every letter-name is a word, every letter-name itself contains consonants and vowel-sounds. Al-Botini now proceeds to group the letter-names according to their primary vowel-sounds. (The words in brackets are supplied by me to give some continuity to this very elliptic passage.)

[4]Al-Botini distinguishes, then, between reading a letter with the primary vowel-sound of its letter-name (e.g., "Y" plus "O") and reading a letter with any other vowel-sound (e.g., "Y" plus "A" or "EI"). The latter is the basis of this chapter.

[5]Look at Fig. 5 and you will see why. Al-Botini regards the "secondary" vowel-sounds as derivative from the "primary." He does not explain this, though the usual theory is that the "secondary" vowel-sounds are "short" while the "primary" sounds are "long."

[6]Al-Botini now proceeds to the heart of his chapter: the "movement" (Heb., ni'nu'a, sometimes: tenu'a) of the letters by the vowels. To understand this, the reader must know: (1) that the symbol for each vowel has a shape, and (2) that this shape indicates how to move one's head while pronouncing the vowel. The instructions are not difficult; try to follow them.

[7]Note who is included here.

use the holy Names—or when you, the "worker," "mention" any letter vocalized with a ḤOLAM ["O"; it looks like this: וֹ], direct and awaken your heart and your inner intellect, and move your head as if drawing the vowel-sound as follows: Do not move your head at all, not to the right, nor to the left, nor up, nor down. Rather, set your head into equipoise as though it were in the balance dish of a scale, in the manner in which [you would set it] if you were talking to someone as tall as you, equally, face to face. Afterwards, as you draw out the "movement" of the letter while "mentioning" it, move your head upwards toward heaven. Close your eyes and open your mouth so that your words radiate light. Clear your throat of all phlegm so that it not interrupt the "mentioning" of the letter. The upward movement shall be according to the extent of your breath such that your breath and your head-movement cease together. Thus, the movement for the ḤOLAM ["O"] is to move your head continually upwards as if you were proclaiming your Creator as King far above all the supernal beings.[8]

The QAMEṢ ["A"] is like a straight line, written by a scribe from left to right, and under the line is a dot [it looks like this: ⫶]. When you "mention" it with any letter, move your head first toward your left shoulder and pronounce the letter in a beautiful tone and with a pleasant voice. Then move your head from left to right, in [one] plane, in the form of a straight line, as the vocalizer set it down. Then move your head back to face the East, which is in front of you, toward which you are "mentioning" the Name, for your face must be toward the East, or toward the Sanctuary, as one who recites the Silent Devotion. Then bow your head down a little, so this downward movement corresponds to the dot which is under the line of the aforementioned QAMEṢ. Do the whole aforementioned movement in one breath as I instructed you above. The result is that the movement of the QAMEṢ is from left to right, after which the head returns to the middle and bows slightly as if you were proclaiming your Creator as King from the North to the South and over the nethermost beings.[9]

The ṢEIRE ["EI"] has two dots, [one] sitting over on the right and one on the left [. .]. When you "mention" it with any letter, begin "mention-

---

[8]The instructions, then, are as follows: (1) Set your face directly forward. (2) Clear your throat, take a not-too-deep breath, and close your eyes. (3) Begin pronouncing the letter "O". (4) Continue pronouncing the sound "O" *and* move your head upwards. (5) Continue pronouncing and moving until you run out of breath. (6) Return to "start" position, with face directly forward. You must practice it privately a few times. When you can do it without too much concentration on the mechanics, add the most important ingredient: Proclaim God as King in the upper worlds.

[9]Steps (1), (2), and (6) are the same. The instructions for steps (3)–(5) are clear. When you have mastered the mechanics, add the spiritual, inner, mental dynamics. Note that the "start" position faces East.

ing'' the letter by moving your head from right to left, the opposite of the straight line of the QAMEṢ, for the QAMEṢ is [really] ''the great QAMEṢ,'' while the ṢEIRE is [really] ''the minor QAMEṢ.'' The result is as if you were proclaiming God to be King from the South to the North.

The ḤIRIQ [''Y''] is one dot underneath a letter [·], and when you ''mention'' it with any letter, move your head downward in the form of a bow before God, may He be praised, with Whom you speak and Who stands before you. [This is] the opposite of the [movement for the] ḤOLAM, and it is as if you were proclaiming Him King over the nethermost beings.

The SHURUQ [''OO''], which is composed of a dot in the middle of the letter [VAV], and which is called ''the mouthful'' [looks like thisּ]. When you ''mention'' it with any letter, set yourself straight [forward] and start to move your head, evenly, forward. From the setting of yourself straight [forward] until the finishing of the movement of your neck backwards, [do it all] as evenly as you can. Neither raise your head nor lower it. Do not move it to the right or to the left; only forward and backward, in a straight line as if you were proclaiming God, may He be praised, as King from East to West. The result is that, with the ''movements'' of these five vowel-sounds, you have proclaimed your Creator as King in the six directions of the Cosmos: East, West, North, South, Above, and Below—above and below in forming the vowel sounds ''O'' and ''I,'' front and back in forming the ''OO'', and right and left in forming ''A'' and ''EI''.

The PATAḤ[10] [''A''; it looks like this: —] is, in its movement, like the straight line of the QAMEṢ from left to right. The SHEVA, which is two dots, one above the other [:], has two types of movements: the upper dot follows the rule of the ḤOLAM [i.e., upward], and the lower dot [follows the rule of] the ḤIRIQ [i.e., downward]. The SEGOL [which looks like this: ·.·] has two dots sitting one to the right and one to the left, and they follow the rule of the ṢEIRE from right to left, [while] the third dot, which is beneath them, follows the rule of the ḤIRIQ, to bow downward. [As to] the SHURUQ, which is of three dots one above the other in a diagonal line [·.·]: the uppermost dot follows the rule of the ḤOLAM [i.e., upward], the middle dot follows the rule of the SHURUQ made up of one dot [in the letter, VAV], i.e., frontward and backward, and the lowest dot follows the rule of ḤIRIQ [i.e., downward]. All these movements have been well explained.

The following is an important rule for you to have in hand when ''moving'' these vowel-sounds to [help] you remember and not to err:

---

[10]Al-Botini now proceeds to the ''secondary'' vowel-sounds. He does not use them later, however.

You must do the movements of the vowel-sound as the scribe has written it. It is known that the scribe begins the line of the QAMEṢ and the PATAḤ from left to right; that for the two dots of the ṢEIRE and the SEGOL, he writes the right one first, then the left, and then the one beneath them [for the SEGOL]; that for the SHEVA, he writes the upper dot first and then the lower; and that for the SHURUQ, which is of three dots, he orders and writes them from the top to the bottom.

Having explained to you the Ways of the vowel-sounds and their [accompanying] "movements," I shall make known to you a deep and great secret concerning the "mentioning" of the form of its enunciation—the "compounding" of the vowel-sound with it [i.e., the letter]—as I have found it written in the books of the kabbalists and those "who isolate themselves."[11] I shall begin to "compound" the vowel-sounds of the word [which is] a Name of God, 'ADONAY, divided into two units of two letters, forwards and backwards according to the sequence NŌṬĀRĒĪYĪQŌŌN which is the proper recitatioh. The secret is that if we were to "compound" [the sounds of] three letters, the permutation would yield a large number, and even more so, were we to "compound" [the sounds of] all of the four letters of the Name ['DNY], many books would not be sufficient [to contain all the permutations].[12] The purpose [here] is only to comment upon the roots [of the matter], and then, automatically, the branches thereof will be known to those who understand.

[As in the preceding chapter, the text here continues with several lines of permutations. Once again, in order to make this material accessible to the reader, I have arranged it in tabular form with an introductory explanation. The narrative resumes on p. 62.]

1. The "Movement" of 'DNY: Introductory Note

Al-Botini's method here is the following: (1) He takes the four letters 'DNY and divides them into pairs: 'D and NY. (2) He then manipulates each pair "forwards and backwards" so: 'D and D' plus NY and YN, generating thereby four pairs of letters. (3) He then combines each pair of letters with the five primary vowel-sounds: "O," "A," "EI," "I," and

---

[11]Having learned the "movements" of the vowel-sounds, we must now learn how to combine vowel-sound movements with consonant-letters. Al-Botini could use, for demonstration purposes, any set of letters with any set of vowel-sound movements. He chooses, however, a set of letters which forms a word, and a special word at that. He chooses the letters 'DNY, which form the word 'Adonay, which is one of God's Names. (Note: the letter " ' " is a glottal stop, which is a slight constriction of the throat before emitting a sound. It is the position of the throat between the two "O's" in "cooperation" or before beginning the word "order".) Note the Maimonidean term, "who isolate themselves."
[12]See next page.

"OO." (4) He does this by varying one vowel-sound in each pair while keeping the other vowel-sound constant (see line 1 below). (5) He then rotates the constant vowel-sound until all possible combinations have been expressed (see lines 2–5 below). (6) He then takes a new pair of letters and begins all over again (see lines 6–10). (7) He continues until all possible vowel-sound combinations and letter-consonant pairs have been expressed. (For the original Hebrew version of the chart, see Fig. 6.)

Given al-Botini's rules here, there are 4×5^2 ($= 100$) possible combinations. Were he, however, to change the rules from: combining the letters 'DNY in pairs "forwards and backwards," to: combining 'DNY in all possible four-letter combinations, he would have $4^4 \times 5^5$ ($= 800,000$) possible combinations. As he has just said, "many books would not be sufficient [to contain all the permutations]." (At 100 combinations per chart, it would take 8,000 charts! Even my very understanding publisher would not agree to that.)

In all this, the reader must remember that this chart is to be recited!! The mathematics is incidental. To recite it, start with the letter "'" (i.e., with a glottal stop) and follow the steps for the "movement" of the vowel-sound "O." Then start again with the letter "D" and follow the steps for "O." You have "moved" the letters of one pair. Now do 'O and then DA (using the qameṣ, the long "a"). Continue with 'O and DEI. And so on, for all one hundred pairs. (It does take time.) Don't forget to "proclaim God as King" in each of the proper directions, i.e., don't get so tangled up in the mechanics that you forget the inner mystical dynamics. Later, al-Botini adds in the breathing instructions and guidance on what to do when you make an error.

Text

[letters: 'D]*
  'ODO 'ODA 'ODEI 'ODI 'ODOO
  'ADA 'ADEI 'ADI 'ADOO 'ADO
  'EIDEI 'EIDI 'EIDOO 'EIDO 'EIDA
  'IDI 'IDOO 'IDO 'IDA 'IDEI
  'OODOO 'OODO 'OODA 'OODEI 'OODI

[letters: D']
  DO'O DO'A DO'EI DO'I DO'OO
  DA'A DA'EI DA'I DA'OO DA'O
  DEI'EI DEI'I DEI'OO DEI'O DEI'A
  DI'I DI'OO DI'O DI'A DI'EI
  DOO'OO DOO'O DOO'A DOO'EI DOO'I

---

*For the Hebrew, see Fig. 6.

The "Movement" of 'DNY

	אֹד אָד אֵד אִד אֻד	דֹא דָא דֵא דִא דֻא
	אָד אֵד אִד אֻד אֹד	דָא דֵא דִא דֻא דֹא
	אֵד אִד אֻד אֹד אָד	דֵא דִא דֻא דֹא דָא
	אִד אֻד אֹד אָד אֵד	דִא דֻא דֹא דָא דֵא
	אֻד אֹד אָד אֵד אִד	דֻא דֹא דָא דֵא דִא
	נֹי נָי נֵי נִי נֻי	ינ ינ ינ ינ ינ
	נָי ני ני ני ני	ינ ינ ינ ינ ינ
סוד	ני ני ני ני ני	ינ ינ ינ ינ ינ
כדלעיל	ני ני ני ני ני	ינ ינ ינ ינ ינ
	ני ני ני ני ני	ינ ינ ינ ינ ינ

The "Transformation" of the Tetragrammaton

צורת הזכרת א׳ עם אות הראשון של השם הא׳ פנים ואחור.

אֹי אָי אֵי אִי אֻי [17]	יֹא יָא יא יא יא
אי אי אי אי אי	יא יא יא יא יא
אי אי אי אי אי	יא יא יא יא יא
אי אי אי אי אי	יא יא יא יא יא
אי אי אי אי אי	יא יא יא יא יא

צורת הזכרת אל״ף עם ה״א פנים ואחור

אֹה אה אה אה אה	הא הא הא הא הא
אה אה אה אה אה	הא הא הא הא הא
אה אה אה אה אה	הא הא הא הא הא
אה אה אה אה אה	הא הא הא הא הא
אה אה אה אה אה	הא הא הא הא הא

צורת הזכרת אלף עם וא״ו פנים ואחור והנקו׳ כדלעיל

אֹו אָו או או או	וא וא וא וא וא
או או או או או	וא וא וא וא וא
או או או או או	וא וא וא וא וא
או או או או או	וא וא וא וא וא
או או או או או	וא וא וא וא וא

[14ב] צורת הרכבת א׳ עם הא אחרונה פנים ואחור והנקו׳ כנז׳

אֹה אָה אה אה אה	הא הא הא הא הא
אה אה אה אה אה	הא הא׳הא הא הא
אה אה אה אה אה	הא הא הא הא הא
אה אה אה אה אה	הא הא הא הא הא
אה אה אה אה אה	הא הא הא הא הא

Fig. 6. THE ORIGINAL HEBREW CHARTS

[letters: NY]
  NOYO   NOYA   NOYEI   NOYI   NOYOO
  NAYA   NAYEI   NAYI   NAYOO   NAYO
  NEIYEI   NEIYI   NEIYOO   NEIYO   NEIYA
  NIYI   NIYOO   NIYO   NIYA   NIYEI
  NOOYOO   NOOYO   NOOYA   NOOYEI   NOOYI

[letters: YN]
  YONO   YONA   YONEI   YONI   YONOO
  YANA   YANEI   YANI   YANOO   YANO
  YEINEI   YEINI   YEINOO   YEINO   YEINA
  YINI   YINOO   YINO   YINA   YINEI
  YOONOO   YOONO   YOONA   YOONEI   YOONI

*   *   *   *   *

Thus, the Way of the root and the beginning of vocalization is complete
in compounding two letters to build two "words," for you know from
Chapter One that two letters build two words. And by "compounding"
upon them [i.e., the two letters] the vowel-sounds of the five units of the
aforementioned NŌṬĀRĒĪYĪQŌŌN [O, A, EI, I, OO], fifty "words"
have been built: twenty-five forwards and twenty-five backwards, and no
one is the same as any other. Know that this sequence contains the secret
of the "transformation" of the Ineffable Name. I mean that the first
"transformation" and "permutation" of the Name of Four Letters which
appears in the Torah is done also according to the sequence of these five
aforementioned vowel-sounds and units of NŌṬĀRĒĪYĪQŌŌN.[13] The
secret of "mentioning" it is to "transform" the letter 'ALEPH, which
points to true unity, into each one of the four letters of the Ineffable
Name, forwards and backwards, in the following manner.

[Here too I have provided a tabular arrangement of the material with
introductory explanation. The narrative resumes on p.64.]

2. The "Transformation" of the Tetragrammaton: Introductory Note

Al-Botini's method here is the following: (1) He takes the four letters of
the Tetragrammaton, YHVH, and combines each of them with the letter
aleph, ', so: 'Y, 'H, 'V, 'H. (2) He then manipulates them "forwards and
backwards," so: 'Y and Y'; 'H and H' and so on, generating eight pairs.

13Just as al-Botini drew up the material shown on p. 61 with the four letters of God's
Name 'Adonay, so, he says, we could draw up such a chart with the four letters of God's
most holy Name, the Tetragrammaton: YHVH. He, however, immediately moves away
from this suggestion and makes another. (This other suggestion is explained below.)

The technical term for this integration of the mystical letter aleph (= 1) with each of the letters of the Name of God is "transformation" (Heb., *gilgul*). (3) He then combines each pair of letters with the primary vowel-sounds and varies them as he did in the previous chart. (4) He continues until all the possible permutations and combinations have been expressed. Using the rule of pairs, al-Botini has 8×5^2 (= 200) possible combinations. Using the rule of all possible combinations, al-Botini would have $5^5 \times 5^5$ (= 9,765,625) possible combinations. Again, however, the mathematics is irrelevant. This is meant to be recited, syllable by syllable, pair by pair, line by line, group by group—and always with the proper "movements," breath control, and inner mystical dynamics.

Text

[letters: 'Y and Y']*
```
'OYO   'OYA   'OYEI   'OYI   'OYOO
'AYA   'Y   'Y   'Y   'Y
'EIYEI   'Y   'Y   'Y   'Y
'IYI   'Y   'Y   'Y   'Y
'OOYOO   'Y   'Y   'Y   'Y

YO'O   YO'A   YO'EI   YO'I   YO'OO
YA'A   Y'   Y'   Y'   Y'
YEI'EI   Y'   Y'   Y'   Y'
YI'I   Y'   Y'   Y'   Y'
YOO'OO   Y'   Y'   Y'   Y'
```

[letters: 'H and H']
```
'OHO   'OHA   'OHEI   'OHI   'OHOO
'AHA   'H   'H   'H   'H
'EIHEI   'H   'H   'H   'H
'IHI   'H   'H   'H   'H
'OOHOO   'H   'H   'H   'H

HO'O   HO'A   HO'EI   HO'I   HO'OO
HA'A   H'   H'   H'   H'
HEI'EI   H'   H'   H'   H'
HI'I   H'   H'   H'   H'
HOO'OO   H'   H'   H'   H'
```

---

*After the first line of each of these "blocks," the reader must supply the vowels following the proper sequence. For the Hebrew, see Fig. 6.

[letters: 'V and V']
  'OVO 'OVA 'OVEI 'OVI 'OVOO
  'AVA 'V 'V 'V 'V
  'EIVEI 'V 'V 'V 'V
  'IVI 'V 'V 'V 'V
  'OVOO 'V 'V 'V 'V

  VO'O VO'A VO'EI VO'I VO'OO
  VA'A V' V' V' V'
  VEI'EI V' V' V' V'
  VI'I V' V' V' V'
  VOO'OO V' V' V' V'

[letters: 'H and H']
(as above, the second "block")

* * * *

Thus for the secret of the permutation of this Name, know that the four general "mentionings" [*hazkarot*] which I have written down are jointly [compounded] of the aforementioned Ineffable Name and the letter 'ALEPH which, as mentioned earlier, is not part of the Name [itself] but points to the secret of [true] unity. I did not write out the above-mentioned permutation with the halves of the very Name itself [which would be] with YH and finally with VH, although it would be proper to transmute and permute it in this manner, so that the secret not be revealed to the masses in sensible form. Rather, I have left the matter hinted at to the enlightened ones. They will become radiant and will understand that, as I drew out the four forms from the four letters of the Name 'ADONAY, permuted above forwards and backwards, two letters by two, just so is the form, also from the very same vowel-sounds, for each half of the Ineffable Name, forwards and backwards thus: YH, HY and VH, HV.[14]

There is another thing which remains concerning which I might inform you to complete the secret of the "intention" of the aforementioned "mentioning" as follows: When you want to "mention" the first, revered Name 'ADONAY, or to "mention" the Ineffable Name of Four Letters either with the permutation of [the added] 'ALEPH as illustrated above or with half of the Tetragrammaton as I hinted at above, according to the above-mentioned sequence of vowel-sounds, it is fitting that, first, you dress yourself decoratively and that you isolate yourself in a special place

---

[14]This, as the purest and most holy of God's Names, would be the most efficacious Name to "mention." Al-Botini now goes on to describe briefly how one sets the stage, so to speak, for such activity. He does this more fully in Chapter Ten.

where no one can hear your voice. Then, purify your heart, soul, and thought from all thoughts of this world and think that now your soul is going to separate itself from your body, that you will die to this world and be alive in the supernal world, which is the source of life and [which is] the simple, spiritual Intelligence[15] of which all stand in awe—an awe of height and glory, and an awe of love. When your knowledge and intellect come to adhere to His knowledge (which, in turn, gives you your knowledge and intellect), your knowledge must remove from within it the yoke of all other knowledge of all other subjects. [Your knowledge must preserve] only that knowledge which is common to you and to Him according to His revered and awesome Name. When you wish to begin "mentioning" [this Name], set your face toward the East, for from there light goes forth to the world. Put on clean, washed, white clothing; wrap yourself in your prayer-shawl; and put phylacteries on your head and arm. Then begin to "mention" the Name, enunciating it in this manner:[16]

When you "mention" the letter 'ALEPH with whatever vocalization, it being a pointer toward the secret of unity, do not prolong [the pronunciation of the vowel-sound] more than for the length of one breath, without allowing any-size stop at all, until you complete its pronunciation. And prolong that particular breath as long as you are able to prolong one breath. Raise your voice a little in melody with a sweet tone and pleasing pronunciation, when you "mention" the aforementioned letter [i.e., 'ALEPH] or any of the other letters of the Name which you are "mentioning," with joy of soul and a good heart. Move your head with it [i.e., the vowel-sound], the form of the "movement" being the shape of the vowel-sound of the letter, as I have instructed you, such that you complete the movement of the head of the above-mentioned vowel-sound together with the completion of the recitation of the pronunciation of the letter, as I explained above.

Know that you are permitted to stop and to take, between the completion of the recitation of the 'ALEPH and the letter after it and similarly, between any [two] letters, only one short or long breath which you breathe between them. Then you must immediately return to "mention" the second letter which is adjacent to it and comes after it. But between each name of the aforementioned two letters [i.e., after each two-syllable unit], whether it be in the forward or backward [arrangement], for example between 'D and 'D or between D' and D' of the Name 'DNY or between 'Y and 'Y or between Y' and Y' of the aforementioned [ex-

---

[15]The Agent Intelligence (Active Intellect), which is the Tenth of the Intelligences, is meant. Note the return to the vocabulary of philosophic mysticism.

[16]Al-Botini, having instructed us on the technique of "moving" the consonants and vowels, now sets forth the rules for breathing.

panded form of the] Tetragrammaton, you may take only two breaths, no more, and you may not speak or think of anything. Do not let your attention be distracted from the matter you are occupied with. At the completion of each row of names [i.e., after five two-syllable units] as formed above, you may take five breaths only, no more, although you may take less.[17] If you make a mistake in the "mentioning" of one of these rows, go back to the beginning of that row until you say it properly and in order. Furthermore, between the block of [']Y and that of [']H or between the block of [']H and that of [']V or between that of [']V and that of the final [']H of the ["transformed"] Tetragrammaton [i.e., after each block of fifty names], you may take twenty-five breaths, no more than this, on the condition that you not break [the breathing and concentration] with speech or thought as I have warned you. If you wish to take less than twenty-five breaths, you may.

You[18] can see from that which I have written that the letter is something like matter, while the vowel-sound is something like form and spirit, which give motion to matter. And the comprehension of the moving [agent] and of that which is moved, as mentioned above, is the [Agent] Intelligence. It is called "Agent" because it "works" ["causes to act"] in the above-mentioned form and matter. Furthermore, the pleasure that he who comprehends receives in that which he comprehends is called the final [cause]. These, then, are the four causes: the material, the formal, the active [agent], and the final. The least of them is the material; the greatest and most elevated of them is the final; the active is close to the final, and the formal is close to the material.

Now that we have come this far, it is proper for us to write a warning[19] which has been issued by the greatest of the scholars and Kabbalists concerning the "mentioning" of Names, to wit: that it is proper and [indeed] obligatory upon every being born of woman not to make use of the crown of His kingdom. Similarly, the Sages, may their memory be a

---

[17]The first line of the chart on p. 60 reads: 'ODO 'ODA 'ODEI 'ODI 'ODOO. Using a slash to indicate one breath, that line should be written as follows: 'O/DO // 'O/DA // 'O/DEI // 'O/DI // 'O/DOO /////—i.e., one breath between "syllables," two breaths between "words," and five breaths at the end of each "line." As we shall see in a moment, one may take twenty-five breaths between "blocks" of letters.

[18]Al-Botini returns to the philosophic mystical vocabulary, interpreting the common matter-form dichotomy and the equally common four-causes-of-motion.

[19]Al-Botini, in these next paragraphs, deals with an issue which is very difficult for him. On the one hand, he knows (from experience?) that the mystic can perform so-called supernatural feats and also receive direct communication from God while in a trance. On the other hand, it is forbidden to pronounce the Tetragrammaton and certainly to use it magically. It is also the case that the Sages of Israel, who (for al-Botini) had such powers, did not in fact use them. May one, then, use the names in a trance, or not?

blessing, have warned us,[20] "He who pronounces the [Ineffable] Name according to its letters [has no share] in the World-to-Come," and, *a fortiori*, if sanctification of the Supernal Name [is intended]. Similarly, they warned us [that] Rabbi Ḥananiah ben Teradyon used to pronounce the Name in holiness and purity [in order] to learn, to teach, and to understand His ways, may He be praised, and not in order to use it, and nevertheless he was punished. What, then, can we who are poor, impoverished, and lacking in heart and knowledge do?

Do you not know that the Sages, may their memory be a blessing, possessed a true tradition from the prophets concerning the holy Names,[21] for example [concerning] the Name of Seventy-Two [letters] and the Name of Forty-Two [letters], as it is said in [the Talmud] *Kiddushin,* [and yet] they transmitted it only very rarely [and only] to a worthy and fitting person? Similarly, they were expert in the knowledge of the other Names, [for example] the Name of Twelve [letters, and they knew] the permutation of the Name of Four [letters] which is the source and fountain for all the other Names and titles [and which is the source] of the entire Torah. So much so that they had the power to innovate signs and wonders with them [i.e., the Names], and with them they could create a new heaven and a new earth, as [indeed] they, may their memories be a blessing, testified of Bezalel that he knew how to permute letters by which the heavens and the earth were created. Yet they never used them [i.e., the Names] for their own needs, only for an exceptional and great need, for example to sanctify God, may He be praised, in public and to save all Israel from severe decrees, as Moses, peace be upon him, stepped into the gap before Him to turn His anger from destruction. I mean to say that Moses, our Rabbi, saw the place of the gap and [saw] the destruction that was to come to destroy Israel, as it is written [Ps. 106:23], "And He had said He would destroy them, had it not been for Moses, His chosen one, who stepped into the gap," and [who], with the power of the Names of the Holy One, blessed be He, which he "mentioned" in his prayer,

---

[20]The two quotations are drawn from Talmud, *Avodah Zarah* 17b–18a, and they "prove" that one may not pronounce the Tetragrammaton. Rabbi Ḥananiah ben Teradyon was burned.

[21]There are four "Names" here: (1) the Tetragrammaton (YHVH), (2) the Name of Twelve Letters (Talmud, *Kiddushin* 71a; lost), (3) the Name of Forty-Two Letters (ibid.; said to be preserved in an extant forty-two-letter prayer), and (4) the Name of Seventy-Two Letters. This last Name is not talmudic but is from a slightly later period. It is formed by combining the letters of Exodus 14:19–21 (cf. Kasher, *Torah Sheleymah* 14:67 and 284–286 for a full chart of these combinations). On Bezalel, the architect of the Tabernacle, and his magical powers, cf. Talmud, *Berakhot* 55a. Al-Botini's point here is that there was such a tradition of the use of Names, but as he notes just below, there was also a tradition that one may not use them.

"turned His anger and wrath back to their place," lest they go forth to swallow, to destroy, and to annihilate the people of Israel. And even this, one is not permitted to do until after one knows (first) that the will of the Holy One, blessed be He, is such.

Know that the Ten Martyrs[22] could have saved themselves, and that they did not want [to die] until they [had] asked God. They [i.e., the angels] replied from behind the [heavenly] curtain to Rabbi Yishma'el, the High Priest, that they [i.e., the Ten Martyrs] were trapped in this, and then they martyred themselves. And who was greater than the craftsmen and smiths who went into exile with Jehoiachim, the King of Judah, during First Temple [times], and how many great teachers were there at the destruction of the Second Temple who could have saved Israel, Jerusalem, and the Temple from the hands of Nebuchadnezzar and Titus by their knowledge of, and "mentioning" of, the revered and awesome Name? Yet when they saw that it was the will of God, may He be praised, that the respective destructions [take place] in order to collect the debt of those who had rebelled against Him and His Torah, and who had rejected and refused to walk in the way of His statutes and judgments, they kept silent and responded no more. It is now clear to you that even for so great a thing as the saving of Israel, Jerusalem, and the Temple, [even] to keep the Shekhina from going into Exile, those righteous and pious men did not wish to use the Names of the Praised One, for they knew that it was not His Will, may He be praised, that it be so. For otherwise He, may He be praised, would never collect the debt of the wicked. This is hinted at in the verse, "I adjure you, daughters of Jerusalem, not to awaken or to arouse the love . . ." [Song of Songs 3:5] that even [concerning] the arousal of the coming of the Messiah, which is also a great, exceptional, and necessary matter for all the worlds, He has adjured the Sages and the righteous who know the secret of the Names of the Holy One, blessed be He, not to arouse this matter until they know that the will and desire of God, may He be praised, is that it be so.[23]

It is, therefore, fitting for anyone who draws near to this "Holy Work," after he has done all the fitting preparations that will be explained in the next chapter, and after he has attained the degree of "isolatedness" in the supernal [world], that he ask—and he will be answered yes when that is

---

[22]More examples of men who could have used the Names and did not. For the story of the Ten Martyrs, cf. *Encyclopaedia Judaica,* s.v. "Ten Martyrs, the." The rabbis understood "the craftsmen and smiths" who went into exile with Jehoiachim (II Kings 24:14) to be scholars.

[23]Not even the coming of the Messiah may be expedited through magic. What, then, may one do? Al-Botini proceeds with his answer. Note the philosophic mystical elements: "passionate desire to adhere" and, especially, that intellectual knowledge precedes, and yet is integral to, mysticism.

the answer, and no when that is the answer—concerning that which is true, modest, and just. Then he must ask [further], examine, and try to comprehend by means of a question—whether in a dream [state] or awake—whether he is permitted by heaven to "mention" the holy Names of the Holy One, blessed be He. And when he knows that it is His will, may He be praised, that it be so, then he may enter the Paradise of the "mentioning" of the aforementioned holy Names, after he has attained knowledge and understanding of the matter of the [true] existence of each Name, of the [true] intent of the essence of each Name, and of that to which it points, for this is that which will bring him to know and to recognize the grandeur of Him Who spoke and the world came into being. He will then be terrified, overawed before Him, and he will yearn, long, and passionately desire to adhere to Him, may He be praised, from within the knowledge of His Names. He will then be near to God, may He be praised. His prayer will be accepted, and of him one can recite the verse, "I exalt him because he has known My Name" [Ps. 91:14]. The verse does not say "because he 'mentions' My Name" but "because he has 'known' [My Name]." Learn from this that "knowing" the Names—their [true] existence, their essence, and their intent—is the principal matter. For after knowing this, with a little intellectual reflection upon them in thought only, without "mentioning" them, then, when he needs to do any "work" with the will of God, may He be praised, for His service or to sanctify His Name, then they will answer him immediately from heaven, as it is said, "He calls upon Me and I answer him" [Ps. 91:15], and it is written, "Before they call, I shall answer" [Isa. 65:24]. I mean to say that they will answer him even because of the thought he thinks and the concentration he has on the Name without his having "mentioned" it. And if he still must "mention" it, then the principles and matters we have written in this short work will be of help to him. And it is fitting that he know this, for this is a great principle and root in this matter. Know it.[24]

---

[24]One must have modest demands. One must have permission. And one's demands must be in the service of God. Only then may one "mention" the holy Names, i.e., recite the vowel and consonant permutations with the appropriate movements and inner spiritual dynamics. If one is very worthy, one need only concentrate one's thought on the question, without having to "mention" any Names.

THE TENTH CHAPTER on the explanation of the Ways of seclusion (*hitbodedut*) and adhesion (*devekut*), and [on] the preparations which are fitting for one who secludes himself such that he achieve the utmost in devotion, causing his soul to adhere to the Agent Intelligence *in actu* and the holy spirit to rest upon him.[1]

Know that the proper and necessary preparations for one who secludes himself so that he "find desirable things" [Eccl. 12:10], consist in making himself simple (*hafshata*)—i.e., that his intellect simplify itself from the material in all its aspects. First:[2] in the matter of the body, one needs to diminish the corporeal desires. In the matter of eating [for example], one should make it a practice to eat that which is small—small in quantity and great in quality—and to diminish the kinds of boiled foods and excess wine, as our rabbis, of blessed memory, have said, "Such is the way of the Torah," and so on [*Pirkei Avot* 6:4]. The intention is not that he shall have a life of pain [which would] trouble him. On the contrary, such things would keep him from achieving completeness. Rather, the intention is that, even if he have great wealth and extended reserves, it is proper that he not enjoy it except to support [the existence of] the soul in the body. He should also deprive his animalistic forces and not give them what they desire because, in their weakening, the soul will prevail and the intellect will leave the imprisonment of the animalistic forces and be actualized and will adhere to its Creator. Also in the matter of intercourse, it is proper to make oneself distant, as our rabbis, of blessed memory, have said, "A man should not be found [near] his wife as is a rooster" [Talmud, *Berakhot* 22a]. Rather, he should fulfill the commandment of cohabitation every Sabbath eve in great cleanliness and much purity. Furthermore, all his thoughts at that moment should be [directed toward] worshipping his Creator and adhering to the highest [form of] "joining" (*hibbūr*) as the wise men of the Kabbalah have explained [concerning] the secret of the "joining" and the unification of male and female in this matter.[3] For when his thought is of adhesion to the Highest, and it is as it is written in the Torah "and you shall walk in His ways" [Deut. 28:9], then that "joining" and his keeping that commandment in this way brings him to a high level

---

[1]Having devoted Chapter Eight to numerological and alphabetological techniques, and having devoted Chapter Nine to intonation and breathing techniques, al-Botini is now ready to present the full range of his special type of mysticism. He calls it the Way of Seclusion (or Self-isolation) and Adhesion. He begins by noting that it is composed of a series of steps for "simplifying" oneself. Note throughout the philosophic mystical terminology.

[2]The first step on this Way is "simplifying" the bodily needs. It is called "Separation" (*perishut*). Note that asceticism, which al-Botini advocates, includes, in traditional Jewish fashion, the regular satisfaction, at minimal level, of all bodily needs, even the need for sexual relations. All self-inflicted pain, celibacy, etc., is rejected.

[3]This usage is distinctly medieval, and it appears to originate in a Zohar-type milieu.

with great illumination. One [who secludes himself] also needs the purification of the body, [i.e.] immersion in the waters of the ritual bath, even though he has fulfilled the commandment of "joining" as it should be done, because it is not fitting that one draw near to the Work of Holiness except in purification and cleanliness.

When[4] [such a person] will have led his body and his corporeal forces along this Way and will have continued in this for a long time—not a day and not two days and not only a month, rather, for a long time—until he reaches the point when his corporeal forces do not grieve him by asking of him that which they used to ask of him previously, then he will also be moved to make a few necessary improvements in his soul, i.e., to train his characteristics *(tikkūn ha-middōt)* to the highest degrees and particularly to remove from himself the characteristics of anger and worry and permitted requests, for these are the characteristics which drive one away from reaching the ascent. In this manner, he will ascend to the degree of "equanimity" *(hishtavvūt)*, as the wise man used to say to his student: When he asked him to teach him the matter of the Merkabah, he replied, "Have you achieved equanimity?" The pupil did not know what he had said to him until he explained the matter to him, saying, "Have you achieved equanimity in your characteristics?" [It is as if] he said to him: "If any man abuses you and takes something of yours, would you be angry and aggravated in your soul because of this? Or if he did to you the opposite, for example, he honored you and gave you many presents, would you be happy and would you feel joy and stirring in your soul from this?" The student said to him, of course he would feel in his soul that he was moved by the two opposites. His teacher said to him, "Then you still have not reached the realm of equanimity, that is, to be equal, such that you will not be moved by the honor or by its opposite. Since that is so, how will you rise to the height of seclusion, since that is the height that comes after equanimity? For improvement of the body is the same as 'separation' *(perīshūt)*, and it leads to the purification of one's forces and to cleanliness of one's characteristics. [Then], equanimity leads to seclusion of the soul, and seclusion leads to the holy spirit, which leads to prophecy, which is the highest step." Thus, one of the main, compelling, and necessary principles for one who follows the Way of seclusion is that he have a beginning of a degree of equanimity—that he not be moved by any matter. On the contrary, it is necessary that he have inner happiness; that he be happy with his portion; that he think in his heart that he himself is alone and he rules all this lowly world; that there is not any man, near or

---

[4]The second step on the Way of Seclusion is "simplifying" the emotions. It is called "training one's characteristics," and it is accomplished when one has attained "equanimity" or "indifference" *(hishtavvūt)*. The master-disciple story cited below is a well-known Sufi story, as Scholem notes to the Hebrew text.

far, about whom he should worry or who will cause him any evil, any injury or anxiety, nor any good, for all the good of the world, and all his wealth, is in his hand, and he does not need anything. About this our teachers, of blessed memory, said: "Prophecy settles upon no one unless he be wise, brave, and rich" [Talmud, *Shabbat* 92a]; and, "Who is he who is a wealthy man? He who is happy with his portion" [*Pirkei Avot* 4:1]; and it is written, "And it came to pass, when the minstrel played, that the Lord came upon him" [II Kings 3:15].

Then,[5] when he will have perservered in acquiring this behavior, he should choose for himself a house and should dwell in it—he himself alone. If he have a house where his voice cannot be heard outside, it will be better for him. [This is] connected (to the fact that) first, he needs to adorn this house with nice decorations, the most important that he has, and with kinds of spices which have a nice fragrance. He also should have shrubs and fresh grass in the house. These are very good because, having secluded himself, his vegetative soul, which is connected with his vital soul, shall find pleasure in all these things. He should then advance to playing music on all kinds of instruments, if he has some or if he knows how to play them; and if not, he should make music with his mouth and voice, [chanting] the psalms of song and of the desire for the Torah, in order to give pleasure to the vital soul, which is connected with the speaking and rational soul. If he do this during the day, it is all right, although it is necessary that he be in a slightly darkened house, and indeed, it is better that he do it at night. In this case, however, he should have many lighted candles in the house. He should dress in beautiful, clean clothes, and it is good if they are white because all this adds to the intention of reverence and love.

After he has all these things prepared, then at the same hour that you prepare yourself to speak with your Creator, be careful to turn your thoughts from all the vanities of the world, wrap yourself in your prayer-shawl, and put the phylacteries on your hand and on your head, if you are able, in order that you be pious and reverent before the Presence Which is with you. Then, at that time and afterwards, sit and take ink, pen, and paper in your hand and start to permute letters, quickly and in great passion as I have taught you in the preceding chapters and particularly in the Eighth Chapter, which speaks of the matters of "skipping and jumping," because all this is necessary in order to separate the soul, to

---

[5] Al-Botini now begins the description of the third step of mystic praxis: "seclusion" (or "self-isolation"), *hitbōdedūt*. It is composed of two stages: a preparatory stage with several phases, and a properly mystical stage with several phases. Note the presence of visionary seizures at various points in this process. It is in this section, too, that the author seems to copy out sections of Abulafia's mystic manual, and you will notice it by the change in pronoun.

cleanse it from all the forms and material things which previously were part of it, and to make oneself simple [in respect] to them so that one direct one's heart and one's thoughts, one's intellect and one's soul, to the intellected image, or to the knowledge or to the question which one asks or wants to know from Him, blessed be He.[6]

When he has done this, he should prepare his true thoughts to make an image in his heart and in his intellect as if[7] he were sitting above in the heaven of heavens before the Holy One, blessed be He, in the midst of brightness and radiance and the majesty of His Presence; and as if you could see that the Holy One, blessed be He, sits like a king, exalted and elevated, and all the host of the heavens and the messengers and the cherubs and the fiery angels, and he [i.e., the initiate] also stands in the midst of them and hopes, like a messenger, that the King and His servants would want to send him; and he is ready to hear the message from the mouth of whichever of them he will hear it, whether from the King or from one of His workers. And then, in that situation, he should shut his eyes tightly and he should shut them with great strength and trembling and shaking. His whole body will shake violently, "his knees will knock together" [Dan. 5:6], and he will prolong his breath as much as he can until all of his limbs are almost prostrate, the outer ones and the inner ones. He will ascend, unite, and cause his soul and his thoughts to adhere from step to step in these spiritual matters, as much as is possible according to his strength in adhesion and in ascension upward from the world of spheres to the world of the separated Intelligences to the hidden world of the highest Emanation such that he will almost be, at that time, as if he were actualized intellect.[8] He then will not have any feeling for any material things because he has left the realm of humanity and entered the realm of the divine. It is then that, if he commands, his will is done.[9]

Know that if he is, at that time, intending to perform any action, [or if] it is his intention to ask when awake, i.e., that an answer come to him when awake, or if it is his intention to pronounce one of His holy Names, whether the Name of Seventy-Two [letters] or Forty-Two or any of the

---

[6]These, then, are the phases of the preparatory stage of the third step: (1) pacification of the vegetative and vital souls, (2) emptying one's thoughts from the vanities of the world, (3) permutation of letters, and most important (4) forming a clear idea in the mind of the magical act or question which one wants to accomplish during the next stage. Note that the mystic is not completely passive in the determination of the outcome of the divine influx. Having detached himself from matter and having formed a clear idea of what he wants to accomplish, the initiate should continue.

[7]This "as if" is very strange. It seems like a kind of internal psychodrama. Note, too, the Merkabah imagery in the next lines and then the description of the (first) trance seizure.

[8]The activity is done by the intellect. It is intellectual. And it follows the philosophic hierarchy, which for al-Botini includes the heavens, the Intelligences, and the Zoharic sefirot (see above, pp. 40–41). To meditate this way is to "actualize" one's intellect.

[9]This is the point of magic, of supernatural power. Maimonides would object violently.

rest of the Names, then he should pronounce each and every letter of that honored and revered Name which he calls to mind with great devotion, and with fear and shaking. He should move his head in pronouncing [each] letter, according to the vowel which points that letter, as you learned the movements in Chapter Nine. All these movements must be done with a quick, strong motion which warms the thought and makes the passion and the happiness greater until all his corporeal strength be abolished from him. Also, his intellect will become [completely] actualized in this way, and he will fall to the earth, almost as if dead, and he will lie down and fall into a deep sleep.[10]

Then, if he is worthy and proper before his Creator, He will let loose a spirit from heaven upon him and abundance will come to him from the Lord, blessed be He, and He will make known to him the answer to his questions—either in words, or by a verse, or a command. He may hear a voice speaking to him or He may appear to him in an appearance and a vision which he will behold. Furthermore, it will appear to him, in the time of the descent of abundance on him, as if they had anointed him with the "oil of anointing" from his head to his feet. This will be a signal and a great sign that his deeds have made him acceptable and that the divine abundance has begun to descend upon him, "like good oil which is on the head [and which] descends onto the beard" [Ps. 133:2], according to his virtues, because without doubt, at that time he leaves the human realm and enters into the divine realm.

At that time, his soul is made simple and enjoys its self-adhesion (hitdabbeḳūt) to the Root of the Source from which it was hewn.[11] It can even happen that his soul, at this time of being made simple from everything, be separated [from his body] and he will [then] remain dead—a death like that being excellent, for it is as if it were close to "the death by a kiss." In this way, the soul of Ben Azai, who saw and died [Talmud, Ḥagiga 14b], was separated because his soul was happy in its beholding the Source from which it was hewn. It wanted to adhere to it and to remain there and not to return to his body. Of his death it was said, "Dear in the eyes of the Lord is the death of His righteous ones" [Ps.

---

[10]These, then, are the phases of the mystical stages of the third step: (1) the forming of an image of the heavenly scene which includes the initiate, (2) a visionary seizure, (3) the ascent through the supernal realms, (4) the pronunciation of the magical Names and the submission of a question, and (5) a second visionary seizure. The phase between the seizures, which is the time of magical action, is called "the time of acting." (On the various Names, cf. the preceding chapter with the notes). We return now to the description of the ecstasy which follows upon the second visionary seizure, which is the complete actualization of the intellect.

[11]Note the mixture of Zoharic, Maimonidean, talmudic, and Biblical images. In medieval literature, this is a virtue.

109:7]. Some of the possessors of wisdom who have entered into this activity have said that: Whoever does not want to have his soul separated from him at the time of that vision, should, before then, near that act, but when he still has his power and his humanity, cause his soul to swear an oath or [cause it] to swear by the great and awesome Name, that during the time of the appearance and vision when he is not in his [own] power, it should not separate and go to join with the Source, rather that it return to its subject as in the beginning [I Chron. 21:27]. This it will do because it will not violate its oath.[12]

After all this, you should return to the matters of the body. Rise and eat a very little and drink a little, and sniff a pleasant fragrance, and return your spirit to its subject. Rejoice and make your heart glad with your portion and with that which God, blessed be He, has bestowed upon you. Know that the Lord, your God, loves you; He is the one Who "teaches you to do what is efficacious" [Isa. 48:17].

Now,[13] when you will be skilled in the matter of the choice of this life, and [when] you will have tried it many times until this thing be firmly and strongly in your hand, know that the more you continue this thing, the easier it will be for you to do. You will acquire preparedness to see the things which you wish to see without great fears, as at the beginning, until you are able to reach the level at which the angels who inaugurate you will come to you, to speak with you and to teach you wisdom and knowledge. But know that not every man has the permission, even though he be worthy, to be drawn quickly near to the Work, the Work of Holiness, which is the pronouncing of the holy Names at the "time of acting," unless he already be regular and experienced many times in these and other matters, and they are these: First, that he be very skilled in the art of "permutation" and in the art of "skipping," which I have explained in Chapter Eight. Then he should practice many times this Way of seclusion, "permuting" [any] of the verses of the Torah which he wants to "transmute." And he should persevere in this many times—a month or less or more, as he wishes—and he will see, in his doing of it, that he is complete in that activity. Then he should advance in seclusion, always having ready questions to ask at the "time of acting," which is explained above— questions whether in a dream at first and for many times, or afterwards when awake—until he sees that in "acting," there are many effects. He should try this thing many times, be answered, and try again. However, he should only ask for things that concern the worship of God, blessed be He, and the completeness of his soul, and not for material things, for the

---

[12]Very strange. Why would one want to return at all? Al-Botini now explains how one emerges from the mystical trance.

[13]Al-Botini continues with words of advice and encouragement.

needs of the body. After his being skilled and experienced in the matter of the questions, and his seeing that each time he is given from heaven answers of truth and justice, then he should ask of Him, blessed be He, at the "time of acting," that he be given permission to pronounce the honored and revered Name in its many letters, such as the Name of Seventy-Two [letters], or Twenty-Two, or Forty-Two, or Twelve, or the rest of the Names with their vowels and vowel-sounds and movements as he was taught and as he has received from the authentic Tradition. Then, if they say to him from heaven that he may do it, he should know that he is worthwhile. Then he should pronounce them, and if he is answered, he will know for certain that he is wanted. Concerning such a person it is said, "I will set him on high because he has known My Name" [Ps. 91:14]. According to the knowledge of these holy Names, he is able to do great things which he did not think and which did not spring up in his heart formerly. The Way of knowing and reading the above-mentioned Names is written in the book *Life in the World-to-Come*[14] and I do not need to repeat it here.

Know[15] that in the pronouncing of the letters and in their accompanying "movements," these great things which are the root of all wisdom and knowledge can be comprehended, and they themselves are the material of prophecy. They are seen in prophetic visions as if they were thick bodies, dressing themselves and speaking to man, "mouth to mouth" [Num. 12:8], according to the intensity of the imaging of the intellect which is "thought in the heart." This hidden thing concerning the letters is a thing which the intellect pushes away at first glance. But when one tries and plumbs the depths in proportion to one's comprehension of the matter, one comes to know that they are the "angels" who teach the prophet, in the vision of prophecy, wisdom, and knowledge, in a manner for which there is not any doubt. This thing is clear and known to the possessors of that wisdom, because by them [i.e., the letters] all creatures were created, as it is written in the *Sefer Yetsira,* "There are three mother-letters, seven double-letters, and twelve simple-letters," and so on. This is a simple thing, and there is no doubt about it at all.

Know, too, that the matter of "adhesion" (*devēkūt*) which is mentioned

---

[14]This is Abulafia's book. It has not yet been published or translated.

[15]Al-Botini here integrates his philosophic mysticism with his theory of prophecy (as Maimonides did). He maintains, following Maimonides, that prophecy is mystical experience par excellence. More specifically, Al-Botini teaches that prophecy consists in direct communication, accomplished in a trance state, in which one sees live, solid letters. These letters are also called "angels." The imaging (and then the decoding) process is done by the intellect. His theory may seem strange, but quoting *Sefer Yetsira,* chaps. 2–5 (cf. *Understanding Jewish Mysticism,* Vol. I, pp. 21 ff.), al-Botini maintains that he has discovered the true nature of the prophetic experience.

in this chapter is a wonderful thing, a ladder to the level of prophecy, as follows: When the righteous and pure man causes his thoughts to adhere to the highest realm, and when he meditates and causes his soul and intellect to ascend to the highest realm as much as possible according to his given ability and his strength in simplifying thought from material things, and when he causes them to adhere to spiritual things of the highest rank by the strength of the great thought which he conceives in his intellect and according to his strengths, then know that each thing and matter that he thinks and intends at that hour will be fulfilled immediately, whether for good or for bad, according to the secret [power] of prayer and the secret [power] of the sacrifices which is adhesion and drawing close to the highest.[16] The reason why his thoughts are fulfilled immediately at that time is that when his soul and his thoughts adhere to the Agent Intelligence—I mean to the *middā* of Malkhut—which is the judge and the conductor of the world, then whether it [i.e., the result] be for the rod and justice or whether it be for kindness, it [i.e., Malkhut] will bring it [i.e., the result] into existence, for his soul, at the time of its adhesion to it, is as if it were a part of it. Therefore, immediately his soul, by itself, accomplishes in the world what his heart desires. Concerning this, our rabbis of blessed memory have said, "Whatever the wise have set their eyes upon, it is for death or for poverty" [Talmud, *Ḥagiga* 5b]. And, "he [i.e., Rav Sheshet] set his eyes upon him [i.e., a Sadducee] and he became a pile of bones" [Talmud, *Berakhot* 58a]. For among our ancestors of blessed memory, there was to be found this great power, for they caused their essences, souls, and thoughts to adhere to that aforementioned *middā* which is the judge and the punisher. Thus, they could punish immediately those whom they wished to punish because they would draw down strength and abundance from on high on whomever they intended to cause evil to, or to cause good to, and immediately their desire was done.[17]

This was part of the matter of Balaam, the wicked, and from him you can see how far the strength of thought will reach, for good or for bad, because when Balaam would cause his thoughts and his soul to ascend and to adhere to the highest and would unite them there, he could draw

---

[16]This is a fusion of Maimonides' "contact" and the Zoharic "adhering." The identification of the Tenth Intelligence and the sefira Malkhut in the next sentence is, as noted above (p. 41), the position of Abulafia and not of al-Botini. The latter must, therefore, be quoting here.

[17]The reason, then, for the magical powers of the mystic is as follows: The mind of the mystic—having been separated from its material substrate (the body), and having ascended through the material, and then the supernal, spiritual levels of the cosmos—mixes, and becomes identical, with those spiritual levels which are responsible for the governing of the material universe (Providence: the Tenth Intelligence/the sefira Malkhut). As such, the mind of the mystic becomes one with an aspect of the mind of God. Therefore, any thought of the mystic, like any thought of God, has creative power—for good and for evil.

down strength on whoever would look and glance at him, and he could do with him as he desired. Therefore, he wanted to glance and to look at all Israel, as it is written, "And he saw Israel abiding in its tents" [Num. 24:2], in order that he make an image of them in his thoughts such that, at the time of his "adhesion," he could curse them with the strength of the thought which he would draw down on them from above, from the *middā* of "strong fear" [Gevura]. God, blessed be He, Who knew the wickedness of his thoughts, changed them from evil to good, and his thought to draw down and to bring abundance from "the Source of the fear and destruction" [Gevura] was changed and a blessing was brought down instead of a curse, as it is said, "But the Lord, your God, turned the curse into a blessing for you" [Deut. 23:6].

Understand this matter because it needs close consideration, for it is impossible to write it down exactly according to its depth; rather, it is proper that it be received mouth from mouth. I have, in this matter, further miraculous explanations about the fulfillment of the thoughts of the righteous man at the time of the preparations, but enough of this. With this, that which I thought to copy and to gather and to collect concerning these "Ways" is completed. Henceforth, pay attention to pronounce and to know the holy Names which are written in the book *Life in the World-to-Come,* as they are written (there) in our book, and then you will succeed in your Ways and you will be enlightened.

Conclusion

Several things are striking about the Abulafian transformation of the Maimonidean philosophic mystical tradition. First, the Abulafian techniques are in themselves startling—decorating houses, using incense, mind-loosening numerological and alphabetological games, body-mysticism involving head movements and controlled breathing, trance seizures, and magical powers. How strange all this seems to the non-mystical rabbinic Jew! One is almost tempted to say that this mysticism is not "Jewish," yet the evidence is plain, and as we shall see, these techniques are still practiced. Where did these techniques come from? Were they original with Abulafia, or did he borrow and adapt them from Islamic or Christian mystics? These questions remain open.

Second, the members of the Abulafian school made a distinct effort to stay within the Maimonidean stream of philosophic mysticism. Abulafia himself wrote a commentary to Maimonides' *Guide of the Perplexed.* Al-Botini wrote a commentary to Maimonides' *Code of Law.* All of them adopted the Maimonidean hierarchy. And all of them adopted the Maimonidean intellectualist bias, with knowledge preceding, and being a necessary part of, mysticism. Why was this so? There is nothing inherent in the techniques that would necessitate the intellectualist structure. One could practice the "permutations" and "movements" without the Maimonidean hierarchy. Yet the facts are that to the men of this tradition, the techniques and the ideas were related to one another. Everything, for them, fit into a whole.

What happened to the Abulafian transformation? First, it was preserved ①
in manuscript form, for there exist relatively recent copies of some of the books of this tradition. Second, the techniques are still used by a few ②
well-trained people. Thus, Scholem has written (*Ha-Kabbalah shel Sefer ha-Temunah ve-shel Avraham Abulafia* [Jerusalem: Akademon Press, 1969], p. 163): "The Kabbalists in the Yeshivot of Bel El and Porat Yosef today, 700 years after Abulafia, still practice these head movements during prayer, when they concentrate on Divine Names. These Kabbalists are called *mekhavvenim* [those who focus/concentrate]." Third, ③
the Abulafian techniques were assimilated to those of the Lurianic transformation of the *Zohar.* Again, it is Scholem who has commented (*Major Trends* [1941], p. 278): "I have had occasion in Jerusalem to meet men who to this day adhere to the practice of mystical meditation in prayer, as Luria taught it, for among the 80,000 Jews of Jerusalem there are still thirty or forty masters of mystical prayer who practise it after years of spiritual training. I am bound to say that in the majority of cases a glance is sufficient to recognise the mystical character of their devotion. . . . it is an ecstasy of silent meditation, of a descent of the human will to meet that of God, prayer serving as a kind of a balustrade on which the mystic leans, so as not to be plunged in suddenly or unprepared into an ecstasy in which the holy waters might drown his consciousness." Finally, something of the ecstatic abandon of this tradition may stand behind later Hasidic ecstatic mysticism.

5

GENERAL CONCLUSION

What is the relationship between mind and experience? How did the intellectual systems articulated to explain the world relate to man's consciousness of the numinous? What was the religious heartbeat of philosophy? How was philosophy the handmaiden of theology, and theology the handmaiden of religious experience? These were the questions which were set forth in the General Introduction to Unit I. We are now in a position to answer them, tentatively, for the body of data we have considered—the philosophic mystical stream within the river of Jewish mysticism.

Jewish philosophy and theology developed a philosophic mysticism which served as the driving religious force of the whole system. This philosophic mysticism had four outstanding characteristics.

1. Knowledge, in the philosophic sense of the word, was made a prerequisite of true religious experience. The study of philosophy, and not just ritual observance and traditional knowledge, was made a necessary step toward true worship.
2. One variation or another of the neo-aristotelian hierarchy was accepted as the basic structure of the physical and spiritual universe. The medieval hierarchy was made into the mystical ladder. In these two senses, philosophy was made the handmaiden of theology. It was made into a means for understanding the divine and the created realms.
3. The whole philosophic theological endeavor was then subordinated to religious experience; i.e., intellectual effort, it was taught, led to meditation and contemplation, to "isolating oneself" and "devoting oneself to God," to "being in His presence, alone, after philosophic intellectual effort."
4. Ultimately, philosophic mysticism taught an experience of "contact," or "unification," of the mind of man with the mind of God. This experience was an intellectual bliss, a philosophic communion. It is this experience, given certain variations in structure and technique,

81

which was the heartbeat of Jewish religious philosophy. It is this experience of meeting God mind-to-mind that provided the religious driving force for philosophic mysticism. In these two senses, theology was made a handmaiden of worship.

Philosophic mysticism as a religious dynamic was given its start by Maimonides. As we have seen, in the East, his insight was preserved and modified, primarily by a complexification of the hierarchy in which one had to place oneself, intellectually and experientially. In the West, insofar as scholars dealt with the religious aspect of Maimonides' system, new techniques were introduced—techniques of which Maimonides would probably have disapproved—but the hierarchy and the nature of the experience were preserved, and these were consciously filiated with Maimonides' teachings. Eventually, these methods were even integrated with Zoharic and Lurianic views and methods, incompatible as those views and methods seem to be with Maimonides.

The demise of the geocentric view of the universe meant the end of one of the crucial teachings of the philosophic mystical tradition. The ptolemaic–neo-aristotelian view of things was simply not true. And with the collapse of the hierarchy came the death-blow for the emanationist solution which had explained how the hierarchy worked. All of a sudden, the ladder and its dynamics fell apart. However, several important teachings remained from this tradition: that philosophic inquiry was a prerequisite to true worship, that the results of philosophic inquiry were subordinate to religious experience, and that the ultimate religious experience was mind-to-mind "contact" with God. In the new empirical world-view, men still believed in a great underlying order. It was not a hierarchy in the medieval sense, but it *was* an Order, and the Order bespoke a Power behind itself. This, in turn, was not a Power that acted through emanation, but it *was* a Power, and one could "sense" it in Nature, in Man, and, with sufficient effort, in History. And so the modern period saw a resurgence, in transfigured form, of philosophic mysticism. It was based upon the intellectual teachings of the new order of things. And it had at its core a religious experience, a sensed "contact" with the Power beyond man and the world. Beginning with Spinoza's *amor Dei intellectualis* and continuing in Mordecai Kaplan's "Power that makes for salvation," the tradition of philosophic mysticism has persevered, in much changed form, into the modern period. And as long as men continue to think of the ordering force of the universe as numinous, "mind-ful," and open to "contact," philosophic mysticism will endure.

The death knell of philosophic mysticism, then, did not lie in the call of modern science and the Enlightenment. If it lay anywhere, it lay in the modern teaching that man's emotions are, in and of themselves, valuable;

that true self-fulfillment comes to man by living his emotions passionately. If these emotions generate intellectual inconsistencies, then better to have inconsistencies than to subordinate emotion to reason. Reason became, in this view, a tool at best, and a straitjacket at worst. Rather, it was "the spontaneous overflow of powerful emotion" that was desirable. Or as one thinker put it: "The medium of thought is feeling." In the field of religion, this shift in valuating human experience, known as Romanticism, had the effect of stimulating the imaginative, ritual, symbolic, and feeling side of religious culture. It also had the effect of justifying a conception of God as anthropopathic, as involved actively in individual human lives and in society. It was this resurgence of the Biblical-rabbinic conception of God as *engagé* that, potentially, signaled the end of the philosophic mystical tradition, for it was no longer necessary to be intellectually informed in order to reach the heights of religious experience. It was no longer the experience of mind-to-mind contact with God that was ultimate. It was, rather, a passionate, personal involvement that was required. It was an all-consuming fire that was desirable. The understanding of the numinous had shifted, and with this shift, the very core of the philosophic mystical tradition was brought under attack.

In Jewish tradition, this change in the understanding of the numinous from the mind to the heart took place in the early years of the eighteenth century, in a remote corner of Poland. Its founder, the Baal Shem Tov, rejected the intellectualism of his milieu and founded a new movement with its own, new understanding of the numinous. It is to this movement, Hasidism, that we now turn.

Unit Two

The Hasidic Tradition

6
GENERAL INTRODUCTION

Of all the traditions within Jewish mysticism, it is Hasidism which has attracted the most attention. The Hasidic way of life has drawn to it such literary figures as Sholom Aleichem, Peretz, and more recently Elie Wiesel. It has drawn to it such scholars as G. Scholem, L. Jacobs, and R. Schatz-Uffenheimer. And it has drawn to it such religious thinkers as M. Buber and A. J. Heschel. Large bibliographies exist on various Hasidic motifs, customs, and life-patterns, and photographic essays have appeared in journals far removed from Jewish studies, such as the *National Geographic* and *Natural History*. Something about Hasidism has also made it a popular subject for modern artists—so much so that there is hardly a synagogue, and hardly a Jewish home, without some kind of lithograph or print of dancing Hasidim in it. Furthermore, the range of serious artists, including Chagall, who have tried their hand at painting Hasidim is very great. And who has not, as a tourist, tried to photograph a Hasid on the streets of Jerusalem or New York? Perhaps the greatest testimony to the attraction of Hasidism is the interest shown in this type of Judaism by Jews seeking to return to their heritage. Some of the seekers have become "converts" to Hasidism, adopting the rigorous ritual life and the social patterns of this group, while other seekers have learned something about the religious dimension of Hasidism and have incorporated that into their personal religious lives—in ritual, in study, and/or in song. And which Jewish family does not have its "remote Hasidic ancestor" about whom stories are told (or created)? Given the range of interest in, and openness to, Hasidism, one might even speak of a "neo-Hasidism."

Why? Why all this interest in Hasidism? What is the nature of its attraction to the modern Jew? Why is it the most popular, and most accessible, of the traditions of Jewish mysticism? This is the problem which lies at the heart of this unit. In order to solve it, however, we shall have to ask three questions:

1. What are the forms of the holy as they appear in Hasidism? What are the patterns in which the numinous expresses itself in this tradition?
2. What are the elements of continuity and discontinuity between Hasidism and the traditions which preceded it? What does Hasidism have in common with Rabbinic Judaism, with the Merkabah tradition, with the Zoharic-Lurianic tradition, and with the Maimonidean tradition? Wherein does it differ from these currents within the stream of Judaism?
3. In what way is Hasidism "modern," if at all? How is it continuous with "modernity" and how is it discontinuous with it? Is it recrudescent medievalism or modern spiritualism? What is the future of Hasidism? Is it modern enough to survive, or tough enough to survive modernity?

The answers to these questions are of scholarly interest, for they tell us something about one of the streams of Jewish mysticism, and a contemporary one at that. However, the questions and the answers are also religiously relevant, for Hasidism claims to offer one possibility for Jewish spiritual revival in the contemporary world. This will serve as our bridge into Chapter 11, "Retrospect and Prospect," where the specific problem of contemporary spirituality will be considered more fully.

Scholars and religious thinkers are not in agreement on how to present Hasidism. Some concentrate on stories, some on Hasidic prayer, some on humor, some on the thought of the Hasidic intellectual leadership, and some on the sociological description of Hasidic communities. I have chosen three forms in which the numinous is embodied in a special way in Hasidism. Chapter 7 deals with the Hasidic story. Several are presented, together with a commentary which points out the distinctly "Hasidic" element. Then, suggestions are made on how to write a "Hasidic" story. Chapter 8 deals with Hasidic prayer. In it, I have tried to avoid overly long theoretical discourses and overly short unexplained texts. Furthermore, I have attempted a typology of Hasidic prayer. Chapter 9 deals with the Zaddik and his community. Here, too, I have presented types of Hasidic leaders and described the functions of the leaders and the community. Taken together, these chapters present a picture of the Hasidic tradition. In the General Conclusion, I have tried to answer the questions put forth here. Throughout, however, the reader should bear these questions in mind and try to answer them. Further readings are suggested at the end of the book.

7

THE HASIDIC STORY

Introduction

There are many kinds of Hasidic stories. There are the tales of Rabbi Nahman of Bratslav, which go on for pages and which are extremely complex in their story-within-a-story structure and in their ambiguous symbolism. There are miracle stories. There are short sayings and beautiful parables. There are even Hasidic reworkings of the Boccaccio stories. And then there are the short, incisive, instructive stories that have become so well-known through the efforts of religious teachers and preachers. This is not the place to examine systematically all the genres of the Hasidic story. Nor is it the place to consider the complex processes by which a Hasidic story is created, modified in oral transmission, and canonized. The problems of tradition-formation, literary form-analysis, and historical verification are not of concern to us here. We shall examine, however, several of the short instructive stories, and our question will be: What makes these stories special? "Hasidic?" For that purpose, several stories are presented with commentary, and several are presented only with guiding questions. The conclusion attempts an answer and, to test the hypothesis, presents guidelines on how to write a "Hasidic" story. If the reader develops the analytic skill, she/he will be able to write such a story.

Forgotten, Completely Forgotten

TEXT*

There was great excitement in Strelisk. Hasidim danced in the streets. Rabbi Mendel, the rebbe of Kossov, had arrived to spend a day with his

---

*From A. J. Heschel, *The Earth Is the Lord's*, pp. 77–79.

brother-in-law, Rabbi Uri the Seraph, the rebbe of Strelisk. It was well known that to these two *zaddikim*—saintly men—the gates of heaven were open. The rebbe of Kossov held the key to the celestial Treasury of Sustenance, and whoever received his blessing no longer had to worry about the necessities of life. The Seraph, on the other hand, held the key to the Treasury of Saintliness. As a result, the Hasidim or adherents of the rebbe of Kossov were all well-to-do, some of them even wealthy, while the Hasidim of the Seraph were very saintly, but extremely poor. But a happy folk they were—the Hasidim of the Seraph. They were thrilled to live in his presence and reveled in the joys and ecstasies of prayer and the service of God. Three times a day they would wage the great battle of prayer into which they would throw themselves with undaunted courage, as if they aimed to storm the hidden fortresses of heaven. And when the battle was over, they were exhausted and amazed at the wonder of having survived.

The rebbe of Kossov, the distinguished guest, was shocked at the sight of the extreme poverty in which the Hasidim of the Seraph lived. He had heard of their indigence, but what he saw—the emaciated bodies, the tattered clothes—surpassed his imagination. Angrily he turned to his brother-in-law: "Why do you permit this?" "Believe me, I am not to blame. They do not really feel any want," answered the latter in apology.

This answer did not satisfy the rebbe of Kossov. Late at night, after the great celebration for the honored guest was over and the songs and dances came to an end, he let it be known that all Hasidim of the Seraph should come to see him.

"What, for example, would be your most cherished desire?" he asked them. The Hasidim were embarrassed. Their most cherished desire, of course, was to attain perfect saintliness, to be able to say at least one prayer in the same spirit as their rebbe. But who would even dare to dream of such unattainable aims? So the rebbe of Kossov became specific: "What about sustenance?" This came as a surprise. Yes, they agreed, it would be a good thing not to be in want. They thought of their wives, of dowries for their grown-up daughters. "Listen," the rebbe of Kossov announced, "tomorrow during the morning service whatever you pray for will be fulfilled."

It was a night full of excitement. They spent restless hours repeating to themselves and fixing in their minds the desire for sustenance, lest they forget to pray for it. Here was a chance that might never occur again.

Early next morning the Seraph appeared in the synagogue, roaring like a lion, "Adon Olam—Eternal Lord," and the Hasidim joined in the vehement encounter. Their songs all but tore the world apart, and they almost lost their souls on the way to heaven, in complete oblivion of the theme they had rehearsed the previous night. . . .

After the service, gradually recovering from their exhaustion, they realized to their dismay: "Ah, ah! Forgotten, completely forgotten!"

COMMENT

This tale, related by the late A. J. Heschel in *The Earth Is the Lord's,* was told to him by one of his ancestors. It is an exceptionally beautiful story and deserves close examination.

What does it tell us about the Zaddikim, Rabbi Mendel of Kossov and Rabbi Uri, the Seraph, of Strelisk, and about Zaddikim in general? The story tells us, first, that there are many kinds of genuine spiritual leadership. There is Rabbi Mendel of Kossov, who sees the poverty of his people and is upset by it. How can a Jew worship God when his family is hungry and ill-clad? This rabbi, then, "uses his contacts" to help his followers: He prays for them. He calls God's blessings down upon them. He urges them to employ one another. He urges them to give charity, and so on. Rabbi Mendel of Kossov shoulders the burdens of the physical existence of his people. This is not easy. Rather, it is a very difficult thing to do—to accept responsibility for the well-being of other people. Rabbi Mendel is one type of Zaddik, one archetype of the true spiritual leader.

Then there is Rabbi Uri the Seraph. The seraphim are the fiery angels of heaven, and Rabbi Uri's spirituality was so intense that he was afire with it. This, too, is spiritual leadership: to have such an intense relationship with God that onlookers are swept up in the fervor; to have such a passion for God that bystanders and devotees are lifted out of themselves along with the leader. This passion for God is not an easy thing to achieve, for in some basic way, we are all afraid of the spiritual in us. We are not really afraid of God's punishment, because we know that He is merciful and we do not really believe that we are so bad. But to look Him straight in the Face, to stand clear-headed and open-hearted in His presence, is another matter. Somewhere at the periphery of our awareness is an inkling of what true saintliness, true holiness, true spirituality is like, but we are afraid of it. Nor is this state of saintliness easy to sustain, even if we achieve some small measure of it. One must ever again confront one's fears, one's weaknesses. One must ever again say, "My strength, my energy, my being belong to God. I can do *anything,* in *His* service." One must be prepared to roar like a lion the words "Adon Olam," and to truly assert, with the full weight of one's mind and being, "Lord of the Universe." Rabbi Uri the Seraph, the tale lets us know, had looked deeply—into himself. He had confronted his fears and conquered them. He could roar like a lion the words "Adon Olam." How weak and anemic in comparison is contemporary man's assertion of that phrase! Rabbi Uri, too, is a type of Zaddik, an archetype of the true spiritual leader.

The tale tells us not only about Zaddikim, spiritual leaders, but also about Hasidim, followers of spiritual leaders. The followers of the Rabbi of Kossov are well off, and I should think that they are also pious and observant Jews. They probably study. They certainly give charity to support those who do study, as well as to other good causes. They are good Jews, even very good Jews. And then there are the followers of Rabbi Uri the Seraph. I would guess that they spend four to five hours a day "storming the hidden fortresses of heaven." They don't work a ten-, twelve-, or eighteen-hour day. Their families are ill-fed and ill-clad. Yet what is their most cherished desire? "To be able to say one prayer in the same spirit as their rebbe." To once have his trust in God, to once have his burning love for God; once—to stand only once—in the true presence of God with a mind uncluttered by the mundane, with a heart not weighed down by the tasks and responsibilities and fears of this world; to reach out and touch God, just once.

There is a similar story told of the Hasidim of the Seer of Lublin (*Souls on Fire*, p. 137):

One of them was asked: "Since you [disciples] were so many and so powerful, and had a Master of such outstanding talent, why could you not make the Messiah come?" And the disciple replied, unsmiling: "The question is a valid one, but you see, in Lublin we lived in such ecstasy, we hardly felt the hardship of the exile."

Where is reality? What is *truly* real? The hardship of the exile and the bringing of the Messiah, or the ecstasy of the soul which transcends even the exile? This-worldly concern combined with piety of the Rebbe of Kossov and his Hasidim, or the fiery passion for God Who is Himself all-consuming fire? What is one's most cherished desire? To sustain, to continue the physical existence of the people, without which there is no spirit, or to reach out for the Ultimate and pay the price? Is it the body or is it the soul—if one must choose? And beware of the answer which is the easier way out.

What You Are Doing, You Are Doing Well

TEXT*

In a dream, the Baal Shem glimpsed his future neighbor in paradise. Upon awakening, he decided to pay him a visit. He found a robust and earthy

---

*From E. Wiesel, *Souls on Fire*, pp. 27–28.

man. How well he disguises himself, thought the Baal Shem, and asked to be sheltered for a few days.

The Besht was convinced his host was leading a double life; that he was getting up at night to accomplish God knows what worthy deeds. Wrong: the man slept deeply until the next morning, when he rose early, hastily said his prayers and gulped down a copious breakfast. At lunch he ate even more, and three times as much at dinner. And so it went for several days.

Let us wait for Shabbat, thought the Baal Shem. Perhaps his saintliness coincides with that of the seventh day. Wrong again: his host ate and slept even more than during the week. Unable to contain himself any longer, the Baal Shem spoke to him: "When I came here, I had a question to ask you. I shall not ask it. But now I have another: why do you eat so much?"

"I'll tell you," answered the man. "It has to do with my father. Who was a good Jew, gentle and frail, aspiring only to please the Lord; nothing else interested him. Neither money nor honors, not even health. He lived only for and by the Torah. One day he was on his way to services when he was grabbed by bandits who tied him to a tree and ordered him to kiss a cross. He refused, of course. They beat him mercilessly; still he refused. They then poured kerosene over him and set him on fire. And because my father was so weak and thin, he burned only a moment; almost as soon as he was lit, he was burned out. And I, who saw him, who saw it all, swore that if ever I was put to the same test, I would not let them get away so easily. I would show them that a Jew does not go out like a miserable skinny candle. No. When I burn, I shall burn so long that they will burst with anger. That is why I eat so much; all my energy, all my passion is devoted to eating. Not that I am hungry, you understand . . ." "Yes, I understand," said the Baal Shem, smiling. "Go on, continue; you must. What you are doing, you are doing well."

COMMENT

This tale is related by Elie Wiesel in *Souls on Fire,* and it, too, is a beautiful tale deserving close attention.

What does the tale tell us about Rabbi Israel Baal Shem Tov, the founder of the Hasidic movement? It tells us, actually, a great deal. First, that for him, unlike modern man, life was one continuum, and hence a dream is real and yields real knowledge. A dream is not a compartment of life devoid of significance except perhaps in a psychoanalyst's office. The Baal Shem Tov did not ask for the dream. It was sent. And it was accepted for that which it was—a sent message, concerning some true reality. We also learn about the Baal Shem Tov that he suffered from stereotypes, as do all men. In the story, he cannot believe that the man and his actions are one. He assumes that the man leads a double life, rising "at night to accomplish God knows what worthy deeds." How human to assume that others fit our conceptions of them! But the story also tells us that he was aware of the fact that things are not always what they seem. He knew that something more must be afoot, that God was hiding something from him. And so he waits, observes, and finally asks. Only then does he see the whole; only then is the hidden revealed. The enormity of the sin of jumping to conclusions about people has become clear.

And the Besht's neighbor in paradise? What was his work? We don't know. His social station? His learnedness? We don't know. And the incident? I think a modern therapist might interpret it as follows: the traumatic shock of seeing one's pious father bound to a tree and burned alive is followed by deep aggressive, even murderous, feelings. These feelings must be repressed because of the powerlessness of the Jew, but even in repression they return to the surface in two forms: as a compulsion to eat, to drink of the milk of comfort in the face of the terrifying, and again, in introverted form, as suicidal spite—spite unto death for the barbarous non-Jew who defies human decency and God's law.

In this mode of interpretation, the story is the story of a human being crippled and warped by trauma and powerlessness. How different is the mode of interpretation of the Besht, and the result too! In that mode, the story is of a human being who is raised to great spiritual heights, to sit next to the founder of Hasidism in heaven! His eating is no escape from fear. It is a leap forward, toward God. His spite is not a personal spite. It is the contempt of the religious man for the unspiritual. This man's deep love for his father, which is very clear, his deep regard for the tradition of martyrdom among his forefathers, and his deep love of God transforms his spiteful suicidal wish into a desire to glorify the memory of his father, his forefathers, and to praise God "with all his heart, with all his soul, and with all his might." The tale interprets the man, his acts, and his inner wish in a spiritual mode, and the story becomes a story of piety reaching up to great heights. The story becomes the tale of a saint in the disguise of a human being.

Why Do You Not Raise Them Up Once Again?

TEXT*

"God of Abraham, Isaac and Jacob," said the rabbi of Berditchev, interrupting his prayers, "You ask us—and rightly so—to follow after

---

*From S. Dresner, *Levi-Yitzhak of Berditchev*, pp. 79–80.

Your ways. And indeed, we try to do so. Why then do You not, at times, follow after our ways? Why, for example, do You not treat us in at least the same manner that any simple Jew would? If a simple Jew were to drop his *Tefillin* or notice that they had fallen to the ground, he would at once lift them up, wipe them clean, and kiss them. For the *Tefillin* are the 'glory of Israel,' and in them are written the words: 'Hear, O Israel, the Lord is our God, the Lord is one.'

"Your people, Israel, are the *Tefillin* of Your head, for the *Tefillin* glorify their wearer, and it is through Israel that You are glorified. For what verse is enclosed in your *Tefillin?* It is a verse of David, of Your anointed: 'Who is like Your people, Israel, a unique nation on earth!'

"Lord, Your *Tefillin* have fallen to the ground and have lain in the dust of exile and suffering lo! these two thousand years. Why do You not raise them up once again?"

COMMENT

This story is told of Rabbi Levi Yitzhak of Berditchev, and it is a typical Reb Levi Yitzhak story. One can almost always identify his stories, for Reb Levi Yitzhak is always taking up the cudgels against God on Israel's behalf, and he does so in a shockingly bold way. *Hutzpah* and *Ahavas Yisroel*—courage bordering on the reckless and the love of the Jewish People—are Reb Levi Yitzhak's trademarks. It is he who perfected the art of talking to God in Yiddish. After all, why should God not understand Yiddish!

The story is based upon a series of passages from the Talmud which have been woven together with exquisite artistry to form the background against which the story plays itself out. According to the Talmud, a Jew must put on *Tefillin*, or phylacteries, when reciting certain prayers. These *Tefillin* are small boxes attached to leather straps. The boxes contain parchments upon which the Biblical passages dealing with *Tefillin*, the *Shema*ᶜ among them, are written. Using the leather straps, one of the *Tefillin* is placed on the head, above and between the eyes, and the other is placed on the arm, opposite the heart. Applying a verse from Ezekiel, the Talmud calls the *Tefillin*, "the glory which is set upon your head." Since the *Tefillin* contain the name of God on the parchment, and since they are man's glory, it became custom to retrieve them immediately if they fell and to kiss them upon retrieval as a sign of respect and love. Going a step further, the Talmud speculates that God, as a good parent and king, must set an example for the Jews. And so, God prays, according to the Talmud. What does He say? How does He pray? These questions need not occupy us here. The relevant detail about God's prayers is that He too puts on *Tefillin*. And since a Jew's *Tefillin* contain passages extolling God and His commandments, God's *Tefillin* must, and do, contain passages extolling Israel as His chosen people. Against this talmudic background, Reb Levi Yitzhak now poses his poignant question.

It is a sad question, for in it one hears the echo of the poverty and the humiliation of the Jew in Eastern Europe: the systematic constriction of living space, the systematic deprivation of the means with which to earn a livelihood, not to speak of the whimsical and cruel pogroms that were a common part of life. One hears the sighs and hopes of the "huddled masses yearning to be free." And one hears the echoes of the centuries of Jewish settlement and life in Eastern Europe, which, a scant 130 years after Reb Levi Yitzhak's death, are to be wiped out in the Final Pogrom, for in this tale, as in all tales, the past is present and the present is past. There is no time.

Reb Levi Yitzhak's question is sad for another reason. In it one hears of man's separation from God. There was a time, in Jewish religious historiography, when God was close to man. He, or His presence, was physically located in the Temple. He, or His glory, abided physically among the people. But then the vessels shattered and He escaped. The link was broken, the umbilical cord severed. But in the days of the Messiah, God will come again. Conversation will be resumed. Intimacy will be restored. Not only political peace, but intimacy is the promise of the days of the Messiah. And that longing is in the question.

Reb Levi Yitzhak's question is also a challenge flung at God, not simply a sad question. It has a hidden threat in it, and in fact, one version of the story relates: Then he (Reb Levi Yitzhak) added: "If You will forsake Your way and adopt our way and forgive our sins and redeem us, all will be well. If not, I shall be compelled to reveal publicly that Your *Tefillin* (which have verses praising Israel) are unkosher" (Dresner, p. 80).

What is behind this challenging of God? From where does a man derive the strength to challenge the Ultimate Power? First, the challenge is based on the covenant, on God's love for the Jews. God chose the Jewish people of His own free will. He made a commitment to them, and He must honor it. He is, therefore, accountable for not honoring His commitment. To challenge Him on that basis in an old tradition—Moses did it, David did it in Psalms, so did others.

Second, the challenge—even the threat—is a function of man's love for God. It is an attempt to push Him into doing that which will bring Him glory. To push someone into doing that which is right and good is to push him into doing that which will redound to his credit. To demand the best of someone is ultimately to demand that which will benefit him most. And this is true of God too. To demand that the "Judge of all the earth do justice" is to demand that He be God, at His best. The King must be ultimately royal, and the Father ultimately fatherly. Reb Levi Yitzhak's question is a kind of preventive theodicy.

Third, and perhaps most important, the strength of Reb Levi Yitzhak's challenge derives from the mutuality of the love between man and God. It is not that God loves man and man loves God, and their loves pass each other in the night of existence. On the contrary, their loves meet one another and strengthen one another. God loves Israel and comes down to meet her, and Israel loves God and sets forth to meet Him. And they do meet and they do live together, giving and talking, speaking and listening. Now among the truly loving and the truly loved, the truth is spoken, challengingly, but in love. And this is the strength of Reb Levi Yitzhak of Berditchev.

The Rebbe and the Football Game

TEXT

The story is told of a certain Rabbi David that, one late October afternoon, right after the Sabbath on which the reading of Genesis had taken place, he noticed that the students were distracted from their study of Torah by something called "football." They were known to have spoken of it, often, in whispers—and when the Rebbe and the teachers weren't looking, so word came to the Rebbe, they had even dared to play their version of it. Finally, Rabbi David decided to probe this matter fully and went, with the students, to see such a game. Afterwards, when everyone had returned to the House of Study and was about to take up his books, the Rebbe signaled for attention and said:

"It is written in the reading of the last Sabbath, 'These are the generations of Adam,' and it is taught in this connection that the true meaning of the verse is, 'This is the story of Adam.' What we have just witnessed is truly the story of Adam, the story of every man. Blessed be God, the glory of Whose work can be seen everywhere! This 'football' you prize so highly teaches three lessons about God, about man, and about Torah. It teaches that, in the arena of life, man must assert command over all his forces; that he must use them to strike down the enemy; and that he must seize firmly that which is essential and advance it, each time, as far as he can. Furthermore, this is no light matter. Indeed, it is very difficult, for the enemies of Torah are legion: insecurity, fear of ridicule, laziness, love of distraction, the burdens of daily living, the difficulty of a life dedicated to the Master of the Universe, and the pressures of time. Who commands these forces? They are commanded by the *Yetser ha-ra'*. Who is the *Yetser ha-ra'*? He is our mirror image; he stands opposite, over and against us. He is the impulse in us to resist God, to resist Torah. But the forces of Torah, too, are legion: the love of God, the love of Torah, the love of Israel, and the fear of God's punishment. And who commands them? The *Yetser ha-tov*, the impulse to seek God, the impulse to serve Him and His Torah. Whatever direction a man may take, whatever his path of life may be, let him assert command with his *Yetser ha-tov,* let him strike down his *Yetser ha-ra'* with all its forces, and let him seize firmly that which is essential and advance it ever nearer to the goal of the Messiah-time, may he come speedily in our day. Amen.''

COMMENT

This tale, which on the surface appears somewhat funny, is actually a very good example of Hasidic teaching-through-the-tale. What are its lessons?

First, it is Hasidic doctrine that God can be found everywhere. So thoroughgoing is this doctrine that it borders on pantheism in places—and indeed, some interpreters have seen Hasidism as a form of Jewish pantheism—and it borders on Sabbatianism in other places, for it was the teaching of the false messiah Sabbatai Zvi that even in sin there is a spark of the divine, and therefore the Messiah must commit certain kinds of sins in order to redeem the divine in them. However, though Hasidism borders on the pantheistic and the Sabbatian, it does reject both doctrines while retaining the idea that God and His wisdom can be found everywhere. Thus, Rabbi David takes his students to see a football game under the firm conviction that God is to be found there too. What started as a distraction will become a lesson in religious living.

There is a similarly motivated story told of one of the Rebbes who took his students to see the first railroad train as it passed through town. Everyone was excited to see this wonder of modern technology, but the Rebbe saw God, and a moral: "See what a wonder this train is," he said, "for there are many wagons and they are all dark and lifeless. Yet note that one wagon with a spark and fire pulls all of them along." Here, too, God is everywhere.

There is in the story of Rebbe and the football game another lesson: that life is not a sea of tranquility, an even plane, a rose garden of beauty and peace through which man floats. Life, the Rebbe teaches, is a struggle. Life is a dialogue between the positive and the negative. Life is an ongoing, competitive game. Note how well he contrasts the opposing quarterbacks as mirror images of equal power, with one ascendant and then the other. Furthermore, life is not a steady progress, an ineluctable evolution. There are setbacks, ups-and-downs as we call them. And there is the goal toward which one strives.

I don't think that Rabbi David intended his interpretation to be humorous, but if its gentle humor strikes us, that too is very Hasidic, for humor is of the essence of life. Gentle humor—not raucous, vulgar, or acidic humor—enables us to see ourselves critically and sympathetically at the same time. We can poke fun at our faults and wrong values with humor, if it is gentle, and we can learn from humor. Why, then, is this story gently funny to us? What is the lesson of its humor? The humor lies in the contrast between the value the Rebbe sees in the football game—a moral and religious value—and the value modern man sees in the football game. For modern man, such sports are the epitome of ritualized violence. All of our repressed violence is played out before our eyes. All of our unsatisfied urge for creative decisive action is played out vicariously for us. For modern man, football is also the commercialism before the game, and the beer and sex after—the parties, the escape through alcohol from the reality of frustration which has only been heightened by having to passively watch it violently acted out. For some, perhaps, football is a return to the happier (or, at least, more carefree) days of an earlier period of life. How different is the association—indeed, the vision—of Rabbi David. For him, football is life, football is reality. Life is a struggle of violent forces within Adam, within each person. No sublimation is necessary. No spectator sports are necessary. No vicarious violence is necessary. Rabbi David's gentle humor pokes fun at the values of modern man and shows, at the same time, another way.

A similarly-motivated story is told of Rabbi Levi Yitzhak of Berditchev. One day, after his congregants had recited the Silent Devotion, he went around to each and said, "Shalom Aleichem, Shalom Aleichem!" The congregants were astounded, for they had not left the city, nor had they been away. When questioned, the Rebbe explained, "During the Silent Devotion, man is supposed to think only of God, to stand here in His presence. Yet you were far away, were you not? You were in the grain market of Lodz, and you were on a ship bound for distant ports. When the sounds of the prayer ceased, you returned from your voyages, so I greeted you." Here too the Rebbe pokes fun at the distractions of man. He needles man, gently, for his uninspired, mundane values, and at the same time shows him another way. Humor is a great teacher, and the Divine is everywhere.

The Hasid and the Computer

TEXT*

When speaking of Kavvana[1] and its myriad channels and functions, the story is told of an incident at one of the Hasidic Yeshivot in this modern day and age.

There once was a devout Hasid who was sent outside the Yeshiva to learn computer data-processing in order to help organize the affairs of the Yeshiva and related community. This Hasid had always shown an interest in mathematics, so he was the logical one to send. He continued his regular studies at the Yeshiva in addition to his computer work.

All continued smoothly until, one day, his fellow Yeshiva-mates noticed some strange actions on the part of the Hasid. They noticed he was spending more and more time at the computer lab and less and less time at their daily Torah-study. He would wander through the halls murmuring strange things that the others did not understand—ISAM, VMOS, SNOBOL—almost as if he were speaking another language. Or for no apparent reason he would break out with, "Why the format must be wrong!" And continue with his calculations. In his room at night, he would pace back and forth trying to debug his programs. "But I'm so close," he often exclaimed, in apparent agony.

When asked by one of his friends who was concerned over his neglected study and wandering concentration, the Hasid hastened to reply that he wasn't neglecting his study, but rather, redirecting its form.

Word soon came to the Rebbe of the apparent transformation of the young Hasid. He called the Hasid into his study and told him: "Your friends say that you are engrossed in some sort of project, and the teachers complain that you have missed classes and do not seem to be preparing as thoroughly as you used to. Tell me, what is taking up so much of your attention? Are you overloaded with work from your computer class?"

"Oh no," the Hasid replied. "The projects in class are not overwhelming. Everything fits into place quite logically and I haven't had much trouble doing the work required for class."

"The truth is," the Hasid continued hesitantly, "I've been working on my own separate project. I want to use the computer as my link to God."

The Rebbe seemed slightly surprised at this statement but nodded with interest and asked the Hasid to explain how he was planning to make this link.

"Well," the Hasid began slowly, "the computer has such amazing capacities. It can store an immense amount of knowledge, and direct and redirect all this knowledge into different patterns, depending upon the program. With a single codeword to the computer, one can prompt a whole memory that can be translated into thousands of uses. Now, when I pray to God, He doesn't always seem to be listening, and I have come to the conclusion that something is wrong with what I am doing—not with my Kavvana itself, perhaps with the order of the Kavvanot. I think it might be a matter of the proper combination, or combinations. I am trying, therefore, to arrange a program that would put my requests and my praise in such a combination, or mixture of combinations, that God would not dare refuse my prayers."

After this explanation the Rebbe was silent for a moment. He sat back, stroked his beard, and then looked at the Hasid and explained gently:

"My son, that is not the task. Man's expression to God is not quantitative, nor is it a mere rearrangement of bits of information. You cannot relate to God in this manner. God cannot be approached through a computer but only through *lev ha-adam,* the heart of every man. The Way to God cannot be found so easily or systematically. It is, rather, through the whole-hearted effort of man's Kavvana that He can be reached."

QUESTIONS

What is the Rebbe's message? What would its implications be for such learned mystical traditions as the Zoharic-Lurianic system? What might the ritual implications be? If learnedness is not the center of Jewish spirituality, what, then, is the center? If "organizing" spirituality is not important, then what is the role of ritual? of mental intention? Do you know a parallel story?

The Rebbe and the Gambler

TEXT*

The story is told that one day, one of the Rebbe's most devout disciples came in appearing drunk, penniless, and ecstatic. The Rebbe asked, "Can you explain to me why you are standing in my presence in such a state?" The disciple answered, "Yes, Rebbe, I have just returned from a village far from this place, in a distant land, where I saw a strange light. And you must go to confirm that which I have spoken. The village is named Malkhut and it is not on any map that I have ever seen. The trip was long, arduous, and confusing for me, but the old man said that you would know how to get there if only I told you the name of the place. The man talked in circles and riddles which I could not understand most of the time. He even said that the trip there would be shorter for you somehow . . . and he would not tell me his name."

In the twinkling of an eye, the Rebbe found himself in the distant, mist-shrouded village of Malkhut. He seemed to be deliberately planted on the doorstep of a very ancient house. The Rebbe knocked on the door, and an old, congenial-looking man appeared, betraying a smile. "I have been expecting you, Rebbe!" The Rebbe then asked the old man his name, and the man replied jestfully, "In this place I have many names, but for you I have the name of a great gambling man—Jacob is my name. Come and spend Shabbat with me, for you are just in time, as a Rebbe should be!" So the Rebbe spent what seemed to be an uneventful, almost

---

*As told by W. Belcher.

overly peaceful Sabbath. As the time passed, the Rebbe grew puzzled as to how he had gotten to the village in the first place. He was generally unimpressed with that which he saw, as the old man never spoke to him except during the prayers. The Rebbe was planning an inconspicuous exit at the end of the Sabbath, and as he was about to quietly leave, the old man Jacob suddenly roared, "Tonight you will find out why you came here! We are going to a very special place in the village!"

That night the old man Jacob walked to the synagogue. The Rebbe remained expressionless and unmoved until they walked through the door of the House of Study. There lay before them a great casino packed with all the men of the village. There was only one game being played, as the Rebbe would soon find out. The old man Jacob gathered all of the men together and began to shuffle and to deal out what appeared to be a most unusual deck of cards. The men played for half the night as the Rebbe sternly watched, many of them gambling away all of their money and possessions. They also drank, and their increasingly drunken behavior also offended him.

Suddenly, an almost overwhelming idea illuminated the Rebbe's consciousness. "At last I know what the old man meant. The reason that I have been sent here is to rid these men of this wicked, drunken gambling. I will arrive at the root of this problem by watching them play several hands. I will then see what it is that obsesses them about this game and will show·them that the power behind the cards is no match for the power of the Creator Who made all things!" "Perhaps these cards are enchanted," he marveled, looking at the intensity of each player in the seemingly spellbound assembly. There was not a soul in the House of Study who was not totally absorbed in the game. Every drunken player's entranced gaze was mindlessly riveted to the cards which he held.

Resolute in the great task which impatiently awaited him, the Rebbe, with great reluctance, wistfully cast his eyes upon the wretched cards. At that very instant, with lightning-quick suddeness, the old man Jacob, the dealer, sprang from his seat. "Aha, Rebbe!" he said glowingly. "Only just now do I perceive that you finally manifest the desire to learn this highly esoteric game which is so drunken with meaning! As a Rebbe, you are already painfully aware that 'Desire is the beginning of Illumination.' You desire, so I shall illuminate!!!" he roared.

"This game of poker represents the life of the Jews before God. God is the dealer Who, before Creation, had all that He could possibly want. But God decided that there should be more, so He gambled and He created man. To each man, He deals out a hand. One man may be truly fortunate and may receive a glorious five-card royal flush. He is like a king, an aristocrat, or a learned scholar or rabbi who holds a high station in life due to the extraordinary gift that God has dealt out to him. Another man may be blessed with a full house—and children are such a blessing from God! Another may receive a five-card regular flush, which means that while he is not as legendary or famous as those men of 'royalty,' he does have some gift which makes him a sought-after person in his lower station of life. Another man may receive a five-card straight, which is a collection of many varied good gifts that make him a lesser, but still respected, person. He is a 'Jack of all trades, but a master of none.'

"But Rebbe," old Jacob lamented, "as you know, not all men are fortunate enough to get these excellent hands. This is a part of the gamble of Creation. Not all men are equally blessed. Thus, some receive three or four of a kind—a single gift that lacks the sought-after divine spark that would light the torch of its full creative potential, giving it completeness in activity. Yet others receive a 'bum hand'—a mixture which is of no consequence. This man may be best off if he chooses to discard what little he has so that he may pick up new 'sparks' from the left-over cards in the deck that may give his menial, rugged existence a new start.

"But every man, Rebbe, must play the game. Every man," explained the old man Jacob with great pathos in his eyes, "must receive, must evaluate, and must commit his heart, his soul, and his might (that is, his wealth) to the great gamble of Creation. Every man must pay the dealer His due. So Rebbe!" roared old Jacob, "why do you not join the rest of my people and gamble . . . or did you not know? You have been playing in this particular poker game all of your life since the day you were born!"

The Rebbe, almost overwhelmed with ecstasy, blurted out his response, "Old Jacob, what an illumination has come to me this night! What? . . . I see that my cards are already arranged in my hand. . . . This game must not be delayed any longer . . . I must pay the dealer immediately!"

The next morning, the Rebbe was bewildered to find himself in the midst of his own synagogue, fervently lost in the depths of a prayer that he could not recall afterwards. His appearance was that of a man who was drunk, penniless, and ecstatic . . .

QUESTIONS

What is the significance of the name of the village? Why is the "unseen dealer" a good image for God, even though it borders on the disrespectful? Is poker a better game to illustrate the point than, say, gin-rummy? Why?

Choose the Man

TEXT

The Rebbe was on his way to pay a call upon a distinguished Rebbe in a nearby city. As was the custom, one of his Hasidim was driving the car. As the vehicle approached the toll-booth, the driver took out the exact change and turned into the lane with the automatic toll-collecting machine. Seeing this, the Rebbe quickly admonished him, "Turn to the other lane, the one with the toll-collector. Given a choice between a machine and a man, one must always choose the man."

QUESTIONS

Why did the Rebbe choose the man? Is he against civilization and technology? How often have you chosen the machine over the man? Can you think of other examples? How might our choice of man-over-machine differ from that of the Rebbe's? Why?

We Shall Overcome

TEXT*

This is a true story. It should have been recorded for all time in the age-old memoir of the venerated Jewish community of Lublin. This community, however, along with all the other communities of a once glorious Polish Jewry, was totally wiped off the face of the earth, and the memoir, together with all the other sacred books of Lublin, was reduced to ashes.

The time was the early days of the extermination campaign launched by the Nazi hordes against the Jews of Poland. The place was Lublin—a "mother city" in Israel. The original reporter of the events was the head of the community, who secretly passed the information along. Later some unknown person risked his life to record in accurate detail all the horrors committed by the enemy. This anonymous writer was fortunate enough to survive the war and to salvage what he had written. After he reached the shores of Israel, he hand-copied the entire record of events, down to the last detail. Since then the story has been kept in the nation's archives, to be retold from generation to generation, to be sung by future poets, and to be held up by future historians as an example of miraculous deeds.

Lublin was a city prominent in Jewish history; the seat of the Council of the Four Countries; the city which later became a center of Torah with the

*From M. Prager, *Sparks of Glory,* pp. 9–13.

rebuilding of the illustrious Yeshiva of Lublin. It was this Lublin that was chosen, through some diabolic design, to be the first place for the Catastrophe to strike. It was there that the first detention camp, or *Reservat,* was erected. And it was there that the first transports of Jews, uprooted from their homes in Western Europe, were sent.

In the streets of Lublin the Germans staged an official public military ceremony, to the accompaniment of a full army band, for the burning of the books of the Great Yeshiva. And it was the Storm Troops' Commander Globochnik, a notoriously sadistic murderer, to whom the sad fate of the Jews of Lublin was entrusted.

The first thing this murderer did was appoint a time of assembly for all the Jews of the city. Young and old, men, women, and children were to come to an assigned place outside the city limits for a demonstration of torture and abuse. A decree was issued: any Jew who did not show up at the given hour would be shot. The frightened Jews considered the alternatives carefully. If they stayed at home, they would be doomed. If they went as ordered, they would be in grave danger, but at least there would be hope. They decided to go.

When the day came the Jews assembled promptly in great numbers. They stood fearful and trembling, prepared for the worst, but secretly praying for Divine intervention.

The assembly was held in an abandoned field on the outskirts of the city, completely surrounded by barbed wire. Armed guards stood everywhere, equipped for the occasion with whips in hand. The Jews stood trembling, their hearts quaking with mounting fear. What was the meaning of this grotesque show? What would the next moment bring?

The armed guards were ordered to form a double file. They were ready for something special to happen, for none other than Globochnik himself, the Commander-in-Chief, was personally overseeing the goings on. Globochnik, as they all knew, knew no bounds when it came to inventing ingenious tortures and clever tricks which he delighted to inflict on his Jewish victims. His troops, trained in brutality and bloodshed waited impatiently for the impending order.

The villainous oppressor was in high spirits. He was laughing uproariously, uncontrollably, without stop. His laughter curdled the blood of the hapless throng. He laughed and laughed as if the whole thing were nothing more than a joke. Even the orders he shouted sounded like nothing but a cruel jest.

"Sing, Jews!" he shouted. "Everyone of you will now sing! Sing, all of you together! Sing a happy song! Sing a Hasidic ditty! Do as I say, quickly!" he kept shrieking, and there was an ominous threat in his voice as he shouted his absurd order.

Sing? Is that all? Is that all the enemy wants? But how? How could these Jews in mortal fear for their lives suddenly burst into happy song? How could they bring themselves to sing a happy Hasidic song to these murderous barbarians?

The Jews remained silent. They could not open their mouths.

"Attack those stubborn Jews!" the commander blurted out, his voice now devoid of laughter. "Beat them with all your might!"

The armed guards followed the order, their ruthlessness matched only by their vehemence.

The Jews bit their tongues to hold back their cries, but could do nothing to stifle their sighs and groans.

"Push back those impudent Jews! Push them! Push them!" the enemy ordered again, shaking with blind fury. "Fast! Push them! Get going!"

The Jews were forced back against the barbed wire. The barbs pierced their flesh, pricking their bones, and the blood began to trickle and run. The Jews huddled and crowded together, stumbling and falling as more kept coming, colliding against the fallen ones and falling with them. Many were trampled under foot as each new wave of retreating people was pushed back.

In the midst of this confusion the shrieking voice of the murderous chief was heard again:

"Sing, arrogant Jews, sing! Sing or you will die! Gunners, aim your machine guns! Now listen, you dirty Jews. Sing or you will die!"

And at that horrifying moment, one man pried himself loose from the frightened mob and broke the conspiracy of total silence. He stood there all alone and began to sing. His song was a Hasidic folk song in which the Hasid poured out his soul before the Almighty:

> "Lomir zich iberbeiten, iberbeiten, avinu shebashamayim,
>   Lomir zich iberbeiten, iberbeiten, iberbeiten—"
> "Let us be reconciled, our Heavenly Father,
>   Let us be reconciled, let us make up—"

A spark of song was kindled, but that spark fell short of its mark. The Jews had been beaten, and recoiled. The voice of the singer did not reach them. His song was silenced. There was no singing.

But something did happen at that moment. A change took place. As soon as the solitary voice was hushed, humbly, another voice picked up the same tune, the same captivating Hasidic tune. Only the words were not the same. New words were being sung. One solitary person in the entire humiliated and downtrodden crowd had become the spokesman of all the Jews. This man had composed the new song on the spot, a song derived from the eternal wellspring of the nation. The melody was the same ancient Hasidic melody; but the words were conceived and distilled through the crucible of affliction:

"Mir velen zey iberleben, iberleben, avinu shebashama—yim,
  Mir velen zey iberleben, iberleben, iberleben—"
"We shall outlive them, our Heavenly Father,
  We shall outlive them, outlive them, outlive them—"

This time the song swept the entire crowd. The new refrain struck like lightning and jolted the multitude. Feet rose rhythmically, as if by themselves. The song heaved and swelled like a tidal wave, arms were joined, and soon all the frightened and despondent Jews were dancing.

As for the commander, at first he clapped his hands in great satisfaction, laughing derisively. "Ha, ha, ha, the Jews are singing and dancing! Ha ha, the Jews have been subdued!" But soon he grew puzzled and confused. What is going on? Is this how subdued people behave? Are they really oppressed and humiliated? They all seem to be fired up by this Hasidic dance, as if they have forgotten all pain, suffering, humiliation, and despair. They have even forgotten about the presence of the Nazi commander. . . .

"Stop, Jews! Stop immediately! Stop the singing and dancing! Stop! Stop immediately!" the oppressor yelled out in a terrible voice, and for the first time his well-disciplined subordinates saw him at a loss, not knowing what to do next.

"Stop! Stop! Stop at once!" the Commander-in-Chief pleaded with his soldiers in a croaking voice.

The Jews, singing and dancing ecstatically, were swept by the flood of their emotions and danced on and on. They paid a high price for it. They were brutally beaten for their strange behavior. But their singing and dancing did not stop.

QUESTIONS

In what way did the Hasidim "outlive" the Nazis? Why did the realization transform them? How did it also transform the Nazis? Does a Psalm come to your mind? There are many stories of deep spiritual heroism from the darkest hours of Jewish history, the Holocaust. (Another good sourcebook is I. Rosenbaum, *Holocaust and Halakha* [New York: KTAV Publishing House, 1976]). From whence did these Hasidim draw their strength? What basic world-view enabled them to confront Hell itself with faith, and even with piety?

Conclusion: How to Write a Hasidic Story

The central element for any Hasidic story, particularly for those of the short instructive type but also for those of the other genres, is God's immediate presence. God is everywhere—in the most likely and in the most unlikely places, in the most obvious and in the most humble and unexpected places. Thus, He can be seen in the life of the Besht and in that of a common Jewish farmer, in a football game, in a computer, on a highway, or in prayer. God is everywhere. Furthermore, He is always sensible, if one but has the bent to think that way. He can always be directly addressed, directly accosted. Thus, He can be addressed in Yiddish in a synagogue, and He can be praised in song from the depths of depravity and death. Most important, *His* reality is what is *truly* real. His presence is what is truly living. He is more real than the problems of sustenance, more real than the dangers of earthly death. He is truer than ritual, and more palpable than the worst this-wordly evil. For the Hasid, then, it is God Who is always central; it is God Who is always the immediate One. The words for this in English are "God-centeredness," "theocentrism," or more plainly: "spirituality." Hasidism is first and foremost an embodiment of the holy in the form of sensed spirituality, of immediate divine presence.

The rest is art. The literary style, the element of surprise, the juxtaposition of contrasting elements, the gentle self-deprecating humor, the problem-solution structure—all these are part of the narrator's art. They are not of the substance of the story. The substance is God: His presence, His compassion, His suffering. The truth is in the substance, and it is heard by the heart. The artifice is in the telling, and it is heard by the ear.

This idea of the singular reality of God is not a simple one, for one could argue: If God is everywhere, then there is no place where God is not. If God is everywhere, then all things, all acts, all words derive from God; indeed, in some way, everything *is* God. This logical extension of the idea of the singular reality of God was, in fact, seen and taught by the masters of Hasidic thought, especially by Dov Baer of Mezeritch, where it was formulated by two phrases: "the fullness of the universe is His glory" (*melo khol ha-aretz kevodo,* Isa. 6:3:) and "there is no place devoid of Him" (*leit atar penui mimei*). Unfortunately, this teaching has been misconstrued by some scholars as a form of pantheism or immanentism. This is not quite right, for Hasidism did not, in any way, deny God's otherness or transcendence. The appropriate formulation is that God is immanent *and* transcendent; that He is truly everywhere, both within the cosmos and beyond it. The term for this belief is "panentheism," and it is central to all Hasidic teaching.

Panentheism, however, does raise certain problems: If God is everywhere, how can one talk of man's free will? Panentheism implies quietism, which is a recognition that it is not man who acts but God Who acts through man. Quietism deemphasizes man's free will. This leads to many questions, among them: What is petitionary prayer in a world-view in which all acts are from God? This type of religious thought, thus, runs counter to traditional Judaism, and the tension between panentheism and

Rabbinic Judaism in Hasidism can be clearly felt. There are other questions too: Is God really everywhere? Is He really in such mundane moments as dishwashing, shopping, diaper-changing, and eating? And is He really in such evil moments as the concentration camp? The Hasidic answer to this question is yes. He really is everywhere. This, in turn, raises psychological problems for modern man, who values his privacy: Do I really want a God Who is everywhere, from Whom there is no escape? To this Hasidism replies: Escape from God? Are you mad? Why escape from that which is ultimately real, if you are fortunate enough to perceive it? God is real, rejoice that you know that. Nothing could be *more* real, *more* meaningful.

To write a "Hasidic" story of the short instructive type, then, the reader need only remember the central insight of Hasidism: God is everywhere and there is no place or moment devoid of Him. Pick a moment in life, any moment, and see it in that perspective. This is not easy for us because we have been trained to think in a secular manner, relying upon psychological generalizations, political instincts, and social perceptions to give us our orientation. Don't use any of those modes of thinking. See the moment from a Hasidic point of view. God is there; one must just look for Him. The rest is art. (Interestingly, Isaac Asimov has claimed that he could write a science fiction story for any given situation. He would analyze the scientific laws involved and then change only one of them in order to generate his story.) Three of the stories in this chapter were written using this method. Can you tell which ones? (The answer is in the section entitled: "For Further Reading and Instruction.")

Story-telling was only one of the forms of the numinous in Hasidism. It was not the most crucial form. The fullest application of Hasidic teaching was to be seen in the Hasidic prayer-life. And it is to that embodiment of the holy that we now turn.

8

THE HASIDIC PRAYER-LIFE

Introduction

When the rabbis of old began to discuss the question of which mitsva is the most important, they found that they could not agree. Some said it was the Sabbath; some said it was study of Torah; some said it was acts of kindness; and some said it was prayer. This very disagreement on the question of what constitutes the center of Judaism reflected the variety of persons who practiced Judaism, and at the same time, it left the doors of variety open to all who would adhere to the rabbinic Way. There was, and is, room for everybody—for the snooty intellectual who would not interrupt his study to pray, for the enrapt pietist who would not interrupt his prayer in order to study, and for the do-gooder whose activity would keep him from prayer and study. Nonetheless, within the rabbinic Way, there have been groups who, as groups, clearly set priorities. Thus, the rabbi-judges emphasized study, the liturgist-mystics emphasized prayer, and so on, though no group abolished entirely the other forms of rabbinic piety. Hasidism, because of its spiritualistic focus, chose prayer as the activity par excellence of the serious Jew. To pray was to be in the presence of God. To pray was to fulfill the verse: "I have set God before me, always" (Ps. 16:8). To pray was to live.

This chapter is, therefore, devoted to the Hasidic prayer-life. It begins with a statement on the nature of Kavvana. Then five types of Hasidic prayer are described through the use of texts and a commentary that explains some of the basic ideas behind the texts. Note that there are several types of Hasidic prayer, not just one; not even one central type. The conclusion deals with the question: What is new and what is old? Throughout, the reader must ponder the phenomenological, as well as the intellectual, aspects of the texts. They must be studied, not read. Then one can raise the question: In which of these types is the holy most present? In which of these forms is God's presence most powerfully felt?

111

Kavvana: The Art of Spiritual Consciousness-Raising

Can you hum a melody and think a thought? Can you dislike a person and yet be polite? Can you knowingly do something wrong? If you can do any of these things (and all of us can do them), then you know what "multiple consciousness" means. It means that we, in the course of our normal lives, can sustain several levels of awareness in us at the same time.

What do you have in mind when you "recite" prayers? What do you think of when you "participate" in a religious service? What do you have in your consciousness when you "pray"? These questions, too, reflect our ability to sustain multiple consciousness—in particular, the multiple consciousness which we call "religious" or "spiritual." To pray is more than to "say one's prayers." It is to raise one's religious consciousness. It is to focus one's spiritual senses.

The traditional Jewish term for spiritual consciousness-raising is *Kavvana*. Kavvana is a consciousness-raising technique; that is, it is a technique for broadening one's awareness of what one is doing. The technique is accomplished by directing one's thoughts and one's awareness to the various aspects of what one is doing. In Hebrew, there is a verb, *lakhavven et ha-lev*, which literally means "to direct the heart" but which can also be translated as "to do (something) with attentiveness." The result of the use of Kavvana, as is the case with all consciousness-raising techniques, is to change an act from a routine, or semi-conscious, act into an experience in which one is more fully present and more fully aware of all the realities touched.

One way to elucidate the nature of Kavvana is by example, and I present here an example of the various modes of Kavvana and the levels internal to each mode as an indication of the range of living religious reality within traditional Rabbinic Judaism.

On certain holidays, the liturgy prescribes the recitation of Psalms 113–118, which together are called *Hallel* ("Praise"). Towards the end of Psalm 118 (verse 25), the Psalmist writes: "Please, Lord, save, please; Please, Lord, grant success, please." This verse can be recited with varying levels of awareness. At the lowest level, it is recited as a matter of routine, in a semi-conscious manner, with the person reciting it being vaguely aware of doing what he is supposed to do. This is called *keva^c* or *she-lo lishma*—that is, mindless prayer. It is prayer without Kavvana.

In one mode of Kavvana, the rabbinic Jew reciting this verse must become aware of the various meanings of the words. He must first become aware of their simple, direct meaning. Then he must become aware of their context within this very beautiful Psalm, which itself speaks of "crying from the straits" and God's response. On a broader level, such a person would have to become aware of the rabbinic regulations regarding the recitation of this verse: that it is recited by the leader first and then the congregation; that on Sukkot there are prescribed movements of the Lulav (palm branch) and Etrog (citron) which accompany the recitation of this verse, and that all movements cease when the word "Lord" is said; and so on. On still a broader level, such a person would have to become aware of the report in the Mishna (*Sukka* 4:5) concerning the circumambulation of the altar during which this verse was recited, and that according to another Sage, a strange metamorphosis of this verse was recited: "I and *ho,* save, please," and that this metamorphosed version occurs in the later liturgy and is reputed to have magical properties. At the outer limits of this mode of Kavvana, the praying rabbinic Jew would be aware of the kabbalistic "unifications" attendant upon recitation of this verse and he would "make" them.

In a different mode of Kavvana, the rabbinic Jew reciting this verse must become aware of what it is he is praying for, of that from which he wishes to be "saved," of that kind of "success" he wishes to have. He must begin with simple personal needs: health, sustenance, strength, love, and insight. He then must broaden his awareness to include the needs of his family, immediate and more remote. More broadly, he must make himself aware of the needs of Jews elsewhere: their need for peace, for security, for freedom. And more broadly still, such a person must make himself aware of the need of mankind for peace, for sustenance, and for life. At the outer limits of this mode of Kavvana, the praying rabbinic Jew would have to become aware of himself and, indeed, of all people, as truly, existentially alone, separated from one another by the silence that separates all being, and that his prayer is a primal cry into eternity for himself, for his children, and for all people everywhere.

In a different mode of Kavvana, the rabbinic Jew reciting this verse must become aware of himself. He must first become aware of his own physical presence; then of his presence in the congregation of worshippers; then of his presence in the greater congregation of worshipping Jews the world over; then of his presence in the greater congregation of worshipping Jews through time; and so on. On a broader level, such a person would have to become aware of those brothers of the flesh and spirit who cannot pray, whose lives were cut off in the crematoria; that they, too, deserve to have their prayers recited; and that through this mode of Kavvana, the praying rabbinic Jew becomes more than himself. His consciousness becomes the instantiation of theirs. His presentness becomes their presentness, and he speaks, or rather cries out, for them too.

In a different mode of Kavvana, the rabbinic Jew reciting this verse must become aware of God. He must become aware of God's absolute transcendence, of the utter power of God, which knows no limits but those which are self-imposed. And he must become aware of God's absolute love of man, of the inalienable bond to which God has committed Himself. More broadly, he must contemplate the types of fear of God and the types of love of God. He must meditate on the essential contingency of all reality upon God—that nothing exceeds God's knowledge, power, and providence. And he must ponder the acts and the Person of God as reflected in the traditional texts. More broadly still, such a person must confront his own real fear of God and his own real love of God. He must confront the reality of his relatedness to God. And then he must consciously broaden his awareness to let the Presence of God into his mind and heart. He must consciously broaden his awareness to permit himself to stand in the Presence of God—person to Person, presence to Presence. At the outer limits of this mode of Kavanna, the praying rabbinic Jew must, in his own awareness, be ready to die, in that moment. He must be ready to immediately cast himself into the abyss. He must be completely ready to give up his soul for God, for His Truth, for His Torah, for His people. And then he must say what he has to say, for whom he has to say it. Then, and only then, the rabbinic Jew may, and indeed must, pray.

Not everyone can achieve or sustain such a broad spectrum of consciousness—in all its modes and levels—but in its full scope (and there is undoubtedly part that I, in my ignorance, have omitted), Kavvana is the key to the range of traditional religious reality, to Jewish piety.

Another way to elucidate the nature of Kavvana is to examine it developmentally, historically. Thus, the early rabbinic texts of late antiquity talk about the need for Kavvana in the doing of any of the commandments, but especially in that of prayer. The verse, "Now Hannah spoke in her heart" (I Sam. 1:13), for example, is understood to teach that "he who prays must direct his heart to heaven." Similarly, there are discussions of the conditions under which one's Kavvana might be inhibited (e.g., if one were working, or traveling, or in danger, etc.). Later, this simple "directing of the heart to God" was very aptly formulated in pietistic and legal works. Thus, Bahya Ibn Paquda, in his *Duties of the Heart* (8:1, cited in L. Jacobs, *Hasidic Prayer*, pp. 71–72), wrote:

When a man is employed in those duties in which both the heart and the limbs are involved such as prayer and praising God, blessed be He, he should empty himself of all matter appertaining to this world or the next and he should empty his heart of every distracting thought, after first cleansing himself and washing away all stains and filth. He should keep himself far from every unpleasant smell and the like. He should then consider to Whom it is the prayers are directed and what he intends to ask and what he intends to speak in the presence of his Creator; pondering on the words of the prayers and their meaning. Know that so far as the language of prayer is concerned the words themselves are like the husk while reflection on the meaning of the words is like the kernel. The prayer itself is like the body while reflection on its meaning is like the spirit, so that, if a man merely utters the words of the prayers with his heart concerned with matters other than prayer, then his prayer is like a body without spirit and a husk without a kernel, because while the body is present when he prays his heart is absent. Of people such as he the Scripture says, "Forasmuch as this people draw near, and with their mouth and with their lips do honour Me, but have removed their heart far from Me" (Isa. 29:13).

Note the stages: emptying one's consciousness of worldly matters, then sensing the presence of God, then determining what one wants to ask, and finally the pondering of the liturgical text. Maimonides, too, following the rabbinic understanding of Kavvana in the section from his *Guide of the Perplexed* cited above (p. 15), gave similar instructions about emptying the mind of worldly concerns, and concentrating on the words and on the presence of God. Earlier, he had formulated these injunctions in his *Code of Law* (*Hilkhot Tefilla* 4:16) as follows: "What is the definition of Kavvana? It means that one should empty one's mind of all thought and see oneself as if one were standing in the presence of the Shekhina." This rabbinic understanding of Kavvana, which consisted in a consciousness of God, of the self, and of the world, was also expounded clearly in the later codes of law and in the exhortatory writings. In fact, it has remained quite consistent in its definition from the earliest period until the present.

The second level of understanding, developmentally speaking, is that of mystical Kavvana. (For an interesting parallel in Christian religion, cf. F. Heiler, *Prayer,* where the author distinguishes "mystical prayer" from what he calls "prophetic prayer.") To be sure, the type of mystical Kavvana varied with the type of mysticism. Thus, when Merkabah mysticism was current, mystical Kavvana consisted in knowing the angel-names and in traversing the ladder, through the palaces. When Zoharic-Lurianic mysticism was current, mystical Kavvana consisted in returning the flow of energy through sefirot and thus aiding in the inner stabilization of God. When the Maimonidean type of mysticism was current, mystical Kavvana consisted in meditation upon the Intelligences and/or the letters. And, when the various forms of Hasidic mysticism became current, mystical Kavvana consisted in that super-added dimension of meditation.

Kavvana, then, is the Jewish term for spiritual consciousness-raising. It is the technique for focusing one's consciousness on the various aspects of religious experience. In its most basic form, it is a focusing upon the presence of God, the meaning of the liturgy, the prayer context, and the communication to be made. In its mystical form, it is a focusing upon the highest mystical experience taught by the current mystical belief-system. As the belief-system varied with time, so did the religious experiential expectation, and hence, so did the mystical Kavvana.

With this in mind, we can now turn to the types of Hasidic teaching and prayer, as well as to the types of Kavvana expected of a Hasid.

The Zoharic-Lurianic-Habad Type of Prayer

Hasidism did not develop in a vacuum. It had at its disposal what W. C. Smith has called the "accumulated tradition"; that is, it had to confront the tradition of mystical thinking and practice which had come down to it. One main element in this accumulated tradition was the Zoharic-Lurianic stream of thought and practice. Hasidism dealt with it in three ways. Some Hasidic thinkers rejected the Zoharic-Lurianic tradition in favor of something new and different (see below pp. 127ff., "The Devekut Type of Prayer"). Some Hasidim preserved the Lurianic system intact, often assigning the study and practice of it only to the Zaddik (see below Chapter 9, "The Zaddik and His Community"). And some Hasidim undertook to modify the Zoharic-Lurianic tradition in accordance with new principles and then to espouse a very intellectualist, contemplative, meditative type of prayer. This last method was particularly followed by the Hasidim of Lubavitch, also known as the Habad Hasidim.

The following reading presents this type of Hasidic prayer-life very well. Note the transformation of the Zoharic-Lurianic tradition through the psychological understanding of the sefirot and through a wholistic, meditative type of Kavvana.

TEXT*

Contemplation, especially during prayer, is an essential feature of the Habad movement in Hasidism. The very name Habad is formed from the initial letters of Hohkmah ("Wisdom"), Binah ("Understanding") and Daat ("Knowledge"). The first two, as we have noted in a previous chapter, are the names of two of the Sefirot, those representing the divine thought. In some Kabbalistic schemes Daat is also one of the Sefirot. In others it is not the name of a Sefirah but of a mediating principle between Hokhmah and Binah. Now according to the basic idea, stressed by Hasidism, that the divine processes are mirrored in man's soul, Hokhmah, Binah and Daat are descriptions, too, of man's contemplative

---

*From L. Jacobs, *Hasidic Prayer*, pp. 82–91.

life. Hokhmah is, in Habad thought, the first flash of intuitive knowledge and awareness, the emergence in the mind of a bare idea not as yet elaborated in thought. Binah denotes reflection on the elaborate details of the idea, the giving of form and content to it in the mind. Daat means an attachment of the mind to the idea so that it is fully grasped by the mind and acquires such a firm lodgement therein that, in turn, it is capable of arousing the emotions. Daat both follows on Hokhmah and Binah and is the motivating power, the essential interest, which propels a man towards Hokhmah and Binah.

As for the material of contemplation, Habad, here and in other areas, treads its own road. Essentially, the Habad Hasid is encouraged to reflect on the detailed Kabbalistic scheme by which creation unfolds. This follows the Lurianic pattern but as reinterpreted by the Habad thinkers. The Hasid has in mind the whole process by which all worlds proceed from En Sof through an increasing coarsening, as it were, of the divine light until the finite world we inhabit comes into being. The true Habad Hasid has to be, in fact, a Kabbalist and his contemplation in prayer consists of a review in his mind of the Lurianic mysteries in their Habad guise. This technique differs from that of the older Lurianic Kabbalists in that it is no longer a sustained reflection on each word of the prayers as referring to one or other of the divine names and their place on the Sefirotic map. Instead, the whole scheme is surveyed in the mind independently at appropriate stages of the prayers, especially when the Shema is recited. . . .

Every idea has its "depth," "length" and "breadth" so that contemplation involves reflection on all three. Reflection on the "breadth" of an idea means that its full implications are uncovered; it is the "width" of the river which has far greater extension than the mere trickle of the brook. Reflection on the "length" of an idea means that an attempt is made so to grasp the subject that it can be conveyed, by means of various illustrations, to one incapable otherwise of grasping it; it is the "length" of the river flowing far from its source. Reflection on the "depth" of an idea means that an attempt is made to grasp the essential point of the subject; it is the "depth" of the river in its underground source. As explained in greater detail by R. Hillel, R. Dov Baer's disciple, the illustration of the river is applied as follows. The underground source of the river represents Hokhmah. The idea springs into the mind spontaneously, from the unconscious, as we would be inclined to say. The first flow of the river above ground represents Binah, the beginning of contemplation proper. Although, at this stage, it is no more than a trickle, it contains within itself the force provided by the subterranean source and, *in potentia,* the whole subsequent flow of the river. The idea has erupted into the mind and its essence is grasped. The breadth of the river refers to the expansion of the waters *near to their source,* i.e. the idea once grasped is pondered on so as to uncover all its implications, so as to understand what it really means in all its details. But if one really understands an idea, one is able to convey it to others by adapting the form in which it is expressed to the intellectual capacity of the recipient. This is the length of the river. The reference is not so much to the actual teaching of the idea to others as to the ability to have the idea so clear in one's own mind as to be able to see how it can be conveyed to others. The Hebrew for "contemplation" (*hitbonanut*) has the same root as Binah. But, R. Dov Baer remarks, *hitbonanut* is an intensive form of the verb and this is to indicate that only prolonged and rigorous reflection in depth qualifies as contemplation.

Furthermore, there are two types of contemplation, represented by the Hebrew terms *binah* and *tevunah.* The man who has grasped the idea in all its details, as above, has attained to the stage of *binah* but he does not reach the more elevated stage of *tevunah* until he is able to use his deductive powers in order to grasp those further ideas that are only implicit in the original idea contemplated. For example, the man who has a complete grasp of a subtle legal theory has attained the stage of *binah* so far as his theory is concerned. But he does not attain to the stage of *tevunah* until he is capable of stating with complete conviction, on the basis of his theory, whether A or B would be culpable in law. Or, to give another example, there is a good deal of difference between a man who has merely read widely about architecture and the professional architect whose reading has been supplemented by his practical skills in which he puts his academic knowledge to use. True contemplation has as its aim the attainment of *tevunah,* not of *binah* alone.

There are thus two stages of contemplation in prayer. The first is that of *binah.* This means reflection with deep concentration on the theme that God "fills all worlds," that all there is has been created by God out of nothing and that it is by His power alone that all things are sustained. It is not sufficient to reflect on the bare idea but to grasp it in all its implications by means of various illustrations and analogies, such as that of the soul giving life to the body or that of the spark emerging from the flame. But it is possible for a man to obtain a theoretical understanding of this idea without being able to "use" it in prayer. Many Hasidim, remarks R. Dov Baer, have a good knowledge of these tremendous themes in an academic way but fail to see of what relevance they are to the life of prayer. This is because they have never tried adequately to apply the themes of their studies to the life of prayer. They are more abstract religious thinkers than true contemplatives. The stage of *tevunah* is reached when the idea has become so much part of man that he can "use" it in his prayers in order to induce the love and fear of God.

There are two methods of contemplation: (a) the general method; (b) the detailed method. The general method is to dwell on the general idea of God's immanence, that all is in God. The detailed method is to reflect on the way in which God is immanent in each creature, on the way in which each is in God, on the divine vitality by which each creature is sustained and in which it has its being, as well as upon all the complex details of the Kabbalah. The worshipper, when adopting this detailed method, has in mind the whole system of divine emanation, from the highest point of the Sefirotic realm down through the whole marvellous chain of being to the lowliest creature in this physical universe. Of the two the detailed method is to be preferred, provided always that the details are connected in thought with the general idea of God's unity. (R. Dov Baer states that his father had told him in the name of the Maggid of Meseritch that this method should also be adopted when studying any detailed exposition of the divine mysteries in the Zohar or in the writings of the Lurianic school.) The fullest comprehension of every detail should only serve to fortify the general idea that all is in God. While the detailed method is to be preferred, R. Dov Baer, nonetheless, advises beginners to adopt, at first, the general method until they have gradually trained themselves to practise the detailed method.

Further, on the detailed method, R. Dov Baer remarks that whenever a man engages in contemplation by this method there are two aspects to his thoughts. In reflecting on each detail he has in mind that the "something-ness" of creatures stems from the divine Nothingness. This can, how-ever, be of two kinds: (a) the reflection that "somethingness" comes out of Nothingness; (b) that it is out of Nothingness that "somethingness" comes. That is to say, in reflection of the type (a) the emphasis is on created things. In reflection of the type (b) the emphasis is rather on the way in which the divine Nothingness has brought them into being. Now the more one engages in reflection of the type (a) the greater the joy in comprehension, since reflection on finite things, albeit in their relation to the divine immanence, is not too difficult for finite man. But reflection of the type (b) is concerned with that which is utterly beyond all human comprehension. That is why the term Nothingness is used. Here the emphasis on the divine Nothingness means that the soul of the contemp-lative can never be satisfied, so that here the more profound and intense the act of contemplation the greater will be the resulting sense of remote-ness and sorrow. When, for instance, man reflects on the myriads of stars in their courses, on the immensity of the space they occupy and on their size in relation to the earth, there is delight in the thought that all these have come into being out of the divine Nothingness. The more man understands the immensity of the miracle of their sheer existence the more he marvels, the greater his sense of wonder that all these came from "nowhere" and the more intense his comprehension of God's majesty.

But when he goes on from there to consider the nature of that divine Nothingness, his mind can only tremble in awe at the overwhelming mystery. Similarly, when a man reflects on the "somethingness" of creatures he senses that he, too, is something. But when he begins to reflect on the divine Nothingness, his total inability to comprehend reduces him to a state of "nothingness," and there is, in the standard Hasidic terminology, "self-annihilation" (*bittul ha-yesh*). These two types of contemplation are, in fact, inseparable. For unless there is joy and wonder in contemplation on the "somethingness" of things, there is little meaning to the idea that they all came from the divine Nothingness. On the other hand, there is little value in contemplation if the mind remains imprisoned in its reflection on the "somethingness" of creatures without gazing beyond them to the divine Nothingness which sustains them all.

R. Dov Baer draws certain conclusions from this for the fuller contemplative exercises. There is both joy and pain when lovers part for a time. These emotions, though conflicting, are, in reality, two sides of the same coin. The very poignancy of the pain they experience is the fruit of love, and that love is more intense than ever before because the pain of parting brings to the lovers a full realisation of what their love means to them. Similarly, the deeper a man's delight in his comprehension of the divine, the greater is his sorrow at his remoteness from the divine. For there is no limit to man's comprehension of the Limitless, there are no confines to man's spiritual ambitions. The nearer man comes to God the greater his sense of remoteness. The more intense his delight, the more powerful his longing and the more profound his sadness. The true test of authenticity in contemplation is whether or not the soul laments her remoteness from God. Where there is only joy, where man enjoys God without any sense of remoteness from Him, the act of contemplation is superficial. Hence R. Dov Baer advises his followers to rise at midnight to weep for their sins, which create a barrier between the soul and God. And it is for this reason that the Maggid of Meseritch taught that the "secrets of the Torah" can only be comprehended by one "whose heart is constantly anxious within him" . . .

Before the *tzimtzum* (God's withdrawal "from Himself into Himself" in order to make "room" for the world) there was only God as He is in Himself. (It should be noted that the Kabbalists think of all these processes as occurring outside time, so that terms like "before" and "after" are not really applicable.) In order for creatures to emerge as the recipients of His bounty, since it is the nature of the All-good to give of His goodness to others, the *tzimtzum* takes place. R. Dov Baer compares it to a profound idea in the mind of a teacher. In order to convey the idea to his pupil, the teacher has to concentrate on the essential point of the matter and has to "withdraw" from his comprehension of the full depth and breadth of the idea. After the *tzimtzum* a "residue" of the divine light penetrated the "empty space" left by the *tzimtzum*. (Again the Kabbalists do not think of "space" in its literal sense but of the primordial "space" into which eventually space and time as we know them emerged.) The light of En Sof (again used in a figurative sense) illumines the "empty space" but no longer fills it. The highest and lowest stages of all the successive degrees by which the light of En Sof is unfolded are called respectively Keter ("Crown") and Malkhut ("Sovereignty"). These are, in fact, the names of the highest and lowest Sefirot but are used, too, at this early stage before the Sefirot have emerged. The "line" of light from En Sof which penetrates the "empty space" in order to illumine it and to sustain whatever is to emerge there, is called Malkhut of En Sof and this, in turn, becomes the Keter of the next stage which is known as Adam Kadmon ("Primordial Man"). In the same way the chain of emanation wends its way downwards by degrees. Malkhut of Adam Kadmon becomes Keter of the World of Emanation, the realm of the Sefirot. Malkhut of the World of Emanation becomes Keter of the World of Creation. Malkhut of this world becomes Keter of the World of Formation. Malkhut of this world becomes Keter of the World of Action. Within the whole process there are countless variations and combinations in which the light of En Sof is contracted and expands, illumines this way and that, so as to sustain all worlds. Much is demanded then of the Habad Hasid who wishes to have *kavvanah* in his prayers. His mind must dwell on all these stages with the aim of seeing all of them as in essence only the infinite light of En Sof.

There is a further idea which is behind the whole doctrine of Habad contemplation. This is that the lowest stage of all the "upper worlds"— Malkhut of the World of Action—reaches back to, and is united with, the highest stage of all—Malkhut of En Sof—and this, in turn, is united with En Sof. Since the actual physical universe is only the lowest and final manifestation of the World of Action, all finite creatures are ultimately united in and embraced by the unity of En Sof. This is the mystical meaning given to the verse: "I am the first, and I am the last" (Isa. 44:6), i.e. from the highest stage of all, the first impulse, as it were, in En Sof, to the final manifestation of the divine creative activity, all are included, as the Habad thinkers are fond of saying, in God's simple unity. The Habad contemplative is expected to become thoroughly familiar with all this, so that when he reflects in his prayers on the details of the process there is an automatic compression of them all into the one great principle of unity. It is for this reason, Habad teaches, that there are no references in the Book of Psalms to the "higher worlds," only to God's majesty as manifested here in the physical universe. For, in reality, there is no "separation" between the processes of the higher realms and those observed in the physical world. They are all part of the same process and are all embraced by the divine unity. The Hasid, trained in the Kabbalah and using it in his prayers, dwells in his thought on all the complex details of the chain of emanation and, through profound reflection on them, learns to perceive that from beginning to end of all the creative processes there is only the divine unity, by the light of which all separate things are illumined and by which they are given the appearance of reality.

The Unifying-the-Letters Type of Prayer

Another element in the "accumulated tradition" of Jewish mystical thought which Hasidism had to confront was the long tradition of letter-mysticism reaching back to the *Sefer Yetsira* and following a line of development through Abulafia's complicated "permuations." Hasidism, on the whole, rejected the magical aspect of letter-mysticism and, as the following passages show, took the words and letters and invested them with spiritual energy, with pneumatic Kavvana. The old tradition thus took on new life.

In the texts which follow, note carefully the interweaving of the new letter-mysticism with allusions to the Zoharic-Lurianic tradition ("unification," "the worlds of emanation," "receive the waters," "the garments of God") and to the Maimonidean tradition ("joy," "delight," "corporeal nature," "burning love"). Note, too, some new terminology ("united with the divine," "Nothingness," "enthusiasm," "attachment," and automatic speech).

TEXT*

We begin with the famous letter (which is generally assumed to be authentic) written by the Baal Shem Tov around 1752 from Rashkov in the Ukraine to his brother-in-law R. Gershon of Kutov who was then in Palestine. The letter was published in the work *Ben Porat Yosef* by the Baal Shem Tov's disciple, R. Jacob Joseph of Pulnoye, at the end of the work, at Koretz in 1781. The section of the letter relevant to our theme reads:

You must have the intention [*tekhavven*] of unifying a name whenever your mouth utters a word at the time you pray and study the Torah. In every letter there are worlds, souls and divinity, which ascend to become bound one to the other. Then the letters become bound and united one to the other to form a word and they become united with a true unification in the divine. You must allow your soul to become united with them at every

---

*From L. Jacobs, *Hasidic Prayer,* pp. 75–78.

stage of the above. Then all the worlds become united as one and they ascend so that there is immeasurable joy and delight. You know how great is the joy when bride and bridegroom unite in this world of smallness and materialism. How much greater, then, is the joy at this lofty stage! God will undoubtedly help you and you will be successful and understand wherever you turn. Give to the wise and he will get further understanding.

The letters of the Hebrew alphabet are, as the Baal Shem Tov understands the matter, not mere symbols but the expression of metaphysical realities. They are the counterpart on earth of God's creative processes and are themselves endowed with creating power. The aim of the Hasid should be to assist the unification of these creative forces and in the process lose himself in the divine. As his mind dwells on each letter separately—Weiss calls this the "atomization" of the letters—so that it embraces "worlds, souls and divinity," his soul becomes absorbed in the unification process. The letters are then formed into words and, by reflecting on this, the mind of the Hasid is embraced in an ever higher unification process. Hasidic prayer is, then, an exercise in assisting the divine unification and participating in it, sharing the joy and delight which attend unification as all worlds and all souls become attached to God. The "plain meaning" of the words of the prayers is entirely ignored. All that matters is the unification theme represented by the letters themselves and the way they are grouped together to form words. One can describe the difference between this kind of contemplation and the practice of the Lurianic *kavvanot* in the following way, apart from the fact that the former is intensely emotional while the latter is severely intellectual. Both techniques depart from the "plain meaning" of the words, but while the Lurianic Kabbalist dwells on the "higher" meaning of the words the Hasid is not interested in the meaning of the words at all, only in the unification process as represented by the letters and words they form.

An oft-quoted Hasidic comment in the same vein as the above is to the verse, "A light shalt thou make to the ark" (Gen. 6:16). The Hebrew word for "ark" (*tevah*) is taken to mean "word." Thus . . .

"A light shalt thou make for the word." This means that the word should be illumined. For in every word there are worlds, souls and divinity. These ascend and become bound and united one to the other and with the divine. Then the letters become united and bound together to form a word and then they become truly united in the divine. A man must allow his soul to be embraced by each stage of the above-mentioned and then all the worlds become united as one and they ascend so that there is immeasurable joy and delight.

Here again is the same theme. The letters of the Hebrew alphabet represent spiritual forces on high (e.g., the letter *alef* is a particular divine potency as it appears in the physical universe). In each letter there are represented the three stages of being: worlds, souls and divinity. The letters, in turn, combine to form words, expressing the further combination of all powers. Since man is the microcosm and the divine realm the macrocosm, then by contemplating the unification theme (the turning of the letters into words, etc.) in his prayers, man raises all these to their source in the divine and he assists the unification process. He repeats, as it were, in his own soul the divine creative activity and so restores the separated universe back to God.

In another passage the technique is described in greater detail:

When he prays a man should put all his strength into the utterances and so he should proceed from letter to letter until he has forgotten his corporeal nature. He should reflect on the idea that the letters become combined and joined one to the other and this is great delight. For if in the material world unification is attended by delight how much more so in the spiritual realms! This is the stage of the world of formation. Afterwards he should reach the stage of having the letters in his thoughts alone so that he no longer hears that which he speaks. At this stage he enters the world of formation. Afterwards he should reach the quality of Nothingness at which all his physical powers are annihilated. This is the stage of the world of emanation, the quality of Wisdom.

This is a remarkable description of the Hasid's ascent of soul in his prayers until self-annihilation is attained. For the understanding of the passage something must be said of the Kabbalistic doctrine of the four worlds.

The doctrine runs that there are four worlds, one higher than the other. The highest of all is the *world of emanation* (*olam ha-atzilut*), the realm of the Sefirot. Beneath it and emerging from it is the *world of creation* (*olam ha-beriah*). Next there is the *world of formation* (*olam ha-yetzirah*). Lowest of all four is the *world of action* (*olam ha-asiyah*). This latter is the origin of the physical universe, which it embraces. The *world of emanation* is identified with the Sefirah Hokhmah ("Wisdom"). In Hasidic thought this Sefirah is called *ayin*, "Nothingness," because of this stage of the divine process nothing can be said; it is utterly beyond all human comprehension. When a man attains to the stage of self-annihilation he can thus be said to have reached the world of the divine Nothingness. Emptied of selfhood his soul has now become attached to the true reality, the divine Nothingness. Thus in our passage the stages of the mystic's ascent in prayer are described in terms of the four worlds which, in fact, are mirrored in his own soul. He begins in the *world of action*, where he stands as he begins to pray. When "he puts all his strength into the utterances" he abandons something of self and begins to ascend to the *world of formation*. The next stage in loss of selfhood is for him to lose the capacity to hear the words he utters. (The tradition of the rabbis has it that the words of the prayers must be voiced so that the Hasid, as an orthodox Jew, is prevented from taking the logical next step of completely silent prayer.) He continues to mouth the words, but his mind has become so preoccupied with the bare thought of the letters that he is no longer conscious of hearing the words he utters. He then reaches the *world of creation*. Finally, "all his physical powers are annihilated." He is no longer conscious even of his thoughts. He has attained to self-annihilation and is completely immersed in the divine Nothingness.

TEXT*

The purpose of all prayer is to uplift the words,
    to return them to their source above.
The world was created
    by the downward flow of letters:
The task of man is to form those letters into words
    and take them back to God.
If you come to know this dual process,
    your prayer may be joined
    to the constant flow of Creation—
    word to word, voice to voice,
    breath to breath, thought to thought.

The words fly upward and come before Him.
As God turns to look at the ascending word,
    life flows through all the worlds
    and prayer receives its answer.
All this happens in an instant
    and all this happens continually;
Time has no meaning in the sight of God.
The divine spring is ever-flowing;
    one who is ready can make himself into a
    channel
    to receive the waters from above.

                   *   *   *   *

When you focus all your thought
    on the power of the words,
    you may begin to see the sparks of light
    that shine within them.

---

*From A. Green, *Your Word Is Fire*, pp. 49, 46, 44, 42.

The sacred letters are the chambers
  into which God pours His flowing light.
The lights within each letter, as they touch,
  ignite one another,
  and new lights are born.

It is of this the Psalmist says:
  "Light is sown for the righteous,
  and joy for the upright in heart."

*   *   *   *

A person should put all his strength into the words,
  proceeding from letter to letter
  with such concentration
  that he loses awareness of his bodily self.
It then seems to him that the letters themselves
  are flowing into one another.
This uniting of the letters is his greatest joy.
If joy is felt as two human bodies come together,
  how much greater must be the joy
  of this union in spirit!

*   *   *   *

Think that the letters of prayer
  are the garments of God.
What a joy to be making a garment
  for the greatest of kings!
Enter into every letter with all your strength.
God dwells within each letter;
  as you enter it, you become one with Him.

TEXT*

It is also an important rule in prayer that a man should allow his intellect
to prevail when he recites the words of the prayers so as to shatter the
barrier which separates [him from God] until he cleaves to God, blessed
be He. For every letter [of the prayers] is a great world extending upwards
ad infinitum and with every letter he utters with his mouth he bestirs those
worlds up above. Consequently, he should recite the words [of his
prayers] with great enthusiasm [*hitlahavut*], with great joy, and with great
attachment [*devekut*]. It is another great rule that in whatsoever he does a

---

*From L. Jacobs, *Hasidic Prayer*, pp. 97–98.

man should intend only to give satisfaction to the Shekhinah. He should
have no thought of self, not even to the slightest degree, for he is vanity
and emptiness so why should he do it for his own pleasure? Even if he
makes many preparations so as to be able to serve God with attachment,
but does this in order to obtain personal delight from his act of worship,
then he is only a self-worshipper. The main thing is that all his worship
should be for the sake of the Shekhinah and there should be nothing of
self in it, not even to the slightest degree. At times a man is like unto a
drunkard in the joy he has of the Torah because a great love burns in his
heart. At times a man is able to recite his prayers at great speed because
the love of God burns so powerfully in his heart and the words emerge
from his mouth automatically.

The Devekut Type of Prayer: Meditative Ecstasy

There are two forms of the devekut type of prayer: the meditative and the
tumultuous. The meditative form, as the term suggests, was intellectual,
intramental. It was a "silent fire"; a burning, yet internal, ecstasy.
Outwardly, it was sedate. In this it followed the general pattern of the
Jewish mystical tradition, particularly the Maimonidean pattern. The
intellectual framework was different, very different, from that of the
previous structures of Jewish mystical thought. But the praxis was a
function of meditation, of the mystical intramental use of the teachings of
a specific world-view. The tumultuous form of the devekut type of prayer,
as the term suggests, was agitated, physical, frenzied. It was a "raging
fire"; a fortissimo; a turbulent, sometimes boisterous, ecstasy. Outwardly, as well as inwardly, it was furious. In this it drew upon precedents
recorded in the early literature. But it was, in large measure, a new form
of worship. Note very carefully, however, two important points: (1) Both
forms of this type of prayer are ecstatic. Both forms led to, and grew out
of, a true mystical ecstasy. They represent two Ways to ecstasy; but both
are ecstatic. And (2) both forms grew out of the same structure of thought.
Both had their ideational and intellectual basis in the same set of ideas, in
the same basic teaching.

   The basic world-view of this type of Hasidic mystical teaching can be
summed up in a few technical terms which make their appearance with
Hasidism or which attain their special transformed meaning with
Hasidism. The first of these terms is *ha-Ayin*, "the Nothing," "Nothingness." The term is a noun derived from the negative particle, and it had
been current in Jewish thought before Hasidism—for example, in the
Hebrew phrase *beriah yesh me-ayin* ("creatio ex nihilo"). In Hasidism,
however, the term came to refer to the ultimately unknowable aspect of
God. For those thinkers who integrated Hasidism with the Zoharic-

Lurianic system, the Ayin was equivalent to, or beyond, the Ein-Sof. For those thinkers who sloughed off the Zoharic-Lurianic system, the Ayin was simply God in His most transcendent, unknowable aspect. Combining this with the Hasidic doctrine that "the fullness of the universe is His glory" and "there is no place devoid of Him," Hasidism arrived at the conclusion that all of reality is God; or, put differently, that there is nothing in the universe but God; or, again, that reality is essentially nothingness. This syllogism—the divine is nothingness, reality is nothingness, and hence all of reality is the divine—is well-known to students of mysticism (although one must add that "reality" here includes transcendence). But it was new in the stream of Jewish mystical thought.

Ha-Ayin has two opposites. The first is *ha-yesh*. This term refers to physical and supermundane reality. For Hasidism, these realms are "created" or "generated"; they are not simply there. In a more subtle sense, however, the opposite of ha-Ayin is *ha-ani*, "the I," "the ego." By an act of providential wisdom, the letters of the word ani (aleph, nun, yod), when rearranged, read Ayin (aleph, yod, nun). This was understood to show the interrelatedness of consciousness, of self-consciousness, and of God.

This bifurcated world-view—with physical reality and the ego on one side and God on the other, yet both closely related, indeed identical in a limited sense of the word—enabled Hasidism to pose the question: How does one bridge this seeming gap? Or, how does one become conscious of the underlying unity of this situation? There are three elements in achieving mystical ecstasy in Hasidism, each of which is designated by a technical term. The first is *hitpashtut ha-gashmiyut*, "the stripping away of materialness." This concept had been known in previous Jewish mystical thought. We have seen it in the Abulafia texts. Hasidic thought, however, took it very seriously and taught the need for shedding one's dependence upon material modes of thought as well as upon material existence.

Stripping away materialness was, however, not enough. *Hitlahavut*, "enthusiasm," "enflamedness," was what was required. Pneumatic, spiritual energy was expected, and it was to be consciously channeled in one's physical demeanor as well as in one's internal thoughts and feelings. Sometimes hitlahavut was more tumultuous; sometimes more meditative (hence the distinction between these two forms of prayer). But always it was a necessary component.

In the final analysis, it was *bittul*, "annihilation," that was the core of both forms of the devekut type of prayer. Bittul was a loss of consciousness of self and a filling with a consciousness of God, ha-Ayin, the Nothing. It was a denial of materiality, of created reality, and of self. And at the completion of the denial was the realized consciousness of God.

(Later, as we shall see in the next chapter, if the Hasid could not annihilate himself into God, he was expected to try to annihilate his self-consciousness into that of the Zaddik.) Again, to the student of comparative mysticism, "enthusiasm" and "annihilation" are commonplace terms. To the rabbinic Jew, and even to the older type of Jewish mystic, these terms, ideas, and experiences were new.

The term *devekut,* "adhering," "clinging," comes from the verses: "And you who adhere to the Lord, your God, you are living this day" (Deut. 4:4), "to go in all His ways and to adhere to him" (Deut. 11:22, also 30:20), and "Him shall you worship and to Him shall you adhere" (Deut. 13:5). But what does it mean to "adhere," or to "cling," to God? (The history of this term has been outlined by Scholem in *The Messianic Idea.*) Hasidism taught that to adhere to God meant: (1) to recognize that all of reality is truly God, and that it is only our self-oriented mode of perception that inhibits us from seeing and responding to this; and (2) to strive to remove the veils of perception, even consciousness of self, so as to be at one with God. Devekut, then, is the adhering to God that is so intense as to be an annihilation of self into God. It is a dying of the self to everlasting life. "I lift up my eyes unto the mountains, (me-ayin) from whence cometh my help?" (Psalm 121:1) must be read: ("me-Ayin) from God, Who is the Nothing, cometh my help." Devekut, then, is a distinct (according to some, the most distinctive) type of Hasidic prayer, and it has two forms: the meditative and the tumultuous.

The selections given here deal with the meditative form of the devekut type of prayer. The most important thing to note is the recurrence of such terms as "attachment," "contemplation," "binding of the inner self," "binding of the soul," "cleaving with one's roots," "silent fire," and "a burning and awesome love." Note, too, the occasional anti-Lurianic comments and, toward the end of the selections, the phenomenon of automatic speech that was reported to have existed among the Hasidic masters.

TEXT*

I have heard in the name of the holy R. Abraham, son of the Rabbi, the Maggid, his soul is in Eden, that a new method of divine worship was suggested to him by the battles of Frederick [the Great]. This is the matter of "attackieren." It appears that they do not array themselves, as in former times, to attack each other but, on the contrary, they fly from the enemy and then surround him until he is compelled to surrender. Similarly, divine worship in former times consisted in a war with evil. Man

*From L. Jacobs, *Hasidic Prayer,* pp. 99–100.

coerced his traits of character by means of that type of contemplation that leads to ecstasy. But he [the "Angel"] discovered a new method by means of which man becomes attached to the category of the divine itself. This is achieved by means of contemplation on the profound mysteries of the higher Partzufim ["Configurations"] or the [mystical] reasons for the divine commandments. These have no connection whatever with ecstasy of love and yet the divine light is drawn down from above to surround the evil until it is automatically vanquished. He [the "Angel"] stated further that there is another difference. According to the earlier methods of divine worship, the battle was joined in one detail at a time. For instance, when a man engaged in contemplation on those matters which concerned ecstasy of love he attained to an ecstasy of love and by this means he transformed evil loves. Similarly, when he engaged in contemplation on those matters which concerned fear he attained to an ecstasy of divine fear and by this means he transformed evil fears. But according to the present method man's attachment to the divine itself, in a general manner, effects both the conquest of evil and its transformation in all details at once. Now although this way is very lofty, it is essential for the lowly souls of this generation who cannot prevail at all over the evil within and who fall into a melancholy state when they desire to search for the "how" and the "why" in their innermost heart. And even if they do not search within but simply attach themselves in that form of contemplation which concerns divine love and fear, no love and fear result from it, as is explained fully in the *Tanya* [the classic work of R. Shneor Zalman]. Consequently, our master and teacher, his soul is in Eden, counselled that one should engage in no other form of contemplation than that of the divine itself, in profound reflection, and then, automatically, "all the workers of iniquity will be scattered" and humbled.

TEXT*

Every day we mention the redemption from Egypt [in the liturgy], for by means of these letters we can unite our inner life force [to God], but first we have to detach our life force from material thoughts and from the being of ourselves, in order to enter the gate of Nothingness. Then we shall easily cleave with our roots unto the Cause of all causes. This is the meaning of the redemption from Egypt. For as long as our intellect is concerned with our selves it remains in the realm of being and the activity of our mind is limited and finite, but when we come to the root then it enlarges [to infinity].

---

*From R. Schatz, "Contemplative Prayer in Hasidism," pp. 216–217.

COMMENT

Note the philosophic term, "Cause of all the causes."

TEXT*

In our generation it is improper for a man to have in mind the *kavvanot* of prayer handed down to us in the Prayer Book of the Ari [i.e., Luria], of blessed memory, whether from the written text or whether he has learnt them and has them in mind by heart. So did I hear it from my master and teacher, the holy rabbi, the godly man, head of all the exile, our teacher Elimelech, may the memory of the righteous and holy be for a blessing. He said that a man should not have in mind thoughts or reflections on the *kavvanot* of the divine names. Instead he should bind both his external and his inner self, that is his vital force, his spirit and his soul, to En Sof, blessed be He. As a result, he binds all the revealed worlds and all the inner aspects of the worlds to Him, blessed be He. His thought should be so attached to the pleasantness of the Lord that he has no time, not even for a moment, to have the [Lurianic] *kavvanot* in mind. When a man's prayers are of this order the [Lurianic] *kavvanot* and unifications are effected automatically.

*   *   *   *

. . . The wise will increase his knowledge to discover further detailed *kavvanot* by labouring hard in the study of the Zohar and the writings of the Ari. It all really comes to the same thing, namely, the comprehension of the simple unity alone. He should not attempt to climb up on the ladder of *kavvanot*, divine names and their unification, as is the practice of the Kabbalists, for God has no desire for these. All He wants is the single *kavvanah* in which man binds his soul to His true essence, blessed be He, alone. . . . God searches out all hearts. There are some whose sole aim is to achieve deep *kavvanah* and the unification in accordance with the Kabbalah alone so that he can say, "I know the mystery, I know the mystery." And his heart is not truly firm and sincere to be directed solely towards His essence, blessed be He, alone.

COMMENT

Note the anti-Lurianic, pro-devekut stance of these passages.

---

*From L. Jacobs, *Hasidic Prayer*, pp. 80–81, 91–92.

TEXT*

Do not think that the words of prayer
   as you say them
   go up to God.
It is not the words themselves that ascend;
   it is rather the burning desire of your heart
   that rises like smoke toward heaven.
If your prayer consists only of words and letters,
   and does not contain your heart's desire—
   how can it rise up to God?

*   *   *   *

A person should be so absorbed in prayer
   that he is no longer
   aware of his own self.
There is nothing for him but the flow of Life;
   all his thoughts are with God.
He who still knows how intensely he is praying
   has not yet overcome the bonds of self.

*   *   *   *

You must forget yourself in prayer.
Think of yourself as nothing
   and pray only for the sake of God.
In such prayer you may come to transcend time,
   entering the highest realms
   of the World of Thought.
There all things are as one;
Distinctions between "life" and "death,"
   "land" and "sea,"
   have lost their meaning.
But none of this can happen
   as long as you remain attached
   to the reality of the material world.
Here you are bound to the distinctions
   between good and evil
   that emerge only in the lower realms of God.
How can one who remains attached to his own self
   go beyond time to the world where all is one?

*   *   *   *

---

*From A. Green, *Your Word Is Fire,* pp. 51, 55–59.

The human body is always finite;
It is the spirit that is boundless.
Before he begins to pray,
   a person should cast aside that which limits him
   and enter the endless world of Nothing.
In prayer he should turn to God alone
   and have no thoughts of himself at all.
Nothing but God exists for him;
   he himself has ceased to be.
The true redemption of man's soul can only happen
   as he steps outside the body's limits.

* * * *

In prayer seek to make yourself into a vessel
   for God's Presence.
God, however, is without limit;
"Endless" is His name.
How can any finite vessel hope to contain
   the endless God?
Therefore, see yourself as nothing:
   only one who is nothing
   can contain the fulness
   of the Presence.

* * * *

As long as you can still say the words
   "Blessed art Thou"
   by your own will,
   know that you have not yet reached
   the deeper levels of prayer.
Be so stripped of selfhood that you have
   neither the awareness
   nor the power
   to say a single word on your own.

TEXT*

Before you begin to pray,
   decide that you are ready to die
   in that very prayer.
There are some people so intense in their worship,
   who give up so much of their strength to prayer,

---

*From A. Green, *Your Word Is Fire,* pp. 33, 64, 83–85.

that if not for a miracle they would die
    after uttering only two or three words.
It is only through God's great kindness
    that such people live,
    that their soul does not leave them
    as they are joined to Him in prayer.

*   *   *   *

There are two rungs of service
    that a person can come to know.
The first is called *Qatnut,* "the lesser service."
In this state you may know
    that there are many heavens encircling you,
    that the earth on which you stand is
    but a tiny point,
    and that all the world is nothing
    before the Endless God—
    but even knowing all these things,
    you yourself cannot ascend.
This is still the "lesser" service.
It is of this state the prophet says:
    "from afar God appears to me."

But he who serves in *Gadlut,* "the greater service,"
    takes hold of himself with all his strength
    and his mind soars upward,
    breaking through the heavens all at once,
    rising higher,
    higher than the angels.

*   *   *   *

"When God is seated upon his throne,
    a fire of silence falls upon
    the heavenly beings."

When a person says the words of prayer
    so that they become a throne for God
    an awesome silent fire takes hold of him.
Then he knows not where he is;
    he cannot see, he cannot hear.
All this happens in the flash of an instant—
    as he ascends beyond the world of time.

*   *   *   *

It is possible to pray in such a way
  that no other person
  can know of your devotion.
Though you make no movement of your body,
  your soul is all aflame within you,
And when you cry out in the ecstasy of that
  moment—
  your cry will be a whisper.

         *   *   *   *

There are times when a person's body
  may remain completely still
  while the soul serves God in silent prayer.
In such moments your prayer may be filled
  with a burning and awesome love,
  though one who sees you
  might never guess the depth
  of your inner service.
Only those who are already at one with God
  may attain this prayer
  of inner flame and outer stillness.
Such worship has greater power
  than devotion which can be seen by others.
The "shells" of evil which feed upon wayward
  prayers
  cannot reach this silent prayer,
  for it is deeply hidden within the self.

COMMENT

Note the descriptions of meditative ecstasy.

TEXT*

There are times when the love of God
  burns so powerfully within your heart
  that the words of prayer seem to rush forth,
  quickly and without deliberation.
At such times it is not you yourself who speak;
  rather it is *through* you
  that the words are spoken.

         *   *   *   *

---

*From A. Green, *Your Word Is Fire*, pp. 62–63.

When you speak, think that the World of Speech is
  at work within you,
  for without that presence,
  you would not be able to speak at all.
Similarly, you would not think at all were it not
  for the World of Thought within you.
Man is like a ram's horn;
  the only sound he makes is
  that which is blown through him.
Were there no one blowing into the horn,
  there would be no sound at all.

COMMENT

The issue of automatic speech is discussed by Jacobs, chap. 10, and
Schatz, chap. 8.

The Devekut Type of Prayer: Tumultuous Ecstasy

How smart does a mystic have to be? How educated? This question,
which is general to the field of mystical religion, was answered by Jewish
tradition with the affirmation that mystical thought and praxis was a
function of the educated elite. Jewish mysticism, from its beginnings, was
highly esoteric, requiring years of study and practice. In fact, the Jewish
mystical tradition was so intellectually elitist as to be inaccessible to the
masses. Hasidism as a pneumatic movement was, as almost all scholars
have pointed out, an attempt to reverse this trend. It was a determined
effort to see God everywhere, to make the consciousness of Him directly
available to all. Hasidism, though it did have its distinctly intellectual
side, was an attempt at mysticism for the masses.
    What can the common person do? He can understand short, instructive
stories. He can practice ritual. He can, as we shall see in the next chapter,
believe in a leader. And he can sing, dance, clap hands, recite the liturgy,
yell, make love, eat, and so on. He can, too, if instructed and encouraged,
do all this at multiple levels of consciousness; that is, he can do all this and
have God in mind at the same time. In the terms of the tradition, he can do
all this with Kavvana. He can sing and think of God. He can dance and
think of God. He can even recite the liturgy and think of God. All with
only a rudimentary education, all without being part of the intellectual
elite of Jewish history. Hasidism did not boast of ignorance, but it did not
reject the unlearned. Hasidism did not cultivate empty-headedness, but it
did not stigmatize the anti-intellectual. Hasidism encouraged awareness.
Hasidism cultivated consciousness. It educated toward consciousness of

God, first and foremost. But any awakening of mankind's most human capacity was a moment of early spring, an anticipation of a fullness yet to come.

In the tumultuous form of the devekut type of prayer, Hasidism reached out to the masses with pneumatic power. In this form, the people came to know and to experience God. In this form, the spirit of man and the Holy Spirit touched each other. And after such a moment, no person was the same. It might be years before a person would have another such experience. It might never happen again. But the memory of the first moment kept one going, striving to be with God again. In a basic way, this was the secret of Hasidism: through intramental focusing of consciousness (Kavvana), even the simple person achieved an intense awareness of God, and forever after that person tried to recreate that moment.

The texts selected here are of several types. Some are reports of individual or group ecstatic experiences. Some are didactic. And some represent what the critics of this aspect of Hasidism had to say, for such tumult was, in other traditional circles, scandalous. Note, however, throughout, that it is the presence of the pneumatic, the holy, which is the unifying and meaning-giving factor.

TEXT*

Jiri Langer describes his first personal encounter with prayer at the Hasidic court of Belz on a Friday evening in the second decade of this century. The old rabbi of Belz had advanced to the reading desk in order to lead the Hasidim in the recital of the psalms to welcome the sabbath.

It is as though an electric spark has suddenly entered those present. The crowd which till now has been completely quiet, almost cowed, suddenly bursts forth in a wild shout. None stays in his place. The tall black figures run hither and thither round the synagogue, flashing past the lights of the sabbath candles. Gesticulating wildly, and throwing their whole bodies about, they shout out the words of the Psalms. They knock into each other unconcernedly, for all their cares have been cast aside; everything has ceased to exist for them. They are seized by an indescribable ecstasy . . . The old man throws himself about as though seized by convulsions. Each shudder of his powerful body, each contraction of his muscles is permeated with the glory of the Most High. Every so often he claps the palms of his hands together symbolically.

---

*From L. Jacobs, *Hasidic Prayer*, pp. 80–81, 91–92.

Herbert Weiner describes his visit to the Hasidic centre, in the Meah Shearim district in Jerusalem, of the followers of the Hasidic master R. Arele Roth.

"Amen," shrieked the man next to me. He was doubled over, his face red, yelling at the top of his lungs, "Amen—may His great Name be blessed for ever, and ever, and ever." For a moment I thought he was ill, but then I saw that all the worshippers were carrying on in the same way. The room resounded with a cacophony of shouts. My guide noticed my bewilderment. One of R. Arele's teachings is that the response, "Amen, may His great Name . . ." be recited, as the Talmud suggests, in an utter abandonment of soul, as if one were willing at that moment to die in sanctification of the name . . .

R. Arele himself, in his ethical will, advised his followers on how to conduct themselves during their prayers.

It is a fundamental principle in connection with prayer that a man should not be embarrassed, God forbid, because people laugh at it. For consider and reflect, my beloved child, that you are engaged in putting right the world, and all worlds and all angels desire every word and every utterance in which you express your nostalgia for the Creator in love and longing. Why should you be concerned with a foolish, brutish and stupid person who cannot discern between his right hand and his left! For all that, when you are among people who are unaccustomed to worship, then you must try to limit it as far as you can so as not to encourage scoffers to pour scorn. And you should not make any peculiar and crazy gestures, God forbid. All the members of our group are fully aware how strict I am about this, and this way is not our way, God forbid. What you should do is to toil with might and self-sacrifice, with the inner and outer organs, and to exercise the mind in toil, in the category of, "Nay, but for Thy sake are we killed all the day" [Ps. 44: 23], which, as is well known, refers to prayer. But as for that which cannot be limited, do not bother to look at the whole world, God forbid, to prevent your giving satisfaction to your Creator. Thus have I seen it written in the work of one of the members of the king's palace, the disciples of the Baal Shem Tov, may his merit shield us and all Israel.

R. Arele's reference to the verse in Psalms is clearly intended to call attention to the Hasidic doctrine of self-annihilation in prayer.

R. Arele's letters of spiritual counsel have been collected and published. In one of them he expresses his strong disapproval of peculiar gesticulation in prayer but not of swaying or of shouting aloud in prayer.

This was the reply I gave to a certain famous man, of the great and famous, who asked me about the peculiar gestures he had observed among some of my disciples. I replied that in reality this was not my way at all but it can be attributed to one of two things. Either the disciple who behaves in this way is a tyro in God's service and then one must allow him the freedom to pursue his own way if, beforehand, he was an inferior person and a sinner, God forfend [i.e. and he behaves in this way in order to escape from his past]. Or else he is an immature disciple who left me after having stayed only for a short time. He acquired some warmth through his association with our company and so forth, but he has not learned a sense of balance so as to be able to assess accurately the type of gesture he makes. This is intelligible. But after he has spent a year or two in beginning to serve God he must then choose a circumspect and moderate way, though inwardly it should be with a spirit of real self-sacrifice, uncomplicated and true. Now I do not mean by this any spirit of indifference, God forbid, such as to cancel out self-sacrifice and toil in prayer with all one's might. This must never be given up even if the whole world protests. For it is like a railway line, from which the train must not be derailed, God forbid. For it is this which brings sanctity and purity to body and soul and which draws down godly vitality to all the limbs and muscles. I refer only to a few imbeciles who make strange noises in their prayers and shake their heads about in a way different from that of the rest of the world, I mean of the world of those who worship God with self-sacrifice. I refer to such strange conduct as glazing the eyes or making odd gestures with other parts of the body. If one notices that sometimes a certain Zaddik does these things one should not copy him—for he does so at times because God's fire burns within him. However, as for swaying in the ordinary way, even with all one's strength and in a spirit of real self-sacrifice, and as for reciting the prayers in a loud voice and with effort, with regard to this it is said: "Nay, but for Thy sake are we killed all the day" (Ps. 44: 23). Now how is it possible for a man to kill himself every day? The sacred books of old explain that the verse refers to prayer in a spirit of self-sacrifice and with all one's strength. As it is said [in those books]: How far should the power of prayer reach? Until one [virtually] expires. May the Lord help us to sacrifice ourselves to Him, blessed be He, and to sanctify His name continually. Amen.

COMMENT

Compare the last line with the "kiss of death" ecstasy in Maimonides (above, p. 20–21).

TEXT*

The Hasidim who gathered under the shade of his son, our holy master, our teacher and mentor, R. Issachar Dov, may the memory of the righteous be for a blessing, of Belza, say that his sensations and *hitlahavut* on the Days of Awe were indescribable. The mood of elevation reached its peak when he recited "Out of the depths" (Ps. 130) before the *shofar* was sounded. He would recite one verse while weeping bitterly so that no one present could fail to have his heart melt like water. Immediately afterwards, he would recite the next verse with such joy and exultation that it was hard to believe that only a moment before he was in tears. The pouring out of his soul in prayer like a son longing for his father went straight to the heart of every one of the worshippers who, at that moment, reached a spiritual degree he could never have attained through his own efforts.

COMMENT

For the Zoharic interpretations of the verse from Psalm 130, cf. Volume I, pp. 121–125. Note that the worshipper is carried along by the Kavvana of the Rebbe. Also, that tears are contagious. My father reported similar experiences from his youth, and many of us can recall similar experiences from our own lives.

TEXT†

This is from the Baal Shem Tov, may his memory be for a blessing, "From my own flesh I behold God." Just as no child can be born as a result of physical copulation unless this is performed with a vitalised organ and with joy and desire, so it is with spiritual copulation, that is, the study of the Torah and prayer. When it is performed with a vitalised organ and with joy and delight then does it give birth. . . .

Prayer is copulation with the Shekhinah. Just as there is swaying when copulation begins so, too, a man must sway at first and then he can remain immobile and attached to the Shekhinah with great attachment. As a result of his swaying man is able to attain a powerful stage of arousal. For he will ask himself: Why do I sway my body? Presumably it is because the Shekhinah stands over against me. And as a result he will attain to a stage of great enthusiasm.

---

*From L. Jacobs, *Hasidic Prayer*, p. 96.
†From L. Jacobs, *Hasidic Prayer*, p. 60, and A. Green, *Your Word Is Fire,* pp. 80, 96.

* * * *

Prayer is union with the Divine Presence.
Just as two people will move their bodies
    back and forth as they begin the act of love,
    so must a person accompany
    the beginning of his prayer
    with the rhythmic swaying of his body.
But as he reaches the heights of union
    with the Presence,
    the movement of his body ceases.

* * * *

Do not laugh at one who moves his body,
    even violently, during prayer.
If a man is drowning in a river,
    he makes all kinds of motions
    to try to save himself.
This is not a time for others to laugh.

COMMENT

Some readers may be shocked by these texts, but there is no reason for it. After all, sex is part of Creation, and it, too, can be a Way to God. In earlier Jewish mystical tradition, sexual union represented processes within God (cf. Vol. I, pp. 149–153). In Hasidism, it is (as A. Green has pointed out in his note, ad loc.) "God and the worshipper who are locked in the embrace of intimacy."

Other acts, too, can be transformed into Ways to God by the use of Kavvana. Thus, for instance, some Hasidim drink rather considerable quantities of alcohol. Unlike Western man, who drinks and withdraws into his sullen self, the Hasid drinks and slowly removes the inhibitions to the perception of God. I once knew a Hasidic young man who told me that he had seen a great light in such an intoxicated state. It is not hard to do: just drink and think of *God!*

Another common activity that can be transformed by Kavvana is singing. What *do* you have in mind when you sing the national anthem? your favorite hymn? any song you know? Sometimes we think of the music or the words. But if we know those well, we think of other things *while* we sing. Hasidism teaches that one should sing with *God* in mind. The melody may be sorrowful or joyous, fast or slow, but one must focus one's consciousness on God while singing it. Clapping one's hands helps. Closing one's eyes is especially helpful. And don't worry if it is not quite in tune. It is not hard to do: just sing and think of God.

TEXT*

At one-thirty I arose, and taking a towel and the phylacteries which orthodox Jews don for morning prayers, hurried toward my appointment. Summer nights in Jerusalem can be cool and moist with heavy dew, and I regretted not wearing heavier clothes. A half moon silvered the stone surfaces and dark windows of the buildings. The only sounds came from the scraping of my shoes on the unpaved rock and gravel streets that connected my home to Meah She'arim.

Gedaliah was waiting for me on the steps of the synagogue, and we started toward Zephaniah Street, where we were to pick up a young man who was going with us. His name, Gedaliah told me, was Yaakov, and he had been born in Jerusalem to Bratzlaver forebears; he worked as a *sofer,* a scribe who copied scrolls of the Holy Torah on parchment. Yaakov's home was on the ground floor of a small apartment house surrounded by a stone wall. Gedaliah knocked several times softly on the door at the side of the house. "Yaakov," he whispered. Yaakov was recently married, and Gedaliah didn't want to disturb his wife's sleep. In a few moments the door opened, and a fragile looking young man with a blonde beard and warmly gleaming eyes, framed by metal spectacles, invited us in. He was dressed in the yellow and black striped robe which is still worn by Jerusalemites descended from the "old community." Yaakov asked if there was anything I might like in the way of refreshments and insisted that I take at least a glass of soda water. I looked over the rows of books on the upper shelves of a buffet-like piece of furniture that occupied one side of the small room; it was the standard library of an Orthodox Jew: a set of the Talmud; *midrashim* and other classical commentaries on the Bible; commentaries, legalistic works of later rabbinic authorities; and a special Pentateuch used by scribes for their copying work.

"It takes a *sofer* about a year to write a Torah, and the going price these days is about three or four thousand dollars," Gedaliah said as he saw me looking at the scribe's Pentateuch. "Would you like to see the parchment on which I'm working?" He opened a drawer at the bottom of the buffet and took out some sheets of white parchment with gleaming, freshly inscribed black letters, decorated with the fine lines called *tagin.* It is the clarity of the letters, plus the accuracy and elaboration of these *tagin* that mark the work of a good *sofer.*

I expressed surprise at the length of time it took to write a Torah. "My grandfather would take much longer," Yaakov replied. "Each time he came to the Name of God, he would first go to the *mikveh* and purify himself. Well, shall we start?"

---

*From H. Weiner, *9½ Mystics,* pp. 243–249.

We left the house and walked rapidly for about ten minutes until the paved streets merged into an empty field. This was Tel Arza, the Hill of the Cedar. Whatever association with trees it might have had in the past, the Tel Arza I saw was now a stony plot of land with hillocks and valleys that merged into a vaguely defined no-man's-land.

"Incidentally," I asked, "how far away is Jordan?"

Gedaliah pointed to some lights on a hill directly on the other side of the valley.

"It seems very close," I said. "In fact, isn't that the muezzin we hear?" An undulating wail calling Moslems to early morning prayer sounded as if only yards away, but my companions didn't appear to share my concern about our proximity to enemy territory.

"Well, here we are," Gedaliah said, after we had made our way single file along a rocky path that twisted and turned between large boulders and small caves. "Now it's time for work, and we can each go our separate ways."

"Yes, here we can cry out and nobody minds," Yaakov said, turning to me with an encouraging smile. Then, sensing my need for more orientation, he offered me a brief introduction to the philosophy of early morning *hisbod'dus*.

"The rebbe says that pure *emunah*, faith, is natural to every Jew, a part of his blood. Through his sins, however, a person can cloud its original purity. Then come doubts and problems. But a man's most natural condition is one of complete faith; the young child believes what he is told until he learns about lies. To recover this original condition of faith, the rebbe recommended *hisbod'dus* at night in an open field. There, away from the noise of the day and people, in the pure air, he can dig into himself, pierce through the surface layers of doubt to his natural faith. That is the purpose of *hisbod'dus:* to ask for a lighting up of the darkness, so that we can see with the clarity of a child, and rediscover the goodness of God, the holiness of his commandments, and the wisdom of his saints. And we do this simply by crying out our questions and doubts. But now, it's a little late and we have to begin."

With that Yaakov turned and walked off into the darkness.

"Come, let's find a good place for you," Gedaliah took over. I followed him to a small cave whose entrance was blocked by some refuse and a rusted bedspring.

"This might do." He pointed to some steps which had been carved out of the rock alongside the cave. "You can sit here if you want, or walk about. Incidentally, you may see some little animals with bushy tails, jackals. If they come close, just throw a few rocks or stamp on the ground. I'll come back in about three quarters of an hour," he assured me and suddenly was gone.

It took me only a few moments to realize that I was going to have a difficult time just talking aloud, let alone crying out. For one thing, there were a number of practical considerations which immediately occupied my attention. For example, the jackals. True, jackals aren't supposed to attack human beings, but still, I decided to pick up a few stones. This act somehow led me to think of scorpions and the likelihood of their being encountered under stones. My fear of scorpions was an old phobia; I had once heard a man screaming for hours after being bitten by one. I then began wondering about snakes, since they are known to inhabit the kind of cave near which I was stationed. Shoes would have been more sensible than open sandals for this excursion, and perhaps it would be just as well to get away from the cave and into the open field. But there was still the muezzin, or rather the record which is used nowadays instead of a muezzin, continuing its melancholy wail. Why offer too clear a target for any adventurous Arab soldiers? Recently, there had been a number of attacks by terrorist bands in border areas, and there were also Israeli border guards who, seeing some figures strolling near no-man's-land at three in the morning. . . .

Suddenly there was a series of groans emerging from some place over the hill. I couldn't make out the words, but it was a man's voice crying like a child, imploring, sobbing. It was, I realized, one of my comrades in the midst of his *hisbod'dus,* while I was worrying about all kinds of nonsense. Of course, I knew who was responsible for raising all these obstacles to my *hisbod'dus*—who but the *Baal Davar,* the Master of the Thing, as Hasidim call Satan, the Obstructor? It is well known to Bratzlaver Hasidim that as soon as one begins to approach truth, this Master of the Thing begins throwing up obstacles. Well, I wasn't going to let "him" spoil this experience; with an effort I wrenched my attention away from the "terrors that fly by night" to the beauties of the dark sky. The stars were out, slightly clouded by the early morning mist, and the moon was clearly visible in the lower quarter of the sky.

"Lift up your eyes and see who has created these." I decided to launch my *hisbod'dus* with this phrase of the psalmist but immediately encountered a serious obstacle, a heresy that I had frequently heard from my old teacher, Dr. Henry Slonimsky. The power and mystery of the cosmic design as expressed in the starry heavens was a good thing, he used to say, "but what has it to do with the Jewish assertion that the Power which made the heavens was also interested in love and justice?" I thought of Slonimsky, who liked to call himself the "last of the Manicheans," because a huge black cloud was beginning to send probing black wisps over the face of the moon. Then the moon completely disappeared. And since every struggle above mirrors one below, was not this conflict between moon and clouds a symbolic representation of the old Manichean claim that the world was divided between good and evil, God and Satan?

A new series of groans from Yaakov's direction reminded me that such doubts were supposed to be cleared up by crying them out in the predawn air. But could one cry out about a semiphilosophical problem? A groan like Yaakov's could only come from a more personal, more specific kind of question. There was a renewed wail of anguish from one of my invisible companions, and then across the valley the muezzin brought his elongated chant to a wavering end. Wasn't his call also something of a crying out, a call for light where there was darkness? The next moment I was singing to myself, repeating the words "to light up." It was only a home-composed melody, and not much of a groan. In fact, it turned out to be a rather cheery little tune calling for a "lighting up" in whatever area came to mind—Vietnam, my home, the soul. Then the moon emerged out of the clouds for a moment, and I entertained the possibility that my singing had some influence on this fact. It probably wasn't very impressive by Bratzlaver standards, but it was the best I could do; I was even rather disappointed to find Gedaliah's silhouette ahead of me. But it was time to leave: the sky above the hills was now that faint green and red which the ancients took as a signal for beginning their prayers. We would have to hurry if we were going to make the *mikveh* and emerge in time to coordinate the silent prayer with the sunrise.

We saw Yaakov waiting for us on the path ahead.

"Now a *rikkud,* a dance," he suggested pleasantly, holding out his hands. "Lift up your eyes and see who has created these," he and Gedaliah chanted as we circled about. I would have been more startled by the coincidence of his selecting the phrase I had used for my *hisbod'dus* if I were not concentrating on not stumbling on the rocky field.

After a few more moments of circling, leaving me slightly dizzy, we began to walk rapidly back to Meah She'arim. The streets were already beginning to lighten, and there was no time to lose. As we walked, I confessed my difficulty in working up a good, loud *hisbod'dus*. Yaakov was consoling.

"Of course. There are many kinds of *hisbod'dus*. The *hisbod'dus* which prays, 'God, open Thou my lips' is also good."

Gedaliah agreed. As far as he was concerned, the important thing was simply to cry out one's problems every night; then, having deposited the burdens with God, go about happily for the rest of the day.

But why should this sort of nightly meditation lead only to joy and faith, I asked. Couldn't it also suggest illness and tragedy, or remind us of the holocaust, clouding rather than clarifying our faith?

My companions hastened to disagree. God's ways were often obscure, but they were surely good in their ultimate intent.

"The important thing," Yaakov suggested, "is to remember that the world is only a passing illusion. There is a teaching—that when a person awakes in the morning, he must quickly think of the first and second letters of the alphabet. The first *aleph* is like the Aramaic *aluf,* which means learn. The second *bet* stands for the number two. We are to learn and remember that there are two worlds, and this world—what is it but suffering and certain death? The best we can hope for is an easy exit.''

I had already encountered the Bratzlaver attitude to death. But how, I asked, could such reflections be reconciled with the constant state of joy that Hasidism commanded?

"That's easy," Yaakov assured me. "It's like somebody who is riding on a crowded bus and has no seat. As long as he knows that he will soon get off, why should he feel badly? It's only if he knows that he can't get off, but will have to stand and stand, that he would have cause for worry. Since all our problems in the world are so temporary, why be sad about them?"

His answer didn't satisfy me, but we had arrived at the synagogue containing the *mikveh,* and I was worried about the next activity on our busy agenda.

COMMENT

This is a different kind of ecstasy, a tumult of its own. Something rather like a primal groan. Note the spiritually inhibited character of the narrator in contrast to his companions.

TEXT*

I trembled when I heard only recently that a new sect of foolish Hasidim had arisen in Volhynia and Podolia, some of whom have come to this country, whose sole occupation is to study moral and Kabbalistic works. They prolong their prayers for half the day, far longer than the Hasidim of old who used to spend no more than an hour in prayer itself. Moreover, these men perform strange movements, weird and ugly, in the prayer of the Eighteen Benedictions. They clap their hands and shake sideways with their head turned backwards and their face and eyes turned upwards, contrary to the ruling of the rabbis that the eyes should be directed downwards and the heart upwards. The Tanhuma only advocates that the eyes should be directed upwards when the Kedushah is recited and even then they should be closed. R. Menahem Azariah in a Responsum forbids any movement at all in prayer. I stormed the battlements time and again in order to discover some compromise whereby some slight and gentle motion of the body to and fro might be permitted, and this alone is

---

*From L. Jacobs, *Hasidic Prayer*, p. 57, and R. Schatz, "Contemplative Prayer in Hasidism," p. 223.

permitted in order to bestir the vital powers. The teachers of old used to recite their prayers without any physical sensation. There is a maxim, based on the Zohar, "When they stood, they let down their wings" [Ezek. 1:24]. But these men make wings for themselves wherewith to fly in the heavens. Ask yourself if they would dare to do so in the presence of a king of flesh and blood. Why, he would have them thrown out so that their limbs would be shattered and their bones broken. Verily, if I ever see those who do these things, which our fathers, of blessed memory, the true Hasidim, never dreamed of doing, I shall break their legs with a bar of iron.

* * * *

The Maggid, and before him the Besht, repeatedly emphasized the value of the "prayer of quiet":

In prayer a person can offer to God the service of orison, in such manner that his service is not at all apparent to others. He will not make any movement with his body, but inwardly in his soul his heart will be aflame and he will shout in silence, owing to his enthusiasm. In this way his internal service will be greater than when it would appear outwardly.

The process of severance from speech in prayer is described as follows:

At first he should utter the body of the word [i.e. articulate its letters] and then infuse a soul into the word. To this end he should first arouse himself with all his bodily might, in order that the power of the soul will light up in him . . . Then he will be able to serve [God] also with thought only, without the body. Sometimes, when a person cleaves unto the higher world, unto God, he ought to guard himself not to make any movement with his body so as not to interrupt the contemplative union . . .

COMMENT

These two texts represent critical voices raised against the practices of tumultuous ecstasy outlined in the previous selections. The first comes from the pen of an opponent of Hasidism, a Mitnagged. Note how, in his learned fashion, he tried very hard to find some precedent for such antics but could not. The second text is from a Hasidic master, the Maggid of Mezeritch, the disciple of the Baal Shem Tov. He, too, favored a more moderate, less ostentatious, Way. In its very variety, Hasidism left the door open for each person to experience God in his/her own way.

The Intimate Presence Type of Prayer

In the final analysis, mystical experience is a rare thing. The Zoharic-Lurianic-Habad type of prayer, the unifying-the-letters type of prayer, and the devekut-meditative type of prayer, all required a great deal of education and leisure. They were for a religiously sophisticated elite. Even the devekut-tumultuous type of prayer required concentration, intelligence, and cultivation of very subtle human faculties, and it did not always yield the desired results. Furthermore, even serious religious people were (and still are) often harried by the burdens of daily living, and many were often uninterested (or unsophisticated) in the arts of mystical worship. Yet no matter how distracted or uninterested a person might be, he or she could still sigh, or cry, or smile. She or he could still raise an eye toward heaven with a word of prayer or praise. Each person could still talk to God, without getting tangled up in mystical theology and techniques. Hasidism understood this, and it taught that this was a good and legitimate Way to God. Hasidism cultivated, in the unlettered man and in the Zaddik alike, a willingness and an ability to talk to God in an intimate and personal manner. This Way of conversing with the Intimate Presence was, to be sure, not new. But it was developed by Hasidism into a great art.

The most famous of these stories is of the poor peasant who could not read or write and who, therefore, recited the alphabet, saying to God: "Master of the Universe, You are the source of all words. Please, You arrange the letters of the alphabet in their proper order for me." In another variant, the poor peasant boy put his fingers to his mouth and gave forth a piercing whistle such as he might use for calling his sheep dog, and said to God: "Master of the Universe, I cannot read or write. I don't even know the words of the prayers. Accept, please, my whistle because I love You."

There were, however, other prayers—prayers in which man turned simply to God as Father. They are all deeply touching. The master of this kind of prayer was Rabbi Levi Yitzhak of Berditchev, and most of the selections given here are ascribed to him. Such prayers, however, are not hard to compose, if God's intimate presence is in your consciousness.

TEXT*

He had no illusions about men, yet he loved even the most sinful and ignorant among them. When the notables of Berditchev reproached him

---

*From E. Wiesel, *Souls on Fire,* pp. 99, 108, 110, and S. Dresner, *Levi Yitzhak of Berditchev,* p. 80.

for associating with people of inferior rank, he replied: "When the Messiah will come, God will arrange a feast in his honor, and all our patriarchs and kings, our prophets and sages will of course be invited. As for myself, I shall quietly make my way into one of the last rows and hope not to be noticed. If I am discovered anyway and asked what right I have to attend, I shall say: 'Please be merciful with me, for I have been merciful too.' "

* * * *

One day he noticed a man in the synagogue whose eyes were filled with tears. It was before *Kol Nidre*.

"Why are you crying?" he asked.

"I can't help it. The tears keep coming. I was a pious man and well-to-do. My wife was hospitable and devout. And suddenly He intervened and turned me into a heap of rubble. I lost my wife, my home. And here I am, desperate and destitute, with six children on my arms. That isn't all. I had a prayer book that meant much to me. He burnt that too. I don't know how to pray any more; all I can do is weep."

The Rebbe ordered that the man be given a prayer book just like the one he once had, and then he asked: "Will you pray?"

"Yes."

"Do you forgive Him now?"

"Yes," said the Jew through his tears. "Today is Yom Kippur; I must forgive."

"Well then, it is up to You to do same," roared Levi-Yitzhak. "You, too, must forgive!" And he intoned the somber, solemn melody of *Kol Nidre*.

* * * *

Before *Mussaf* service on Yom Kippur, he cried out: "Today is Judgment Day. David proclaims it in his Psalms. Today all Your creatures stand before You so that You may pass sentence. But I, Levi-Yitzhak, son of Sarah of Berditchev, I say and I proclaim that it is You who shall be judged today! By Your children who suffer for You, who die for You and the sanctification of Your name and Your law and Your promise."

* * * *

"Lord of the Universe," prayed Levi Yitzhak before the sounding of the *Shofar* on Rosh Hashanah, "You have commanded us, 'A day of sounding the *Shofar* shall there be for you.' And because of this commandment in Your Torah, we, Your children, sound a hundred *Shofar* blasts each Rosh Hashanah, and thousands upon thousands of Jews have sounded these hundred blasts for many centuries.

"Now these thousands upon thousands of Jews, Your loyal children, cry out and pray and beseech You, and have beseeched You for these many centuries, to sound but *one* blast for our freedom on the Great *Shofar*.

"Still You have not blown it!"

TEXT*

May it be Thy will, O Lord our God and God of our fathers, Who hears the sound of supplication's cry and Who hearkens to the prayer of Thy people Israel in Thy mercy, to make our heart ready and our thought prepared. Send our prayers into our mouths and let Thine ears hearken to the voice of Thy servants' prayer, as they entreat Thee with the voice of supplication and with a broken heart. And Thou, O God of mercy, in Thy many mercies and in Thy great love, pardon, forgive and grant remission to us and to all who are associated with us and to all Thy people Israel, for all that we have sinned, transgressed, have done wickedly and have rebelled before Thee. For Thou knowest that, perish the thought, it is not in rebellion and with trespass that we have disobeyed Thy commands and the words of Thy Torah and precepts but only because of the power of the evil inclination which burns inside us all the time. It knows no rest and ceases not until it has brought us into the lusts of this lowly world and into its vanities. All the time it confuses our thoughts so that even when we stand to pray before Thee and to entreat for our lives it confuses our thoughts continually with its tricks. We are incapable of offering resistance to it for our minds and intellect have become so weak and we have lost the power to bear it as a result of our worries and lusts and because of the numerous adversities we meet in our times. Therefore, O merciful and compassionate God, do Thou with us as Thou hast promised through the faithful of Thine house, "I will be gracious to whom I will be gracious, and will show mercy on whom I will show mercy," upon which our rabbis comment, "Even if he is unworthy," for that is Thy way to do good both to the bad and to the good. For Thou knowest our cry, our pain and our sighing so that we are incapable of bringing ourselves near to Thy worship and to make our souls cleave to Thee in truth and uprightness. Woe to our souls! Woe, woe to us, our Father in heaven! So now let Thy great compassion and Thy great and numerous mercies be awakened on our

---

*From L. Jacobs, *Hasidic Prayer*, pp. 136–138, 139, and E. Wiesel, *Souls on Fire*, pp. 44, 133.

behalf, to drive away and consume the evil inclination in our midst. Rebuke it, that it turn away and depart from us and let it not entice us so as to push us away from worshipping Thee, far be it from such a thing. Let not any evil thought enter our mind, whether when we are awake or when we dream, far be it from such a thing. Especially when we stand before Thee in prayer and when we study Thy Torah and when we keep Thy precepts, let our thought be pure, clear and refined, and strong in truth and uprightness, because of Thy benevolent will towards us. Awaken our heart and the hearts of all our associates and the hearts of all who desire our company and the hearts of all Thy people Israel, to declare Thy unification in truth and in love, to serve Thee with the perfect service acceptable before the Throne of Thy Glory. Fix firmly in our heart our faith in Thee, at all times without cessation. Let faith in Thee be bound up in our heart like a peg hammered in so that it can never be removed. Banish all the barriers which separate us from Thee our Father in heaven, and save us from every cause of stumbling and error. Forsake us not, leave us not, put us not to shame. Be Thou with our mouth when we speak and with our hands when we toil and with our heart when we engage in contemplation. Father in heaven! God of compassion! Grant us the merit of uniting our heart, thought and action and all our movements, whether conscious or unconscious, whether revealed or hidden, that all be united to Thee in truth and uprightness, without any objectionable thought. Purify our heart and sanctify us. Sprinkle clean water upon us and cleanse us in Thy love and compassion. Plant in our heart always the love and fear of Thee unceasingly. And wherever and whenever we go and when we lie down and when we rise up again let Thy holy spirit burn within us. Let us rely always on Thee, on Thy greatness and love and fear, and on Thy Torah, both Written and Oral, both revealed and secret, and on Thy commandments, that we may unite Thy great and terrible Name. Guard us from ulterior motives, from pride, and from anger, petulance, melancholia, tale-bearing and from all other evil traits and from everything that interferes with Thy holy and pure worship which we love. Allow the grace of Thy holy spirit to flow into us that we may cleave to Thee and that we may long always more and more for Thee. Elevate us from stage to stage that we may have the merit of reaching the degree of our holy forefathers, Abraham, Isaac and Jacob. Let their merit support us that Thou mayest hear the voice of our prayers that we may always be answered when we pray to Thee either on our own behalf or on behalf of any one of Israel, whether on behalf of an individual or of the community. Rejoice in us and be proud of us and let us produce fruit above and a root beneath. Remember not our sins, especially the sins of our youth, as King David, on whom be peace, said, "Remember not the sins of my youth and my transgression." Turn our sins and iniquities into merit and let there flow

always to us from the world of repentance the thought of turning to Thee
with a perfect heart and of putting right the flaws we have made in Thy
holy and pure Names. Save us from being envious of one another and let
not the thought of envying others enter our minds nor envy of us their
minds. On the contrary, put it into our hearts that each of us sees the
virtue of our neighbours and not their fault and that each one behaves to
his neighbour in the way that is upright and acceptable to Thee. And let
not, far be it that such a thing should happen, any hatred of one another
enter our hearts. Strengthen our bonds to Thee in love since it is known to
Thee that all we do is satisfying to Thee for this is our main intention. If
we have insufficient sense to direct our heart to Thee, do Thou teach us to
know in truth Thy good will. And more than all this we offer our
supplications to Thee, O God full of compassion, to accept our prayers in
compassion. Amen. So may it be Thy Will.

*   *   *   *

God of Abraham, of Isaac, and of Jacob! Guard Thy people Israel from all
evil for the sake of Thy praise. As the beloved, holy Sabbath departs, we
pray that in the coming week we should attain to perfect faith, to faith in
the sages, to love of our fellows, to attachment [devekut] to the Creator,
blessed be He. May we believe in Thy thirteen principles of the faith and
in the redemption, may it come speedily in our day, and in the resurrec-
tion of the dead, and in the prophecy of Moses our teacher, on whom be
peace. Sovereign of the universe! Thou art He who gives the weary
strength! Give, then, also to Thy dear Jewish children the strength to love
Thee and to serve Thee alone. And may the week bring with it good
health, good fortune, happiness, blessing, mercy, and children, and life,
and sustenance, for us and for all Israel, and let us say, Amen.

*   *   *   *

"Do you know who rescinded the celestial decree that would have
unleashed catastrophe unto our people?" the Baal Shem asked Rebbe
Nahman of Horodenko. "I'll tell you. Neither I nor you, nor the sages,
nor the great spiritual leaders. Our litanies, our fasting were all in vain.
We were saved by a woman, a woman of our people. This is how it
happened: She came to the synagogue, tears running down her face, and
addressed the Almighty: 'Master of the Universe, are You or are You not
our Father? Why won't You listen to Your children imploring You? You
see, I am a mother. Children I have plenty of: five. And every time they
shed a tear, it breaks my heart. But You, Father, You have so many more.

Every person is Your child, and every one of them is weeping and weeping. Even if Your heart is made of stone, how can You remain indifferent?' And," the Baal Shem concluded, "God decided she was right."

* * * *

His favorite prayer is mine too: "Master of the Universe, know that the children of Israel are suffering too much; they deserve redemption, they need it. But if, for reasons unknown to me, You are not willing, not yet, then redeem all the other nations, but do it soon."

* * * *

Master of the Universe, Master of the Universe, I would like to sing You a You-song:

Where shall I find You? And where shall I not find You?
Where can one find You? And where can one not find You!?

Wherever I go, it is You.
Wherever I stand, it is You.
Only You, Only You;
Either You, or You.

If things are really good, it is You.
And, God forbid, if they are bad, oy, it is You.
You, You.

He Was—You, He is—You, He will be—You.
He was King—You, He is King—You, He will be King—You.
Heaven—You, Earth—You;
Above—You, Below—You.

Wherever I go, wherever I turn—
You, You, You.

COMMENT

This is not properly a "prayer" but a song, a poem, a musical meditation. It is by Rabbi Levi Yitzhak of Berditchev (and is translated from the version given in Dresner, p. 107). It was written in Yiddish, the language of intimate conversation for East European Jews, and the translation misses the shift from liturgical (Hebrew) to intimate (Yiddish) discourse. Does it impress you as joyous or as poignantly pensive?

COMMENTED TEXT*

The document which testifies best to Levi Yitzhak's love of Israel is not a story or a saying but a song, an event that became a poem.

While leading the congregation in prayer one Rosh Hashanah, the Rabbi of Berditchev, grieving over Israel who, despite its sufferings, persisted in sanctifying God's Name, broke from the fixed words of the Hebrew liturgy to cry out in the folk tongue that not only the people, but the Lord as well, understood.

THE KADDISH OF RABBI LEVI YITZHAK

Good morning to You, Lord, Master of the Universe.
I, Levi Yitzhak, son of Sarah of Berditchev,
I come to You with a Din Torah from Your people Israel.

What do You want of Your people Israel?
What have You demanded of Your people Israel?
For everywhere I look it says, "Say to the Children of Israel,"
And every other verse says, "Speak to the Children of Israel,"
And over and over, "Command the Children of Israel."

Father, sweet Father in Heaven,
How many nations are there in the world?
* Persians, Babylonians, Edomites.*

The Russians, what do they say?
* That their Czar is the only ruler.*
The Prussians, what do they say?
* That their Kaiser is supreme.*
And the English, what do they say?
* That George the Third is the sovereign.*

And I, Levi Yitzhak, son of Sarah of Berditchev, say,
"Yisgadal v'yiskadash shmei raboh—
Magnified and sanctified is Thy Name."

And I, Levi Yitzhak, son of Sarah of Berditchev, say,
"From my stand I will not waver,
And from my place I shall not move
Until there be an end to all this.
Yisgadal v'yiskadash shmei raboh—
Magnified and sanctified is only Thy Name."

The soaring strains of this song of divine dissent sounded far beyond the narrow confines of Berditchev, echoing in the hearts of Jews scattered

---

*From S. Dresner, *Levi-Yitzhak of Berditchev*, pp. 85–89.

throughout poverty-stricken, persecution-ridden communities in Eastern Europe and, in time, even in far-off America and Israel. It gave voice at one and the same time to the misery and the grandeur, the tragedy and glory, which inhabited the soul of this people. It was as if the song took on a life of its own, moving from its point of origin in time and space as a millennial outcry from the pit of anguish—irrevocable, unfaltering, eternal. Incredible was the song the Jews continued to sing: Despite all the claims of kings of flesh and blood, there is but one King and one Kingdom—the doxology of Israel.

Nor was the mysterious power of this song understood only by the Jews. There were countless others who were drawn to it because they heard in it the deathless hope of the human soul. Paul Robeson, for example, the noted black singer, sang it following World War II at the great rallies for European Jewry and for the State of Israel during the early years of the young state's struggle for independence and subsistence.

He sang it in 1958 in Moscow at a special concert. The hall was filled to overflowing with military and government officials, persons of influence and culture. Among those present were also a large number of Jews. It was well known that Robeson's repertoire contained many Negro folk songs, African freedom songs, and several Jewish songs. Robeson's procedure was to explain the meaning of each song before he sang it. Conscious of the suffering of the Russian Jews, he had decided to sing the Berditchever's *Kaddish* and listed it on his program. Suddenly he received a note from a member of the sponsoring committee, which read: "No one in the audience understands Yiddish. It would, therefore, be out of place to sing any Jewish songs this evening."

Robeson was perplexed. Yiddish had been listed in the last Russian census as the mother tongue of thirty-five percent of the Jews, who were well represented in the audience. Granting the assumed ignorance of Yiddish, would the African songs that he would sing in the languages of Ghana and the Congo be better understood?

He began his program in his usual manner, explaining each song before it was sung. First he introduced a series of songs from the Congo and Ghana, indicating their anti-colonial character, which reflected the new spirit of the rising nationalism there.

Then he boldly announced, "And now I shall sing an anti-imperialist song for you which you may not have heard in some time. It was written more than one hundred and fifty years ago by a Russian as a protest against the Czar. The name of the author is Levi Yitzhak, and he lived in the city of Berditchev."

So it was that he began to sing Rabbi Levi Yitzhak's *Kaddish*.

When he came to the words:

What do You want of Your people Israel?
What have You demanded of Your people Israel?
For everywhere I look it says, "Say to the Children of Israel,"
And every other verse says, "Speak to the Children of Israel,"
And over and over, "Command the Children of Israel."

Father, sweet Father in Heaven,
How many nations are there in the world?

a tremor passed through the auditorium, scattered sighs and muffled sobs were heard. And when he began to thunder:

And I, Levi Yitzhak, son of Sarah of Berditchev, say,
"From my stand I will not waver,
And from my place I shall not move
Until there be an end to all this. . . ."

weeping could be heard from parts of the auditorium. Tears flowed freely from dozens of faces. The applause, sporadic at first, reached a crescendo which threatened to shake the walls. The song became a rallying cry among the frightened Jews of Moscow for weeks to come.

TEXT*

Only a handful of old timers among the prisoners knew about the cache inside the Nazi labor camp, and about the treasure which was kept inside of it.

The sign above the gate read *Julag,* short for *Juden Lager,* a labor camp for Jews. Such camps were not official extermination camps. There were no gallows, no gas chambers, no crematoria. To judge from the installations, the various buildings and barracks were shops equipped with sophisticated machinery. But the supervision of those camps was entrusted to the Nazi Storm Troopers, the S.S., which came to mean only one thing, and before long the camp became a mass graveyard. Even the strongest Jew could not last there for more than a few months. Small food rations, slave labor—twelve to fourteen hours a day without stop—as well as indescribable tortures—these conditions ultimately equalled the efficiency of the execution methods in even the most efficient concentration camps. The turnover of the prisoners in the camp was continuous. The dead were thrown into a huge pit, and new transports came to take their place. The predetermined fate of the newly arrived was sealed, and the camp authorities were constantly planning ahead for the new arrivals.

Only a few members of the original group of prisoners who had built the

*From M. Prager, *Sparks of Glory,* pp. 62–65.

barracks and installations remained, like solitary sheaves after the harvest. The all-seeing Angel of Death must have overlooked them. Those old timers guarded a deep secret: Somewhere hidden inside the camp was a small box which contained an invaluable treasure, a rare, tiny Torah scroll, made of the thinnest parchment and written in tiny letters. Because it was so small it was easily hidden. An aged rabbi of aristocratic descent, a scion of an ancient rabbinic family, had smuggled it into the camp. Family tradition had it that the scroll came out of Spain with the Jews who were exiled by the Inquisition. The old rabbi did not live long after his arrival, but he did manage to pass his treasure on into safe hands, and it was preserved intact.

In time another sacred object was put into the box. A sexton of a synagogue arrived in one of the transports, and brought with him a shofar. Miraculously, this sexton, though weak and emaciated, survived the rigors of the labor camp. He was sure that he owed his survival to the shofar. Because of it he strove to maintain his position and continue his work as a religious functionary inside the camp. He kept track of the Sabbaths and the holidays. He held secret prayer services. He even took care of the burial of the dead.

"Jews," he whispered to his neighbors in the barracks, "the New Year is approaching. For the sake of the New Year we must form a *minyan* and pray according to our tradition."

"What's the point of a Rosh Hashana prayer without the blowing of the shofar!" one man said with a sigh.

"What's the use of blowing the shofar? What we need is the shofar of the Messiah. Oy, oy, oy, blow the great shofar for our liberation, the great sho-far, oy, oy, for our liberation—"

"We do have a shofar, we have a shofar right here!" The sexton revealed his secret in an excited whisper. "I'll bring it out and if any of you knows how to blow it, I . . ."

"Heaven forbid! No, you can't do it!" a voice of protest was heard. "I know the rules of prayer, and I am telling you that the Law prohibits us from provoking the murderers. The blowing of the shofar is an important commandment, but it does not supersede the Sabbath, and if Rosh Hashana occurs on the Sabbath you don't blow. . . . Well, this is conclusive proof. Praying can be done silently, in a still small voice, but to blow loudly is to risk our lives. Let's not endanger the people's lives by blowing the shofar!"

"But that's just the point," the sexton said with sudden intensity, "precisely because we are lost, because our lives are at the mercy of anyone who will claim them, we must blow the shofar. Our bodies are theirs, but our souls . . . we won't abandon our souls, we won't give in to them. The soul is not theirs! Jews, do you agree?"

"Yes, yes," came the answer. "If we have a shofar it's a good sign. We won't show disrespect to the shofar, heaven forbid. We will blow the shofar no matter what."

The day arrived. The dawn of Rosh Hashana. The first shift of the forced laborers left the barracks and went to work and the second shift came back from an exhausting night of work, ready for sleep. At that time the services for the Days of Awe were taking place in the hut. For this secret service the sexton prepared the shofar, having taken it carefully out of hiding. But the reading of the Torah was dispensed with. They were afraid the scroll might fall into the hands of the enemy and they decided to leave it in the cache. An expert shofar blower was found on the spot. Though he knew he was taking a greater risk than all the rest, he did not hesitate for one moment, but held the shofar firmly in his hand.

When the silent prayer began, they posted guards outside the huts. At that moment the Nazi camp guards were inside their kitchen, busily stuffing themselves with food. The sexton gave the signal, and every one in the hut held his breath.

"*Tekiah!*"

"Too-oo-oo-oo," the sound of the shofar pierced the silence and entered every heart.

"*Shevarim—teruah!*" the sexton called out in a stronger, more daring voice.

"Too-oo too-oo too-oo, tu tu tu tu tu tu tu tu," the shofar grew louder and the sound broke out and was heard throughout the camp.

"*Tekiah, shevarim, teruah!*" the voice of the sexton was heard, loud and strong, as if the sound of the shofar were breaking the arm of the wicked, subduing the villains and freeing the prisoners. . . .

"Too too too, too too too, too-too," the shofar blasted, making a deafening sound which reached the murderers who were busy stuffing themselves.

"*Kreuzdonnerwetter!* What is this? What kind of a strange alarm is this? A riot? An uprising? A signalling to the enemy? *Donnerwetter!*" The murderers jumped up and ran madly, their weapons in hand, toward the hut where the service was held.

"*Halt!* Stop!" the camp commander stormed furiously into the hut. "I caught you this time, you dirty Jews. I caught you red-handed. You are signalling our enemy with secret instruments. This is why we have had so many air raids lately, you . . ."

"Listen, listen!" a quiet and confident voice interrupted him, emanating from the crowd of worshipers.

"Shut up!" the commander shouted.

"This is no secret instrument, this is a shofar! we are praying here," one man tried to explain.

"You can't fool me, you treacherous Jews!" he screamed savagely. "We have suffered serious defeats lately. The situation on the front is very grave. The enemy's bombs hit our most vital points with deadly accuracy. It's all your fault!"

"Did you hear this, Jews? It's true!" the sexton called out, lifting up the shofar which he had taken from the blower. "True! With this shofar we signal and we bring upon you all the curses and the maledictions. I'll tell you everything, everything . . ."

"Tell, dirty Jew, tell!" the head of the murderers blurted out.

"I'll tell, I'll tell," the sexton continued in a slow controlled voice. "With this shofar we don't signal to people but to our Heavenly Father; we alert the jealous and vengeful God! The defeats you have suffered are only the beginning. We are signalling more, more . . ."

"Shut your mouth, Jew!" and in his rage the Nazi pointed his pistol at the speaker. "No, I won't shoot you. It would be a waste, a German bullet. . . . A waste! I won't finish all of you off right here on the spot. We have too few Jews left to finish off. It's a waste of good entertainment . . . you will all get your shares of whipping . . ."

Immediately henchmen attacked the emaciated Jew, and the commander himself led the execution of his orders.

As the Jew twisted and writhed in his terrible suffering, he chanted verses from the prayers of Rosh Hashana in a voice imbued with pain and exaltation.

"The righteous will see and rejoice and the upright will be glad and the pious will sing for joy—and all wickedness will vanish like smoke, for You will have removed the evil kingdom from the earth—"

The rest of the Jews, who were forced to watch his suffering, joined his prayer silently.

"And all wickedness will vanish like smoke, for You will have removed the evil kingdom from the earth—"

Conclusion

"As the deer searches yearningly after streams of water, just so does my soul search yearningly for You, God. My soul thirsts for God, for the living God. When shall I come and be in the presence of God?" These words from Psalms (42:2–3) capture well the heartbeat of the Hasidic prayer-life, for Hasidism was, more than anything else, an intense yearning for God. Sometimes this yearning expressed itself in elegant, complex mystical theology and meditative praxis. Sometimes it expressed itself in powerful emotions, great ecstasies, and intense intimacies. Yet always, Hasidism was a passion for God.

The elements of the previous mystical tradition are clearly visible: the Zoharic-Lurianic structure of thought and meditations, the letter-mysticism, and the various levels of Kavvana. Against this background, the new elements are also clearly visible: the wholistic mystical theology of Habad; the pneumatic Kavvana; the theology of the Ayin (Nothing) and the bittul (annihilation) into it, or the devekut (adhering) to it; and the returning of religious ecstasy to the masses, in its mystical and in its intimate forms. Hasidism was a veritable renaissance of the Holy Spirit.

Typologies of Hasidic prayer based on dichotomies such as "contemplative vs. ecstatic" or "quietistic vs. activist" are not helpful. The picture, as we have seen, is much too varied. There were many types of Hasidic prayer-life. Nor is it helpful to try to give a definitive answer to the question: In which type of Hasidic prayer is the holy most intensely present? Hasidism was too conscious of individual human differences in character and style to allow only one answer to that question. For some, the holy was most intense in bittul, in a loss of all consciousness of self and in an awareness of the totality of the divine. For some, the yearning was most intense in a sigh, accompanied by the single word "Tatenyu" (a diminutive form of the Yiddish word for "father"). Who is to say which is true? If God is immediately present, that is enough.

Hasidism, however, was neither all stories nor all prayer; it was also community. It was leader and follower, Zaddik and Hasid. And it is to this characteristic embodiment of the holy that we now turn.

9

THE ZADDIK AND HIS COMMUNITY

Introduction

One of the revolutions accomplished by Hasidism was a change in the definition of the community leader from the halakhically oriented scholar-rabbi to the Zaddik.* This revolution was even more astounding when one considers that the new figure was not the leader of a small fringe group of mystics but the leader of one of the most significant mass movements within the history of Judaism and that, in a very basic sense, this movement was "orthodox," i.e., within the acceptable rabbinic definition of Judaism. How was this possible? And what might it mean for the future of Rabbinic Judaism?

Much has been written on the rise and decay of "Zaddikism." Most of it, however, was written by the opponents of Zaddikism. Some were Mitnaggedim, rabbinic-orthodox opponents of Hasidism who objected to the halakhic innovations, the social upheaval, and the pneumatic justification. And some were enlightened Jews who objected to the authoritarianism and the absolutism. These prejudices to the contrary notwithstanding, the Zaddik-Hasid relationship is central to an understanding of Hasidism. It is, in fact, one of the major embodiments of the holy in that tradition.

The readings in this chapter deal with two aspects of the Zaddik-Hasid relationship. The first set of selections presents several types of Zaddik, thus bringing home the point that there was no one single leader, not even one single type of leader. Rather, the holy expressed itself in very different forms in each of the men who became its embodiment. The second set of selections presents the strange split in functions which Hasidism assigned to the Zaddik and the Hasid respectively. The responsibilities, powers, and rewards of the former were different from those of the latter. And yet each drew vitality from the other; a true spiritual symbiosis. In studying these selections, the reader will want to ask about the different types of leaders, as well as about the different functions of

---

*The terms "Zaddik" and "Rebbe" are more or less interchangeable and are used here that way.

the leader and the follower. Ultimately, the reader will want to ask: What characterized this institution of the Zaddik? How did it work, and why? How did it respond to people's deepest psychological needs and faith-situation? Remember, too, that the institution of the Zaddik evolved in the nineteenth century. Is it, then, "modern" in some basic way? a response to something about life in modern times?

Variety among the Zaddikim

Hasidism did not have one Zaddik, one prophet, one rabbi, one law-giver. There were, and still are, many Zaddikim. But how does one know if someone is a Zaddik? Is Zaddikism a phenomenon that can be conveyed by heredity? Can it be conferred upon one by a community? These questions have been answered. In early Hasidism, the Zaddik was recognized by consensus on the basis of his spiritual charisma, mystical insight, and esoteric learning. In later Hasidism, the office of Zaddik became hereditary. When there were no heirs, the line either died out or the community chose another leader, usually related to the deceased.

With so many leaders, however, what were the points of continuity and discontinuity? Just how varied could the figure of the Zaddik be, and still be a Zaddik? The selections given here are intended to sketch the beginning of an answer. The first deals with the Baal Shem Tov, called in shortened form: the Besht. He was the founder of Hasidism. The second selection deals with his great disciple, the Maggid from Mezeritch. The remaining three selections deal with other types of Zaddik, although there are many more. The closing comment indicates some parameters of a definition.

The Founder

TEXT*

The works attributed to him—*Shivkhei ha-Besht, Keter Shem Tov, Tzvaat ha-Ribash*—really belong to others. His apocryphal letters—to his children, his disciples—have been questioned more than once. There remains of him no portrait, no document, no signature constituting irrefutable evidence that behind the legend there was a man, a face, a consciousness. Perhaps this was but another way for him to emphasize his contempt for things written. To the disciple who had transposed his verbal teachings to paper, the Master said: "There is nothing of me in your pages; you

---

*From E. Wiesel, *Souls on Fire*, pp. 8–16.

thought you heard what I didn't say." Also: "I said one thing, you heard another, and you wrote a third." For the Baal Shem, imagination gains in impact with each passing moment. Until finally its power is perhaps greater than that of any testimony. The real and the imagined, one like the other, are part of history; one is its shell, the other its core. Not to recognize this is to deny art—any form of art—the right to exist.

Yet it is precisely on the imagination that the Baal-Shem plays—even after his death. Each of his disciples saw him differently; to each he represented something else. Their attitudes toward him, as they emerge from their recollections, throw more light on themselves than on him. This explains the countless contradictory tales relating to him.

The historians may have been troubled, but not the Hasidim. Hasidism does not fear contradictions; Hasidism teaches humility and pride, the fear of God and the love of God, the at once sacred and puerile dimension of life, the Master's role of intermediary between man and God, a role that can and must be disregarded in their I-and-Thou relationship. What does it prove? Only that contradictions are an intrinsic part of man.

But not of historians. Frustrated by his elusiveness, they fight him. Some go so far as to deny his very existence. They would like us to believe that he was—quite simply—invented by his disciples, whose own existence they fortunately do not doubt. Others, to restore the balance, claim that . . . there were actually two Baal Shem Tovs and that the Hasidic movement was founded . . . by the other.

Controversies, confusion of places and dates, paradoxes, the Baal Shem's legend abounds with them. He who had the talent to clarify ideas and concepts appears to have done his utmost to obscure the trails leading to his person.

The exact date of his birth has not been established: 1698 according to some, 1700 according to others—as though it made any difference. There seems to be no disagreement as to the place of his birth: a small village—a fortress perhaps—named Okop. Still, the scholars have some difficulty in agreeing on its precise location. Dubnov believes it to be near Kamenetz, Balaban moves it to the banks of the Dniepr, whereas Schechter prefers to see it in Bukovina. As for Mahler, he simply annexes it to Galicia. Evidently the Baal Shem succeeded in turning even geography into a mystery.

Mystery again in all references to his childhood, his education, his family life, his travels, his wanderings across mountains and valleys to come to the aid of anyone in need of help or love.

His parents—Eliezer and Sarah—were rich and generous, according to some; poor but generous, according to others. Their son—Israel—was given to them as a reward when they were almost one hundred years old. They had shown themselves hospitable and indulgent toward the Prophet

Elijah, according to one version, and toward Satan, according to another. Their son was to be a symbol of promise and consolation, a guiding light to a people in distress.

Eliezer, the father, was so kind, so generous a man, says legend, that it had been decided in heaven to put him to a test. And so, one Friday eve, a stranger dressed in rags, leaning on a staff, a bundle on his back, knocked at the old couple's door just as they were sitting down to celebrate the first meal of Shabbat. Without even the slightest hint of disapproval in their countenance, they warmly received the visitor, though he had transgressed the law. And because they neither offended nor embarrassed the poor prophet, he told them the news: the following year they would no longer be alone.

Another tale describes Eliezer as a victim turned hero. Captured and carried off by barbarians, he makes a career in the royal palace, counseling the sovereign and helping him plan and win his wars. Though the king showers him with honors, Eliezer privately continues to carry out the duties of a good Jew, obeying the laws of Torah. Of course, the king becomes so fond of him that he offers him his daughter in marriage. The marriage takes place, but to the princess' great chagrin, is not consummated. Pleading for her forgiveness, he confesses not only that he is married, but that he is a Jew. Reassured about her charms, she magnanimously helps him leave the kingdom. And because of his faithfulness to his people and to his wife, a son was born to him blessed with all gifts and vested with all powers.

At his death, Eliezer told his heir: "I leave before I can make you into a man who fears God and loves those who fear Him. Remember one thing: God is at your side and He alone is to be feared." Later the Baal Shem was to add: "God sees, God watches. He is in every life, in every thing. The world hinges on His will. It is He who decides how many times the leaf will turn in the dust before the wind blows it away."

Orphaned and destitute, without a friend, he practiced all trades: tutor, beadle, ritual slaughterer. Somewhat clumsy and absent-minded, eccentric, he lived on a meager subsidy from the community. He was still very young when the community took the first opportunity to get him married. But soon after the marriage, his wife died and he reverted to his former marginal, introspective existence, and waited for a sign.

There are countless legends concerning the life he led before his revelation. Some say that he saved schoolboys from werewolves and warlocks. Others, that he could bring mountains together. And that during his walks through the forests, he spun dreams in which ends found their beginnings and the world's song reverberated in God's.

Some sources claim he was a saint who fled the limelight; others describe him as a harmless dunce; still others endow him with enough wisdom and learning to make him into a judge of the rabbinical court: a *Dayan,* an arbiter of the community. It is as such that he is said to have made the acquaintance of Reb Abraham—or is it Ephraim?—Kitiver, who wished to arrange a suitable match for his daughter Hannah. Her age at the time? A few months, according to some texts, much more—since she was already divorced—according to others. No matter, the engagement contract was signed, showing the boy's name as Israel, son of Eliezer, and mentioning no title whatever. Shortly thereafter Hannah's father died.

Years went by, until one day the "bridegroom," dressed in peasant clothes, appeared in Brodi to see Reb Gershon Kitiver, Hannah's brother, who took him for a beggar and offered him alms. "No," said the visitor, "that won't do. There's something I want to say to you alone." Then he added roughly: "I want my wife, give me my wife."

Reb Gershon, one of the town's notables, did not take the jest lightly. Even after he had been shown the agreement signed by his father, he advised his sister against marrying this primitive, clumsy peasant. Hannah chose to obey her late father's wish and a date was set for the wedding. Before the ceremony, the Baal Shem drew Hannah aside and told her: "I am not who you think I am, but you must tell no one." He then described the road he had chosen and predicted the difficulties they would encounter, the obstacles still left to overcome. Hannah declared herself ready to confront them at his side.

Then followed hard, unrewarding days. Reb Gershon was ashamed of his brother-in-law and therefore persuaded the couple to go away, as far away as possible. He bought them an inn with a tavern, and then a horse and cart. Isolated in the Carpathian Mountains, Israel and Hannah lived in misery. They dug the soil and eked out a bare subsistence selling lime in the villages.

One day he was summoned by the local rabbi, who undertook to give him a lesson in Judaism. The Baal Shem, in quick succession, put on and removed his simpleton's mask. The rabbi was perplexed: how could the expression on a face change so rapidly? Stunned, he demanded his visitor tell him the truth.

"So be it," said the Baal Shem. "But you must keep what I tell you to yourself. For the moment."

However, there lived in Brodi a woman who was mad. She saw through all men's masks. Brought face to face with the Baal Shem, she said: "I know who you are and I am not afraid of you. I know that you possess certain powers; I also know that you may not use them before the age of thirty-six."

"Be quiet," he answered, "otherwise I shall convene a court to evict the Dybbuk inside you."

The frightened woman held her tongue—but she knew. The others found out much later. Seven lonely and ascetic years went by before the Baal Shem received the order to reveal himself and assume his destiny.

On that particular Saturday, a pupil of Reb Gershon interrupted a journey to spend Shabbat with Israel and Hannah. It was midnight when he awoke trembling with fright: a huge flame was rising from the hearth. Thinking to prevent a fire, he ran to extinguish it. When, instead, he saw his host flooded in light, he fainted. As he regained consciousness, he heard the Baal Shem scolding him: "One does not look where one should not." After Shabbat, the traveler hurried back to Brodi, where he stormed into the House of Study, shouting the great news: "There is a new source of light close by." The men rushed to the edge of the forest and there built a throne with branches and leaves. The Besht took his seat. "I shall open a new way," he declared.

He was thirty-six.

The madwoman had seen right. She had known before anyone else. Strange: more than any of the town's devout and erudite men, she spoke the language of the young saint in the forest.

Strange, too, the Baal Shem's pilgrimage to the Holy Land. What had moved him to undertake it? Vague desire or well-defined project? One legend tells that bandits somewhere in the Carpathians revealed to him the existence of a tunnel leading to Jerusalem. Another legend claims that he reached the Holy Land by way of Istanbul, accompanied by his scribe Tzvi-Hersh Soifer or—alternately—by his daughter Udil. To simplify matters, a third version insists that he brought both—or then again, that maybe he made the trip . . . twice. A fourth version: his project came to naught; he never went at all.

More enigmas: did he or did he not participate in a public debate with Jacob Frank's followers in Lemberg? Did he or did he not practice healing, distribute amulets to influence fate and drive out demons? Opinions are divided. Even the date of his death is controversial. Some say he died the first day of Shavuot, others affirm it was the second.

Remember: all this confusion centers around a man who lived not in the Middle Ages, but in the eighteenth century. This contemporary of Voltaire and Kant, of Lessing and Diderot, built his empire not in a still far removed and backward Africa, but in the heart of Europe, where man in his quest for enlightenment had begun to reduce history to a human scale. People were striving to learn, to travel, to explore and experience. The word everywhere was becoming challenge, instrument of rebellion, heralding revolutionary changes. Men used it to smash idols and altars— and wanted to make certain that the rest of the world knew. Yet politicians and philanthropists, adventurers and preachers, conquerors and dreamers, all made their way into the chronicles, if not the history, of their times—all except the Baal Shem.

There remains of him nothing but legend, a legend whose profound and lasting reverberations paradoxically gained in strength with time. More than any other Jewish historical figure, with the exception of the Prophet Elijah, the Besht was present in joy as well as in despair; every *shtibel* reflected his light, his warmth. Every Hasid had two Masters: his own and the Baal Shem—each drew his strength from the other. The first was needed to live, the second to believe. Whoever disclaimed kinship with the Baal Shem found himself relegated outside the mainstream of the Hasidic community. The most hauntingly beautiful legends are those in which the Baal Shem is the central—or at least a major—character.

Perhaps then we should say that he was the sum of all tales that were—and still are—told about him and his work. More precisely: that he *is* his legend.

The Preacher

TEXT*

These three stories are characteristic. They show the quality of the pilgrims attracted by Mezeritch and also the diversity of knowledge they drew from it.

"After the death of our Master Israel Baal Shem Tov, the Shekhina herself shouldered her bundle and stick and moved from Medzebozh to Mezeritch," legend tells us by way of several renowned disciples. Authentic or apocryphal, no matter. It illustrates a fact: it was the Maggid who took over. From that moment on he was undisputed head of the rapidly expanding movement, and its center, therefore, shifted elsewhere. Briefly contested at first, his authority soon went unchallenged. Moral guide, teacher, experienced tactician, seasoned organizer and outstanding visionary combined in one person, Rebbe Dov-Ber of Mezeritch counted three hundred disciples, or so they say, of which thirty-nine became leaders and founders of dynasties in their own right.

With him, Hasidism underwent its first structural if not ideological mutation: from the realm of legend to that of history. Even those historians who, for reasons best known to themselves, questioned the physical existence of the Baal Shem, never denied that the Maggid of Mezeritch was his successor.

We know only what we are permitted to know about this spiritual leader who shrouded himself in mystery. While he himself put nothing down on paper, his disciples transcribed his commentaries on Torah and Talmud,

---

*From E. Wiesel, *Souls on Fire*, pp. 56–61, 78.

his interpretation of Zohar, his words of advice and parables, and quoted them abundantly in their own works. Levi-Yitzhak of Berditchev carried his zeal to extremes; he recorded the Master's most trivial remarks. Another disciple, Rebbe Zusia of Onipol, went further yet: he devoted his entire life to scrupulously repeating everything he had heard in Mezeritch.

Thus we know many facts about his origins, his childhood, his life before and after his decisive encounter with the Baal Shem. We know, for example, that in his youth he liked to rise at dawn and walk beside the streams and lakes; he was learning the art of listening. We know that he was nearsighted. That he limped. That he was constantly afflicted by obscure pains. That he trembled before speaking in public. We also know that he ate and slept as little as possible; that under his severe exterior hid a generous man and tender father. But above all, we know his incomparable, unequaled role in the development of Hasidism and the enrichment of the exalted universe that is its own.

In Mezeritch, new center of learning, talented men abounded. Among them were Elimelekh of Lizensk, Zusia of Onipol, Shneur-Zalmen of Ladi, Israel of Kozhenitz, Yaakov-Yoseph of Lublin. One could even meet some of the Baal Shem's companions, such as Pinhas of Koretz or Yaakov-Yoseph of Polnoye. Together and individually, they acknowledged the Maggid as their guide. Each of his disciples received from him whatever he needed to take root and fulfill himself according to his own truth. To some the Maggid taught *Nigla,* the revealed science, to others *Nistar,* the esoteric science reserved for the select few. At the same time, and with equal conviction, he showed the simple uneducated people that merely by reciting the prayer *Sh'ma Israel,* they could be worthy of redemption. For each he found the right word, the needed gesture. In his presence, people realized how much was still to be learned. They suddenly became aware of depths within themselves never recognized before. And that to achieve total awareness, they needed his help. Those who indulged in mortification, he taught that the body is sacred as long as it is alive and that to mutilate it is an offense to God. Those too comfortably ensconced in their existence and neglecting the virtue of fear, he showed what fear could be.

Many whose lives had been transformed by the Baal Shem, and many others who wanted to change theirs, flocked to Mezeritch. The Maggid knew whom to attract and encourage and whom to turn away. His intuition was such that he gave meaning to all waiting and corrected all shortcomings. If we are to believe his admirers, he, like his Master, could accurately describe people simply by looking at an object of their making.

All testimonies concur: the Maggid had mastered the art of winning the absolute loyalty of men by upsetting their equilibrium. His methods relied on surprise and shock. His pronouncements were as unexpected as his silences. To one visitor he made a single comment: "The horse who knows he is a horse, is not. Man's major task is to learn that he is not a horse." To another he said: "Just as there is light and darkness in the world, there is light and darkness in man's mind." On his lips, ordinary sentences took on the weight of confessions. "When the sick Maggid told a simple story," according to Israel of Rizhin, "the bed he rested on would shake violently, and so would the privileged few present." The Baal Shem made people dream, the Maggid made them tremble.

A man, a mystic, came to see him. The visitor had given up food and sleep and was seeking total renunciation. The Maggid first directed his son, Rebbe Avraham, to feed him by force. Then he ordered him to repeat after him, word by word, the ritual confession, the *Vidui: Ashamnu, bagadnu, gazalnu*—We have sinned, we have betrayed, we have stolen. The man fainted. When he came to, the Maggid sent him away, ordering him never to let it happen again: some words are as important as deeds—some words *are* deeds.

Another visitor, a Hasid and noted Talmudic scholar, came to seek his advice. He was afraid he was losing his faith. The Maggid did not engage the man in lengthy philosophical discussions, but instead asked him to repeat with him, over and over again, the very first prayer every Jewish child learns by heart. And that was all.

"One day," Rebbe Wolfe of Zhitomir tells us, "we were all sitting around the table in the House of Study. It was a Friday afternoon. We could hear the Maggid, in his study next door, reading the Sidra, the weekly portion of Scripture customarily read on Shabbat. Suddenly he stopped, the door opened, and there he was, standing motionless in the doorway, staring at us, or perhaps at someone beyond us. His whole being was on fire, but most of all, his face, most of all, his eyes. Seized with panic, Rebbe Pinhas, Rebbe Shmelke, Rebbe Elimelekh and Rebbe Zusia ran into the street. Rebbe Levi-Yitzhak hid under the table. As for me, gripped by a strange exultation, I began to applaud with all my strength—and to this day I regret it."

And do you know how Rebbe Avraham Kalisker came to attach himself to the Maggid's court? For years he had lived in seclusion, refusing to meet people so as not to take time away from Torah. One day he heard a Hasid quote the Maggid's interpretation of *Umala haaretz kinyanekha*, the earth is full of things that permit man to acquire a partnership with God. Rebbe Avraham Kalisker needed no more: he climbed out the nearest window and hurried to Mezeritch. Later he told the famous Gaon of Vilna: "What *I* learned in Mezeritch? One simple truth: *vehai bahem*, Torah is given to man so he may celebrate life and everything that makes life a source of celebration."

The Holy Seer of Lublin testifies: "Once I heard the Maggid say *Ein*

Ke'elokhenu, no God is like our God, the last prayer of the service. At that very moment the skies parted and I saw the words coming alive before my eyes: I *saw* that there is no God like our God."

One day the Maggid invited Rebbe Wolfe of Zhitomir to say grace after the Shabbat meal. Afterward he asked him: "What did you feel?"—"Two hands on my head," said the astonished disciple.—"That was the Prophet Elijah ordaining you a rabbi," said the Maggid.

As for Shneur-Zalmen, the illustrious author of the *Tanya* and founder of the school of Lubavitch, he praised the Maggid's vast erudition. Not his supernatural powers. He would say: "Miracles? In Mezeritch? Who had the time to notice them all?" As for himself, Shneur-Zalmen, he was impressed only by the prodigiously acute and prolific mind of the Maggid. Himself a noted scholar and philosopher, he stated without the slightest hesitation: "Whatever I know is nothing compared with what he knows."

On the other hand, we have the testimony of another great Hasidic figure, the mysterious Leib, son of Sarah, who proclaimed to anyone willing to listen: "I came to the Maggid not to listen to discourses, nor to learn from his wisdom; I came to watch him tie his shoelaces."

In Hasidic vocabulary, the Great Maggid means the one from Mezeritch. What made him great? We shall enlarge on this later; for the moment let us say that the impact of certain Masters must be measured by evaluating the men they inspire. Those who made up the Maggid's "court" were personalities of the first rank. That they chose him to be their leader proves that they, who were known as his peers, believed in his superiority. . . .

And so Mezeritch did not become another Medzebozh. Unlike the Baal Shem, the Great Maggid rarely left Mezeritch and avoided crowds. The Baal Shem had been constantly on the move, showing interest in men of many backgrounds, everywhere; the Maggid addressed himself to a select few. The Baal Shem had told stories; the Maggid made speeches. The Baal Shem celebrated services with the crowd, and the larger it was, the happier he was; the Maggid prayed alone, and only at the end of services were nine privileged disciples invited to join him in a *minyan.*

The Baal Shem had been accessible and always ready to be of service. Anyone could come and see him without having to go through intermediaries. Not so the Maggid. He was the first to appoint a *gabbe* or *shamash* (secretary, servant, guard) to keep intruders away.

More than his Master, the Maggid seems to have had an affinity for drama and staging. The Baal Shem had wandered around dressed alternately as a coachman or a peasant, a woodcutter or a vagabond. The Maggid had a different vision of himself. He assumed the role of high priest and habitually donned the white flowing robes of that office. He inspired respect. The Baal Shem had inspired love.

Toward the end of his life, the Maggid used crutches, which made his already impressive appearance even more awesome. His sickness became one more barrier erected between himself and the outside world.

The Rebbe of Love

TEXT*

A story: The Rebbe notices a coachman, who to save time runs through his morning prayers while greasing his carriage. He does not scold him. Instead, he lifts his eyes to heaven and asks it to be his witness:

"Look at Your people, God of Israel, and be proud. What does this man do while working on his cart? He prays. Tell me, do You know of any other nation that has You so completely in its thoughts?"

Another: On his way to the synagogue to celebrate Shabbat services, he meets an "enlightened" young man who pulls out his pipe in overt defiance and lights it. The Rebbe stops to remind him: "Surely you're forgetting that today is Shabbat?"

"No, I haven't forgotten."

"Then surely you are ignorant of the law that forbids us to smoke on Shabbat?"

"Not at all, I know all your laws," the smoker impudently replies.

The Rebbe looks the young man over. He refuses to be provoked; instead he turns to Him for Whom every being also signifies provocation: "Did you hear? True, he violates certain of Your commandments. But You must admit one thing: nobody will coerce him into telling a lie."

The Rebbe of these anecdotes is of course none other than Levi-Yitzhak Derbaremdiger (the Merciful), better known by the name of his town: Levi-Yitzhak of Berditchev. His stories, dialogues and litanies can be attributed to no one else. His monologues are poems, his poems are legends, and all bear witness for man. Always he appears as our spokesman.

A contemporary of the Great Maggid of Mezeritch, he occupies a very specific place in the Hasidic movement as well as in the life of every Hasid. His popularity equals the Baal Shem's. Even today, today more than ever, he commands our respect and affection. No European Diaspora Master since the Baal Shem has left so profound a mark on the Jewish imagination. . . .

* * * *

---

*From E. Wiesel, *Souls on Fire*, pp. 89–90, 101–103.

His was an impulsive, unpredictable nature. One never knew what to expect from him.

Once he climbed to the roof of a building facing the marketplace. He watched merchants buying and selling, he listened to the screeching horse dealers, and suddenly he began to shout at the top of his lungs: "Good people, do not forget, do not forget that God too is to be feared!"

Every once in a while he dispatched his servant to one or the other of the neighboring synagogues: "Look neither to your right nor to your left, walk straight to the bimah, pound your fist on the pulpit and make the following announcement: 'Know ye, men and women, know that God exists and that He is of this world, of this world too!' "

People resisted him but—in Berditchev—no one mocked him. People listened to him and respected him, though he was odd and clumsy and everything happened to him. He could not light the Hanukkah candles without burning his fingers, nor could he take the ethrog out of the cupboard without breaking the glass door. Attending the Seder of the pedantic Rebbe Barukh of Medzebozh, he tipped over the table. He went to the well and barely missed falling in. Whether absent-minded or in a trance, he seemed to have little sense of reality. Nor was he aware of the disorder he left in his wake. His inner life detached him from real life. When a gang of hoodlums beat him mercilessly, he did not interrupt his prayers for a moment; as though he never felt his wounds. Impervious to the outside world, he was not afraid of suffering; he ignored it. He fought pain in his own way. Accompanying his dead son to the cemetery, he began to dance, crying: "Lord, You entrusted me my son with a pure soul and that is how I give him back to You."

No wonder that Mitnagdim, opposed to anything that smacked of sensationalism, fought him so bitterly and with such determination, especially in the early days. They complained about his manners, his manias—what they called his taste for dramatics—in short, his way of life. In his capacity as official rabbi, he should have, in their opinion, devoted more time to study and less time to services. He did the exact opposite. Like Rabbi Akiba long ago, he worshipped with such abandon that the frightened faithful instinctively moved away. He gesticulated, howled and danced, jumping from one corner to the other, pushing and overturning whatever was in his way. People ceased to exist for him. When he prayed, he himself ceased to exist. Sometimes the faithful became tired of waiting and went home, leaving him alone in the House of Study. This even happened on a Passover eve.

He prayed with fervor because he believed in prayer. A story he liked to tell: "I was there when a thief was being caught. I heard him whisper: 'Too bad, I'll try again, and next time I'll do better.' From this thief I learned that one must always be prepared to try again."

But he believed just as much, if not more, in fervor. His own was boundless. Whatever he did, he did without reservations, with his entire being. He often fainted in the middle of services. The slightest prayer exhausted him; it involved more than his faith, it involved his life.

But above all he believed in the coming of the Messiah. Drawing up his son's engagement contract, the scribe had specified that the marriage was to take place on a certain date in Berditchev. Levi-Yitzhak furiously tore the contract to shreds: "Berditchev? Why Berditchev? This is what you will write: 'The marriage will take place on such a date in Jerusalem, except if the Messiah has not yet come; in which case the ceremony will be performed in Berditchev.' "

The Rebbe of Wealth

TEXT*

Born in 1797, Israel of Rizhin was Hasidism's favorite child and last undisputed leader. Was it because he was the great-grandson of the Maggid of Mezeritch that he enjoyed a special privileged status? Be that as it may, he had no known enemies or even opponents. People loved him, asked nothing more than to love him. They forgave him everything: his predilection for solitude, his lack of erudition, his pride, and in a more general way, the new path he was taking, so different from the one the Baal Shem had opened a century earlier in the Carpathian Mountains.

From the very beginning, he behaved like a spoiled child, a prince entitled to all honors. "I was seven," he said, "when I visited Vienna. There I was received with such pomp that nothing impresses me any more." Nothing but the best was good enough for him. Whatever he wanted, he was given. His every whim was satisfied. His elegant suits were made to measure. He was both handsome and rich, and from the beginning he craved wealth and loved beauty. During the latter part of his reign he owned a palace with servants, musicians and stables. His synagogue in Sadigor accommodated three thousand worshippers. He never went anywhere without a suite of a hundred or so aides, cooks, coachmen, musicians and intimates. On Passover his guests were served on golden dishes. Rizhin was a temple and the Rebbe its royal presence. Every Shabbat brought another attempt to re-create the lost splendors of Jerusalem. The singing was reminiscent of the Levites; the repasts evoked memories of sacrificial ceremonies.

Hasidim, by the thousands, converged upon Rizhin and, later, Sadigor, simply to be in Rizhin and Sadigor, simply to see the prince in his palace, the prince on his throne, the prince and his wealth—and strange as it may

---

*From E. Wiesel, *Souls on Fire*, pp. 143–149.

sound, nobody was shocked, nobody called it scandalous; the Rebbe was above reproach, beyond judgment.

There were great Masters among those who came to see him: Hersh Riminover, Yitzhak-Meir of Ger, Yitzhak of Worke, Haim of Tzanz—and even a rabbi as far removed from Hasidism as Shamshon-Raphael Hirsch of Frankfort. None lifted an eyebrow. All returned to their homes impressed if perhaps not conquered by the Rizhiner's personality.

True, they realized how different his concept of Hasidism was from theirs, from the one they had received from their Masters. Once upon a time, in Medzebozh and Mezeritch, in Tchernobil and Berditchev, the Hasid had tried to overcome poverty by means other than money, to defeat sadness by means other than ostentation. Hasidism in those days mocked appearances and denigrated comfort. The Baal Shem had lived in misery and so had his disciples. They had advocated joy within misery, hope despite misfortune, despite injustice. They had believed in generosity toward others and severity toward themselves. They had lived for each other, for their fellow man; they had helped one another attain knowledge, and above all, self-knowledge. They had lived and survived, fully realizing their needs and desires.

Once upon a time Hasidism had meant emphasis on inner truth and fervor; a return to nature, to genuine beauty, to identification. A Hasid would see a tree and become that tree; he would hear the song of a shepherd and become that song and that shepherd—that was his way of coming closer to the essence of man. He had no need for castles and servants in order to feel at home in God's creation. To possess meant nothing, to be meant everything. Thus, it is no coincidence that the heroes of the Baal Shem's legends were mostly beggars. His way of telling us that it is more important to possess oneself than to possess; more important to be than to appear.

But in Rizhin it was the aristocracy that set the law. In Rizhin, greatness had to be displayed to be recognized. What counted was the mask, not the face; the reflection, not the source.

The question naturally arises; why? What did Israel of Rizhin want to prove, discover or refute? Whom was he challenging? What game was he playing and—most importantly—why was he permitted to play?

The fact is he could have been criticized, castigated for his style of living, for the economic and social gap he was creating between himself and his followers; but he wasn't. He could have been opposed and challenged on the grounds that within Hasidic terms of reference, his extravagance was bordering on heresy. But he wasn't. He was free to do and say whatever he wanted, in any way he chose. As a founder of a dynasty, he was protected, untouchable.

It is said that when Avraham Yehoshua Heschel of Apt proclaimed a day of fasting and prayer out of solidarity with a certain Jewish community, in distress, on that same day the Rizhiner Rebbe summoned his musicians to play for him. Yet the Apter Rebbe did not take it as an affront. His only comment: "No one can understand the ways of the Rizhiner." Other Rebbes adopted the same attitude. Out of respect rather than complacency. He was a Rebbe unlike others, a special case, a destiny apart.

But why such favoritism? Why such privileges? What made him so special? The fact that he was the direct descendant of the Mezeritcher Maggid? Or because he represented, almost from the beginning, a real force within the movement, a force with which other leaders had to reckon? Was there something else, and if so, what was it?

Whatever the reason, the fact remains that his popularity kept growing; his fanatic followers saw to it. His legend exerted a magic appeal on the masses, it captivated their imagination, starved for things sublime. His biography—embellished by popular storytellers—became that of a saint, prophet and prince in Israel. It was said that his soul was among the four Moses brought back with him when he returned to earth at Sinai. The other three being those of Shimon Bar-Yohai, Yitzhak Luria and Israel Baal Shem Tov.

The Rizhiner himself claimed that he had been on earth three times. First as a young prince in the Kingdom of Judea, then as a young priest in the Temple; this was the third time.

Once, when he was five—or ten, opinions vary—his ritual belt slipped and fell to the ground in the presence of his powerful protector, the old Rebbe of Apt. The old Tzaddik bent down, picked it up and girded the youngster's waist, explaining: "This is how one performs the commandment of *Glila,* of girding the scrolls of the Torah." On another occasion he said: "The Rizhiner has forgotten nothing of what the angels taught him before he was born."

Perhaps that explains why, as a child, he refused to study. His tutor reportedly complained that his illustrious pupil was not the most promising of students. Could young Israel's refusal to read the required books, to prepare his homework be ascribed to lack of interest or ambition? That seems unlikely. More probably, it was excessive ambition and a desire to do everything better and faster by taking shortcuts. And also to show he had received the Torah "directly from God." Soon he became so sure of himself that he professed having no need to study. Whatever he said became interesting and important because he said it. To Moshe of Savran, who came to visit, he showed his stable and spoke with pride of his magnificent stallions. All the pious and saintly visitor found to say afterward, in the way of commentary, was: "All this talk of horses was allegorical. Actually, the Rizhiner was referring to the celestial chariots, symbols of the mystical relationship the Creator maintains with creation.''

His more formal discourses, though rare, were not particularly scholarly. A few commentaries on Torah, several ingenious findings on Midrash and Zohar. What people remembered mainly were his sayings. For instance: ''How is one to distinguish the silent sage from the silent fool? The sage doesn't mind being silent.'' Also: ''Look around you. Works of art everywhere are cherished, honored and protected, while man—God's masterpiece—lies in the dust.'' But even his most ardent admirers admit that his personality was his strength; his impact was due to the quality of his presence, not to his scholarship.

A certain Yaakov-Yoseph of Koretz told him of his plans to move to a remote village to be a schoolteacher. ''What?'' exclaimed the Rizhiner. ''Another schoolteacher? No! I want you to become rich!'' And so great was the Hasid's faith in his Rebbe that he went into business and in a few short years amassed an immense fortune.

Was that the Rizhiner's secret? His ability to push his followers to the limits of their potential? And beyond? Perhaps. But then why did he need such pageantry? The Baal Shem in his wooden hut had caused incomparably deeper changes in his faithful. In fact, the Rizhiner's ostentatious wealth should have repelled and offended many a visitor. It didn't. On the contrary. As his fortunes multiplied, more and more poor people flocked to his court. What attracted them? Curiosity? A possibility of sublimation? Escapism? The fact that they liked him, worshipped him, proves that they needed someone like him to admire and idolize. Perhaps they needed to see that it was possible for a Jew to live like a prince; for them he was a reflection of past grandeur, a continuation of ancient and glorious times. He reminded them of what they had once been. There was so much poverty lurking behind every door, so much fear to be contained in every heart, that the sight of a Jew crowned and gratified was enough for them. He was their illusion, their holiday.

Still, it became necessary to invent a plausible explanation that would justify his eccentricities. So they said: ''Poor Rebbe. Beneath his princely robes he is dressed in straw. We honor him, but his heart is in mourning.'' And they would shake their heads: ''Poor, poor Rebbe. His shiny leather shoes are without soles; he walks on snow, his body is bruised. He suffers even while he appears happy.'' The proof? He never ate in public, slept three hours a night, spoke little, sought solitude and eschewed noise. In constant meditation, he moved in other worlds. But what about his properties? His valuables? His riches? He had to accept them. In order to fool Satan. For where would Satan set his traps for the Just? In synagogues, in Houses of Study, in the poorhouse, but surely not in a princely palace, under the golden robes of someone whose demeanor was that of a nobleman, not that of a Tzaddik. Satan covets only the humble; the conceited, the already corrupted leave him indifferent. That is why, they maintained in Rizhin, the Rebbe had to cover himself with gold and show himself proud.

The Rebbe of Madness

TEXT*

One day the king summoned his counselor and told him of his anguish: "I have read in the stars that all those who will eat of the next harvest will be struck with madness. What shall we do, my friend?"

"Nothing could be more simple, Sire," replied the counselor, "we shall not touch it. Last year's harvest is not yet exhausted. You have but to requisition it; it will be ample for you. And me."

"And the others?" scolded the king. "All the subjects of my kingdom? The faithful servants of the crown? The men, the women, the madmen and the beggars, are you forgetting them? Are you forgetting the children, the children too?"

"I am forgetting nobody, Sire. But as your adviser, I must be realistic and take all possibilities into account. We don't have enough reserves, not enough to protect and satisfy everyone. There will be just enough for you. And me."

Thereupon the king's brow darkened, and he said: "Your solution does not please me. Is there no other? Never mind. But I refuse to separate myself from my people and I don't care to remain lucid in the midst of a people gone mad. Therefore we shall all enter madness together. You and I like the others, with the others. When the world is gripped by delirium, it is senseless to watch from the outside: the mad will think that we are mad too. And yet, I should like to safeguard some reflection of our present glory and of our anguish too; I should like to keep alive the memory of this determination, this decision. I should like that when the time comes, you and I shall remain aware of our predicament."

"Whatever for, Sire?"

"It will help us, you'll see. And thus we shall be able to help our friends. Who knows, perhaps thanks to us, men will find the strength to resist later, even if it is too late."

And putting his arm around his friend's shoulders, the king went on: "You and I shall therefore mark each other's foreheads with the seal of madness. And every time we shall look at one another, we shall know, you and I, that we are mad."

* * * *

*From E. Wiesel, *Souls on Fire*, pp. 169–172, 180–182.

In a distant land, a prince lost his mind and imagined himself a rooster. He sought refuge under the table and lived there, naked, refusing to partake of the royal delicacies served in golden dishes—all he wanted and accepted was the grain reserved for the roosters. The king was desperate. He sent for the best physicians, the most famous specialists; all admitted their incompetence. So did the magicians. And the monks, the ascetics, the miracle-makers; all their interventions proved fruitless.

One day an unknown sage presented himself at court. "I think that I could heal the prince," he said shyly. "Will you allow me to try?"

The king consented, and to the surprise of all present, the sage removed his clothes, and joining the prince under the table, began to crow like a rooster.

Suspicious, the prince interrogated him: "Who are you and what are you doing here?"—"And you," replied the sage, "who are you and what are you doing here?"—"Can't you see? I am a rooster!"—"Hmm," said the Sage, "how very strange to meet you here!"—"Why strange?"—"You mean, you don't see? Really not? You don't see that I'm a rooster just like you?"

The two men became friends and swore never to leave each other.

And then the sage undertook to cure the prince by using himself as example. He started by putting on a shirt. The prince couldn't believe his eyes.—"Are you crazy? Are you forgetting who you are? You really want to be a man?"—"You know," said the Sage in a gentle voice, "you mustn't ever believe that a rooster who dresses like a man ceases to be a rooster." The prince had to agree. The next day both dressed in a normal way. The sage sent for some dishes from the palace kitchen. "Wretch! What are you doing?" protested the prince, frightened in the extreme. "Are you going to *eat* like them now?" His friend allayed his fears: "Don't ever think that by eating like man, with man, at his table, a rooster ceases to be what he is; you mustn't ever believe that it is enough for a rooster to behave like a man to become human; you can do anything with man, in his world and even for him, and yet remain the rooster you are."

And the prince was convinced; he resumed his life as a prince.

The author of these tales is Nahman of Bratzlav, whose stories are among the most spellbinding in Hasidic literature. They constitute a universe of their own in which dreamers go beyond their dreams, beyond their desires, swept away by their quest for imagination and salvation and an infinite craving for innocence and wonder.

*   *   *   *

I remember reading these stories as a child and, spellbound, thinking that I had understood them. Now I reread them, and though I am still under their spell, I no longer understand them. Some seem too simple, others too complicated; sometimes both at the same time. Frequently their form is what misleads me; sometimes it is their inner structure. The more I read, the more I get the feeling of being left behind, of being incapable of continuing to the end. And then I fear that there will always remain a zone of silence, a zone of darkness which I shall never pierce. Never will I retrace the steps leading back to the teller; I shall see neither what he saw nor what he refused to see. I shall not live his adventures, though I may sometimes claim those of his heroes and their victims as my own.

His tales? Each contains many others. Imagine a series of concentric circles whose fixed centers are buried in man's innermost being: the I inside the I, conscience become silence and peace, memory inside memory. And all are inhabited by princes and sages. By haunted creatures seeking one another, one in another. By survivors of calamities, refugees, fugitives, messengers and innocent children, orphans and beggars endlessly roaming the world only to meet again in a cave or in a palace, reunited and fulfilled in ways that go beyond the experience they have gone through or been subjected to, perhaps unwittingly. Following them, we plunge into the supernatural, and yet the word miracle is never pronounced. For in the Bratzlaver's universe everything is miraculous, even the most common event. On his lips, the most deprived, most primitive of men are endowed with powers; his objects have the gift of song, just as his forest, his trees, his animals and his morning breezes all have the gift of laughter.

More daring than the most daring of the surrealists, trusting only his intuition, Nahman creates freely, impulsively; he rejects all logic, inductive or deductive; he obeys no law, acknowledges no influence. "Time does not exist," he asserts, meaning his tales as well as the world; he goes so far as to exclude it from primary creation. According to him, God gave man everything—except time.

Thus, the notion of time never enters Rebbe Nahman's work. Neither does the notion of place. Continuity? He prefers unbridled, irresistible and sovereign fantasy disdainful of frontiers, all frontiers; those of the mind as well as those of lands inhabited though cursed. His characters are forever leaving one another: sometimes to hide behind others for no reason. Impossible to know who is playing what role and for how long. The episodes arbitrarily fit into one another, follow one another, becoming inextricably tangled. And then, just as arbitrarily, they reach an abrupt ending, as though the teller had exhausted his patience and wanted to finish quickly in order to start anew. The tone is epic, the pace fast and erratic. Every fable contains ten fables, every scene is a mosaic whose every fragment is a tale, a scene in itself. One easily loses the thread. There are too many *maassioth betokh maassioth,* too many tales inside the tales Rebbe Nahman tells us. One ends up forgetting the main, subterranean plot. Like Nahman's heroes, the reader-listener no longer has any notion where he is or what might be awaiting him at the next step; he is helpless, lost in a strange land.

At first glance, this may seem surprising, for Rebbe Nahman could impose a discipline on himself when he wanted to or deemed it necessary. He was too skilled a craftsman to botch a tale. If he sustains our attention to the end in spite of the dispersion of his characters, it is only because he is a master of his craft. But then, how could he who in the secondary, not to say minor, episodes attached such importance to the smallest intricate pattern, to every detail—the color of a cloud, of twilight; an old man's expression of wonder, a passer-by's sneer—how could he neglect the framework and underestimate the importance of the work's very structure? Why did he leave so many gaps? Threads leading in too many directions at once; action ten times suspended—and seven times resumed? Have they a purpose? The answer is contained in the question. The same failings—or apparent failings—may be found in all his tales, in everything he created; therefore they must be deliberate, translating his concept of creation, of the art of transmitting legends and also of their author.

It is as though he wanted people to understand that it is more important for man to halt and consider the mystery of his own life than that of the world's origins. Danger and evil are not in the walk toward death, but in the digression. Man advances toward more than one goal, lives on more than one level, loves and despairs in more than one way for more than one reason. Yet he does not even know whether his deeds fall into a main or secondary pattern or if his awareness is blessing or curse. The human condition gains in impact at the very moment it breaks apart. Every fragment contains the whole, every fissure bears witness that man is at once the most fragile and the most tenacious of creatures.

Rebbe Nahman is more concerned with man than with mankind. Because he reacts more directly to the individual, his relationship to earth and heaven is filled with as many secrets as are contained by heaven and earth. Rebbe Nahman tightens the episodic events and lets the canvas flutter because he prefers the moment to years, the infinitely small to the infinitely large, the jolts of a life to a lifetime without surprises.

COMMENT

The selections given here are only a shadow of the reality of the Zaddik. And still, there were many more kinds of Zaddik: the Rebbe of Suffering, the Rebbe of Cynicism, the Rebbe who dressed in modern clothes and went to the theater, and so on. And then there are the Rebbes of the Holocaust—those who died as well as those who survived. It is almost as if the holy did not (or could not) take on only one form; as if the holy had to be expressed according to the strengths and weaknesses of each of its embodiments. And upon reflection, how could it have been otherwise. The holy, the pneumatic, is not clay that can be stamped into a mold. It cannot be manufactured. The holy is a fire, and it must only burn intensely. Perhaps because of this, one of the two elements which all the Zaddikim have in common is an intense spirituality, an intense presence of the holy. Without that, a person is not a Zaddik. The other common element is Rabbinic Judaism, for although the Zaddikim made what appeared to their opponents as major modifications, they actually remained very clearly within the parameters of Rabbinic Judaism. The ideals of Torah study, worship, commandments, charity, social cohesion, morality, etc., were strictly adhered to. No Zaddik could, as the false messiahs of the seventeenth and eighteenth centuries did, demand of his Hasidim to violate any basic precept of Rabbinic Judaism. Such a person would have lost his following immediately. Intense spirituality and rabbinic prescription, then, bound the Zaddikim together, while individual character differentiated them.

Split-Level Spirituality

The essence of the rabbinic reworking of Jewish religion was that anyone could be a rabbi. This had not always been so, for in the period preceding the establishment of Rabbinic Judaism, there were priests, levites, etc., and not everyone could be a priest. Not everyone could enter the Holy of Holies. Rabbinic Judaism, however, by understanding the inner sanctum to be Torah, its study and practice, made the holy in its most intense sense open to any person gifted and dedicated enough to become a rabbi. Even rabbinic mysticism, as we have seen all along, was open to anyone, although it required intelligence and spiritual sensitivity. Hasidism did not exactly change all that, but it did modify it by defining two levels of spirituality: one for the Hasid or follower, and one for the Zaddik or leader.

The selections which follow indicate this "split-level" spirituality. The reader should note carefully which functions are limited to (or recommended only for) the Zaddik. Note, too, the special relationship which the Hasid must have to his Zaddik and how this affects both parties. The Conclusion sums up the Zaddik as an institution.

Elevating "Strange Thoughts"

TEXT*

A doctrine of much significance in early Hasidism but one that was eventually abandoned by the majority of later teachers is that of elevating "strange thoughts" (*mahashavot zarot*).

We have noted in the previous chapters how concerned the Hasidim were to avoid thoughts of self during prayer. The ideal for the Hasid was to lose himself in the divine. Yet the Hasid could not help experiencing in his prayers the intrusion not alone of selfhood but of thoughts opposed to the Jewish tradition. These "strange thoughts" were generally of three kinds. In the literature on the subject in Hasidism there are repeated references to "strange love," to "pride" and to "idolatry." "Strange love" refers to thoughts of sexual sin or sexual imaginings. "Pride" refers to thoughts of how wise and pious the Hasid was. "Idolatry" refers to thoughts about irreligion, the denial of Judaism or the attraction of Christianity.

What was the Hasid to do? A dialectic developed in early Hasidism between the conscious attempt to reject the "strange thoughts" by pushing them out of the mind and the attempt to keep them in the mind but to "elevate" them. Elevation in this context means to trace them in the mind to their source in God (since from Him come all things) and so deprive them of their baneful power. For example, if the Hasid suddenly finds that his devotions are being distracted by thoughts about a woman he knows, he begins to dwell on the fact that her beauty, which is the cause of her attraction, is only a very pale reflection of the source of all beauty on high and this helps him to sense the illusory nature of all physical beauty in comparison with the divine. By having this in mind during his prayers the Hasid has managed to cope with the distraction not by rejecting it but by using it and so redeeming it for the holy. Or if the Hasid finds that his thoughts are turning towards a sense of his own importance, he should dwell on pride as a manifestation here on earth of God's majesty and he will then be led on to elevate the pride to its source in God and so transcend the self in the very process of having his attention drawn to it. Or if he finds himself entertaining idolatrous thoughts during his prayers, he should remind himself that the lure of idolatry is occasioned by the desire in the human breast to worship. Very well then, let it lead to the Being alone worthy of human worship. In these ways the "strange thoughts" themselves lead man back to God and are "elevated" rather than rejected. Naturally, this whole doctrine aroused the ire of the

---

*From L. Jacobs, *Hasidic Prayer*, pp. 104–105, 112–114.

Mitnaggedim. Among the Hasidic masters themselves the problem was approached in different ways and various techniques were evolved.

*   *   *   *

Even if lustful imaginings and other strange thoughts enter his mind at the time of his worship, in the study of the Torah or in prayer, he should take no notice of them but should straight away disregard them. He should not be so stupid as to engage in elevating the quality of the strange thought, as is well known, for those matters apply only to the Zaddikim into whose mind there fall not their own strange thoughts but those of other people. But as for a person into whose mind there enter his own strange thoughts, stemming from the evil in his heart and situated in the left ventricle, how can he elevate them if he himself is securely fastened there down below?

*   *   *   *

When strange thoughts and imaginings attack a man but he strengthens himself to prevail over them, then the Holy One, blessed be He, has great delight from it and it is very precious in His eyes. To quote a parable: it sometimes happens that kings on a carnival day arrange for contests between different wild beasts. The kings stand by and witness it and have great pleasure from the contest. In the same way, thought comes from the category of man's vitality [*hiyut*] and holy things are in the category of clean beasts [*hayot*] while evil thoughts are in the category of unclean beasts [*hayot*]. From above these are allowed to struggle with one another and the Holy One, blessed be He, has great delight when man prevails over the unclean beasts and conquers them. The general principle is this: it is quite impossible for a man to have different thoughts in his mind at the same time. Consequently, he can easily drive out evil thoughts simply by doing nothing, that is to say by refusing to think that thought but to think of something else, of the Torah or of worship or even of business. For it is quite impossible for two thoughts to be together in any circumstances. I have already explained that one has no need to engage in battle and wave the head backwards and forwards in order to drive the evil thoughts away, for this has no effect whatsoever. On the contrary, by this means the evil thoughts become stronger. He should rather ignore them completely and simply carry on what he is doing at that time, whether it be studying the Torah or offering his prayers or engaging in business and he should not look behind him at all. The result will be that the strange thoughts will vanish automatically.

*   *   *   *

From the time of the breaking [of the vessels] the sparks fell into all the worlds and they are elevated little by little from one stage to another through the prayers of the Zaddik. When the Zaddik prays and thus attaches himself to that [divine] attribute to which his current spiritual stage corresponds, a strange thought comes into his mind of the same nature as that attribute. When the Zaddik ascends still higher there comes into his mind a strange thought from that higher attribute. The Zaddik must know from which attribute and from which world the strange thought comes and he must know how to elevate it to that attribute and to that world which corresponds to the stage in which he now finds himself. It can happen, however, that the Zaddik desires to elevate it but is incapable of so doing. The reason for this is that the strange thought that comes into his mind belongs to a higher stage than that in which he finds himself at present. Consequently, it is impossible for him to elevate it for there exists for him a lower stage, namely, that in which he finds himself at present.

On Performing Lurianic Kavvanot

TEXT*

The intention of prayers [i.e., the Lurianic Kavvanot] are applicable only to the chosen few, the elevated ones who are few in number, and not to the masses as a whole. For these latter are drunk through the troubles of the exile and are like a drunkard who casts off the yoke of the Torah and accepts the yoke of the world and of business activity. Not so the chosen ones who accept upon themselves the yoke of the Torah. These are called free men, free from the drunkenness of exile. Consequently, it is to them that the intentions and the soul of the prayers are given. It is otherwise with one who engages in business. He is truly called a drunkard as we see with our own eyes and as we know from experience . . . Now God in His mercy, because He desires lovingkindness, gave us the counsel of the 613 precepts of the Torah, known as 613 counsels. And, in any event, the meaning of the word Torah is to show those who keep it the way in which they should walk. Consequently, these two precepts were placed in juxtaposition: "Him shalt thou serve" [Deut. 10:20], this refers to prayer; "And to Him thou shalt cleave" [Deut. 10:20], which means, cleave to scholars. The Torah hints here at a great principle. This is that the body has no vitality unless it is attached to the soul and then the soul vivifies the body. Not so when the body is separate from the soul, which is separation of the masses from the chosen few in each generation. It is in accordance

*From L. Jacobs, *Hasidic Prayer*, pp. 131–132.

with this mystery that the Ari, of blessed memory, ordained that before he prays a man should take upon himself the obligation to love his neighbour as himself, to love in his heart every one of Israel, so that his prayer can be included in the prayers of the faithful believers in Israel who know the intentions of the prayers. This is easy to understand.

Symbiosis and Faith

TEXT*

After the founder—the Baal Shem—and the architect—the Great Maggid—came Elimelekh—the teacher, the practical man who translated abstract concepts into simple language for simple people.

What and who is a Tzaddik according to Lizensk? Rebbe, rabbi, guide, conscience, tutor; he is the sublimation of man's self. He is what man can be, wants to be. He is the chosen one who is refused nothing, in heaven or on earth. God is angry? He can make Him smile. God is severe? He can induce Him to leniency. His followers owe him blind and unconditional allegiance. *Emunat Tzaddikim*, faith in the Rebbe, is one of the basic tenets of Lizensker Hasidism. He who hesitates, who wavers, cannot be helped. To question the Rebbe is worse than sin; it is absurd, for it destroys the very relationship that binds you to him.

If his behavior appears bizarre, it means the Hasid does not possess the required powers of understanding. So complex is Elimelekh's dialectical approach that the Tzaddik's relationship with the "higher spheres" is never clearly defined—yet the common mortal may not question its existence or its efficiency. Whether he chooses to sing or laugh, to smile or be unpleasant, to open up or withdraw into meditation—*he* knows what he is doing; that should be enough. One must not try to understand. One must admire, that's all. Let him choose poverty while accepting donations; let him simulate joy but spend nights in lamentation; let him *boast* of his humility—nobody has the right to take exception. What he does, he does well, and for you. A superior, almost perfect being—meaning that his thirst for perfection is almost perfection—he uses his mysterious powers to redeem the sins of his generation. No matter what the Tzaddik does, he transcends his own person. His suffering confers a meaning upon all suffering; and when he eats, he cleanses the very act of nourishing the body.

"If they had left me alone, if they had left me in peace for two years," said Rebbe Elimelekh, "I would have made the Messiah come."

Like the Baal Shem and the Great Maggid of Mezeritch, Elimelekh

---

*From E. Wiesel, *Souls on Fire*, pp. 122–124.

linked individual salvation to universal redemption. A Tzaddik is called upon to play the most vital role in human drama, just as the Messiah would in cosmic drama. Though the two roles are not identical, they are related. Which explains why, at one point, a Tzaddik *must* assume responsibility for the Messiah's *not* coming. Like his two immediate predecessors, Elimelekh is said to have planned a momentous journey to the Holy Land—and like them, had to abandon the project: times were not propitious as yet. . . .

Once he remarked: "So many people come to me with their pleas. One cries for health, another for bread, a third for a better life. Why do they come to *me?* Because in truth I am responsible for their sickness, their hunger and their misery."

Does that mean the Hasid's own responsibilities are diminished? Surely not. Only shifted. He is responsible for what happens to the Tzaddik—for *his* crises, for *his* spiritual anguish. One needs the other. For the Tzaddik represents man's potential; he is all that every Hasid wishes to become, could become. Granted, it is given to every man to attain perfection. Granted, too, that the Tzaddik owes his position of Tzaddik only to himself. Whoever works on himself long enough, obstinately enough, will in the end break his chains. Ancestry means nothing. A descendant of the Baal Shem is no worthier than any other man. Like the Baal Shem, Elimelekh left his throne not to his sons but to his disciples, none of whom had titles other than those they had acquired themselves. Titles every Hasid can acquire, if only he tries. Failing that, he can set his sights on a secondary project: to labor for salvation by attaching himself to a Tzaddik who thus becomes his other self. If he cannot be Tzaddik, he will be Hasid. And the Tzaddik will be Tzaddik to the extent that the Hasid will be Hasid. Except that a perfect Hasid is worthier than a Tzaddik who no longer is Tzaddik.

The Hasid-Tzaddik relationship, therefore, must exist under the sign of faith, and contrary to what one may think, it reinforces the faith in God. . . .

It is because the Hasid believes in God that he believes in the Tzaddik, who, according to the terms of their tacit agreement, must bring him closer to God. The school of Lizensk illustrates this relationship with the Biblical verse: *Vayaaminu baadoshem uv-Moshe avdo,* and they had faith in God and in his servant Moses. Because they believed in the one, they could believe in the other, thus becoming worthy of the miracle of the Red Sea crossing. And enabling Moses to speak on their behalf—and sing. *Az Yashir Moshe,* and that's when Moses began singing. Singing? He? Wasn't Moses a stutterer? He could sing, Hasidim say, because his people now had faith in him. Thus, faith in one's Tzaddik makes one an active participant in the Tzaddik's work and partly responsible for his being the omnipotent, omniscient figure he is.

The Plot to Bring the Messiah

TEXT*

We are at the beginning of the nineteenth century, right in the middle of the Napoleonic wars. Churning in blood and fury, Europe is turning itself upside down. Frontiers, thrones, loyalties, and systems change overnight. The earth trembles. Nations discover new passions, liberating but deadly. History moves and bursts into flames. And the blood flows. Priests change their styles, kings their thrones. Patriotism, romanticism, nationalism—so many words newly come to life—prove themselves powerful enough to drive men to breaking their visible and invisible chains.

In the rabbinical courts, these events are endowed with a messianic dimension. One speaks of Gog and Magog, of their gigantic, apocalyptic war. The Hasidim are more and more convinced that the real battles are being waged not by emperors and generals but by Tzaddikim, who, unfortunately, are to be found on both sides. If only they could mobilize their powers in support of the same emperor, the same army, the war would come to an end and redemption would be near.

To hasten that event, three great Masters combined their efforts: the Seer of Lublin, the Maggid of Kozhenitz and Rebbe Mendl of Riminov. They drew up a plan of action. The tasks were divided—the roles distributed—the secret well kept. Unfortunately, the mystical plot failed. And the three conspirators, punished by God, died before the year's end.

The Farbrengung

TEXT†

I had been warned to come early to the *farbrengung* if I wanted a seat, but the wooden tables and benches set up in the courtyard adjoining the building were already filled when I arrived. At one end of the courtyard was a long table covered with a white cloth and mounted on a platform. Most of the seats on the dais were still empty, but a row of chairs behind the central table was already occupied by bearded dignitaries of the movement. A microphone had been set up at the center of the table and hooked to loudspeakers at the other end of the courtyard. I saw a few inches of space on one of the rear benches and, following the example of others, climbed from table to table over the backs of the seated people to reach it—the tables and benches had been packed so closely together

---

*From E. Wiesel, *Souls on Fire*, pp. 206–207, 138.
†From H. Wiener, *9½ Mystics*, pp. 165–169.

there was no aisle space left. It was a humid summer evening, and there were beads of sweat on the faces of many of the Hasidim, who wore full jackets or long black coats along with large-brimmed hats. But nobody seemed to mind the heat, and the crowded courtyard was only further proof to the Hasidim of the greatness of their rebbe. . . .

At about nine-thirty the yard suddenly became quiet. There was the sound of the scraping of chairs and benches as people tried to stand, and all eyes turned to the door which led from the courtyard into the main building. Into the yard with quick step walked the seventh rebbe of the Lubavitcher movement, son-in-law of Joseph Isaac and a direct descendant on his father's side of the Alter Rebbe.

Rabbi Menachem Mendel turned out to be a man of average height and build. The most striking feature of his well-formed face was his deep, gentle blue eyes, in which there was little of the *malchus*—imperial sternness—of his predecessor. His complexion was pale, contrasting with his short black beard in which streaks of gray were beginning to appear. His frock coat, hat, and tie were all black and neatly tailored. The brim of the hat was just a bit larger than a conventional brim, but smaller than that of the Orthodox Hasid. I had heard that when Rabbi Menachem Mendel was studying in Paris, he had refused to wear the long black coat which was customary in Hasidic circles. Now he alludes jokingly to his former habit of dress as a device that gave him more hours for study—"Hasidim didn't come to me when I wore a short coat."

. . . As he mounted the dais now and took his chair, Rabbi Menachem Mendel seemed very much at ease in his role. The audience rose when he entered and remained standing until he sat down. Once seated, he turned to receive a bottle of whiskey which he passed over the table to some outstretched hands below. As if by prearranged signal, little paper cups and bottles of whiskey appeared on all tables in the yard.

The students on the bench in front began clapping hands and swaying back and forth in rhythmic accompaniment to a song. Everyone, including the rebbe, participated in the singing. In the middle of one particularly animated melody, the rebbe leaned forward and began beating out the rhythm on the table with his fists, at which the singing of the Hasidim immediately mounted in volume and intensity. The rebbe, a slight smile on his lips, began to sway from side to side and rose from his chair. An almost physical current of excitement ran through the audience and the singing reached a fever pitch. Near a fan in the back of the courtyard a man wearing a hat which came down to his ears was jumping up and down, clapping his hands, his eyes closed as if hypnotized. Behind the rebbe, an elderly man with a long white beard was hopping from leg to leg, waving his arms about. Then the rebbe sat down, and at once the current of excitement subsided.

Rabbi Menachem Mendel cleared his throat and reached for the microphone. The courtyard grew quiet as the rebbe called out several names. One of those called was sitting near me. He leaped to his feet, his face flushed and his hands trembling as he raised his cup to the rebbe and said, "*L'chayim,* to life!" The rebbe, with a faint smile, vigorously nodded his head in return and moved his lips in an answering "*L'chayim.*" After all those he had singled out by name had offered toasts in this fashion, others in the room began to rise from their seats, and as soon as they had succeeded in catching the rebbe's eye they too called out, "To life!" Near me, a youngster was unable to hide a grimace of distaste as he downed his cup of strong liquor. These exchanges between the rebbe and his Hasidim continued for about an hour, and then they began singing a slow melody with Yiddish words that sounded like "*Essen est zich, shlofen shloft zich, ober davenin davent zich nisht*" ("Eating and drinking take care of themselves, but not prayer").

Only one person in the room seemed not to be singing, and that was the red-bearded rabbi standing at the rebbe's right. He stood immobilized, staring fixedly at a spot on the table before the rebbe. I was told that this was Rabbi Mintlik who had the honor of being the rabbi's cup-bearer; his feeling for the rebbe was so intense that it had reached the level of *hitbatlut,* self-extinction. The act of extinguishing oneself before the will and personality of the rebbe was evidently considered one of the summits of Hasidic devotion.

After the singing was over, the rebbe reached for the microphone and cleared his throat with a nervous little cough. As one, the *farbrengung* rose, and my neighbor informed me that we were about to be instructed in Torah.

Conclusion

We are now in a position to answer the question: How did the institution of the Zaddik work? How did the Zaddik-Hasid relationship respond to the deepest psychological and faith needs of its participants?

The responsibilities of the Zaddik can be summed up as follows:

1. The Zaddik had to be knowledgeable in the tradition—the legal and mystical traditions and the traditions of Hasidic lore and interpretation. He did not have to be learned, though it was desirable, because he could always have experts as part of his entourage. For instance, frequently a Rebbe had a Rabbi, i.e., an expert in Jewish law who handed down decisions for the community. But he did have to be informed.
2. The Zaddik had to set an example of piety. He had to be observant. He had to pray with fervor. Devekut had to be visible in him. And he was

also expected to be able to perform the various Lurianic Kavvanot and elevations.

3. The Zaddik was expected to teach, to preach, and often to train disciples. He could not be a hermit.

4. Most important, the Zaddik had to understand his power and to use it. His powers were exceptional: He could command charity, he could make marriages, he could direct lives, some could perform miracles, he could determine penances, and so on. In part, this was due to the absolute loyalty that he commanded from his Hasidim. But the greater one's power, the greater one's responsibility. People often forget this, but it is basic Biblical teaching that power and responsibility go hand in hand; that even God, while omnipotent, is also omni-responsible. So, too the Zaddik—his powers were extraordinary, but so were his responsibilities. He was expected to give advice as a counsellor, as a political leader, and as a spiritual leader. He was expected to take upon himself the burdens of his flock—their problems of sustenance, family strife, even of doubt and perplexity. If the Hasid had faith in the Rebbe, the Rebbe had to bear the burden of that faith. In its ultimate sense, the exercise of responsibility by the Zaddik meant being an intercessor with God on behalf of individuals and on behalf of the Jewish people. The Zaddik was man's representative to God, with the whole burden of Jewish life and history upon his shoulders. He was Moses on the mountain.

In return for bearing these responsibilities, the Zaddik not only had unusual powers, he also was given enormous latitude in his personal behavior. He could be rich or poor, learned or almost ignorant, social or rather withdrawn, even eccentric. Yet his Hasidim remained loyal, as long as he stayed within the broad framework of Rabbinic Judaism.

The responsibilities of the Hasid can also be summed up. First, he had to be an observant rabbinic Jew. He was expected to observe the commandments and, in some areas, even to study. Second, he had to belong to the community: to learn the lore, to tell the stories, to do his own kind of preaching and teaching. Third, and most important, he was expected to have faith in his Rebbe. This was called, as we have seen, *Emunat Zaddikim,* and it expressed itself in three ways.

1. The Hasid gave absolute obedience to the Zaddik. If the Rebbe was late for prayers, everyone waited. (I have been in such a synagogue where we waited two and one-half hours.) If the Rebbe said to do such-and-such in his business, the Hasid did it. If the Rebbe said to go to Paris and marry so-and-so, the Hasid did it. When, after the Israelis

crossed the Suez Canal in 1973, the Lubavitcher Rebbe told his Hasidim to take printing presses across the Canal and to print an edition of the *Tanya* there, it was done (just before the withdrawal). When the Rebbe said to go into the streets of New York in mobile vans (called "mitsva-tanks") to urge Jews to be observant (there is no mission to the non-Jew), it was done. And so on.

2. The Hasid made a pilgrimage to the "court" of his Rebbe. (I remember one such Rebbe coming to Europe from Israel, and for the entire time he was there, thousands of Hasidim flocked to the otherwise exclusive resort town where the Rebbe was.) So strong is the need for contact with the Rebbe that the Lubavitcher Hasidim have a worldwide radio-telephone network upon which the Rebbe's speeches are broadcast. The pilgrimage alone, however, was not enough. When there, one had to greet the Rebbe with *Lehayyim* over wine or drink. One had to eat of the food the Rebbe had tasted (*shirayim*). And one really ought to have consulted privately with the Rebbe (*yehidus*).

3. All doubt, all hesitancies had to be transferred to the Rebbe. There could be no existential or intellectual split between the Hasid and his Rebbe. If the Hasid had doubts, he had to assume that the Rebbe had thought through these matters, and he had to have faith in the Rebbe's mind and heart. He had to have faith in the Rebbe's faith. It was not really a blind faith because the Hasid knew that the Zaddik, too, was circumscribed by Torah (by Rabbinic Judaism); but it was, and is, a personal faith and trust in a pneumatic, charismatic leader.

This faith of the Hasid in his Zaddik, with all that it entailed for both the Hasid and the Zaddik, was very strange to the democratic structures of Rabbinic Judaism and the modern world. And so it was vigorously fought by the opponents of Hasidism, rabbinic and enlightened. Yet, in a basic way, it was one of the secrets of the success of Hasidism, because the masses could participate in the holy, if not directly then indirectly through their Rebbe. Also, Zaddikism relieved one of some of the terrible burdens of existence and made life more spiritual, either by vicarious spirituality or because, when one gives oneself completely to a cause, one is whole. The Hasid-Zaddik relationship enabled the Hasid to free himself from the fear of being Jewish and to enter without reserve into the propagation of God's will on earth. The very absolutism of it was liberating. The very intensity of the loyalties demanded was meaning-giving. While, at the same time, the presence of the pneumatic and of the rabbinic parameters was limiting, comforting. There were, to be sure, some abuses, but on the whole, the system worked well.

Was the liberating absolutism of Hasidism a foreshadowing of the ideological absolutisms that were to bring modernity to the brink of moral ruin? Was it the fact that these ideological absolutisms lacked the pneumatic-rabbinic component that enabled them to turn evil? These questions have a haunting quality, and we will consider them in the General Conclusion.

10
GENERAL CONCLUSION

In the General Introduction to Unit II, I suggested some questions that would direct our inquiry. We are now in a position to propose some answers.

What was the heartbeat of this unusual mystical movement? The answer to this question is quite simple: it was the immediate sense of the divine. The divine was, as we have seen, sensed everywhere—in prayer, in labor, in humor, in evil, in the mundane, and in the sublime. Sometimes, the divine was sensed with an intensity that was all-consuming, and sometimes it was sensed simply as part of the background of human existence. Hasidism was not all ecstasy, but from those moments stemmed its basic world-view of life as an ecstasy of the divine presence. Hasidism was not all spirituality, but "spiritualization" is probably the best word for the reworking of Judaism and life which Hasidism effected. Messianism was spiritualized; prayer was spiritualized; the rabbinate was spiritualized; study was spiritualized; even prayer was spiritualized. The pneumatic became the lifeblood of Judaism, the rain that brought vitality to everything. The immediate sense of the divine became that which gave meaning to life. In Hasidism the holy became real, more real, as we have seen, than that which we sometimes call life.

What were the forms of the holy as they appeared in Hasidism? There were three: stories of various kinds, prayer of various types, and the Zaddik-Hasid relationship. The varieties and types of these manifestations have already been explained.

What were the elements of continuity and discontinuity between Hasidism and the previous rabbinic and mystical traditions?

1. Hasidism was fully rabbinic. The values of observance, Halakha, Torah-study, even of the rabbinate were never seriously questioned (as they were by the forms of modern secular Judaism). True, Hasidism spiritualized these values. True, Hasidism, as a social movement, disrupted the local orientation of the Jewish community in favor of the

trans-local Hasidic community whose loyalties were oriented toward
the Rebbe's court wherever it might be. But Hasidism, even in its most
outrageous forms, was circumscribed by Rabbinic Judaism.

2. Theoretical Hasidism, in part, continued the Zoharic-Lurianic tradition
   of thought. The sefirot, the Kavvanot, the theories of the soul, etc.,
   were all preserved. True, they were reinterpreted in a psychological
   vein, with God's personality reflecting man's. True, this type of
   esoterica was reserved for the elite. But it was present, and it did form
   one of the basic rubrics of Hasidic thought. (Scholem, Tishby, Jacobs,
   Schatz, and others have written extensively on the Hasidic development of Lurianic thought.)

3. Hasidism continued the intellectual, contemplative type of mystical
   "contact" with the divine set forth in the Maimonidean tradition. True,
   the special hierarchy of Intelligences, etc., was, in large measure,
   ignored, but the approach to God through intellectual meditation was, in
   certain sectors, preserved.

4. Hasidism revived the simple, anthropopathic way of talking about God
   which had been current in the Bible and especially in the midrash. In this
   way, the intimate, personal dimension of the holy was recovered for
   Jewish mysticism. It took on its most poignant forms in the stories and in
   the personal prayers, usually in the vernacular, addressed to God.

In several important ways, however, the Hasidic reworking of Rabbinic
Judaism was rather radical:

1. The immediate sense of the divine, which was the heartbeat of
   Hasidism and which enabled it to spiritualize many elements in Rabbinic Judaism, also enabled Hasidism to envision true mystical union
   with God. In a certain sense, bittul (annihilation into the divine, directly
   or indirectly through the Zaddik, and not just "contact"), for the first
   time, became a true religious option. Furthermore, this became an
   option not only for the mystical fringe but for the masses, not only for
   the elite but for the simple.

2. The phenomenology of bittul sprang from, and in turn generated, the
   definition of God as ha-Ayin, the Nothing. This emphasis was new.
   Furthermore, the same phenomenology generated some rather extreme
   mystical techniques, including bodily movement, dance, the use of
   alcohol, and even a type of primal groan.

3. The need to give some social structure to this ongoing ecstasy created
   the institution of the Zaddik and, hence, the Zaddik-Hasid relationship. Such a form of discipleship was not unheard-of, but the absolute
   loyalty demanded and given became a true religious option for the first
   time in Hasidism.

These elements existed earlier, but they were galvanized into new form in Hasidism.

In what way was Hasidism "modern"? This is the most difficult question to answer because there is no universally accepted definition of modernity. Four elements in Hasidism, however, impress me as being "modern":

1. Hasidism, insofar as it left behind the Merkabah, the Zoharic-Lurianic, and the Maimonidean world-views—i.e., insofar as it freed itself from the previous Jewish mystical tradition—was intellectually anti-hierarchical. Hasidism, insofar as it was new—and not all of Hasidism was "new" in this sense—rejected the older hierarchies of celestial palaces, of Intelligences, of hypostases, of sefirot. In this, Hasidism broke with the medieval intellectual tradition, which was, in its very essence, hierarchical. With Hasidism, man had direct access to what had been the top of the hierarchy. With Hasidism, man had direct access to God, either in intimate personal form or as the Nothing. It is interesting to note too that J. Katz, in his study of the social history of the late medieval and early modern periods, has made the same observation in the social realm: that Hasidism, by orienting the Jew away from his local rabbi and toward his Rebbe, who might be on the other side of the world, undermined the carefully cultivated hierarchical socio-political structure of the medieval Jewish community. The Jewish "estate" was thus challenged by Hasidism, socially as well as religiously and intellectually. This anti-hierarchical trend, then, is part of Hasidism's modernity.

2. Hasidism, insofar as it shifted the center of Jewish identity from the mind to the heart, was "romantic." Hasidism, insofar as it saw the justification of Jewish existence not in the exercise of the intellect but in the vividness of personal experience, was "modern." Passionate personal involvement, "the spontaneous overflow of powerful emotion," existential engagement—the very rallying calls of Romanticism against the intellectualism of the Enlightenment—all became central to Hasidism. In this, Hasidism broke with the intellectualist and legalistic traditions of medieval Judaism. Justifying religious living by religious experience was central to modernity and to Hasidism.

3. Hasidism was "democratic" or "humanistic," not in the social-contract sense of the word, not in the political sense of the word, but in a spiritual and moral way. When Hasidism taught that the "language of God is man," it was teaching that even the poor, the ignorant, and the oppressed were "equal before God." When Hasidism taught that ecstasy was available to the simple and the uneducated, it was being "democratic." When Hasidism took the side of the underdog, when it spoke for the misery of the masses, it was being "humanistic." But were these expressions of "modernity"? Were they products of some

process at work in history? If so, what was that process? Was it the beginning of capitalism? Or was it the internal collapse of medievalism? Was the "democratic-humanistic" tendency of Hasidism, perhaps, really the result of the renaissance of the divine in Jewish history, of a return of the prophetic spirit to Jewish religion? *Why was* Hasidism anti-hierarchical, feeling-oriented, and pro-"humanist"? To put it differently: Can "modernity" be found without its economic and political concomitants? Can one speak of "modernity" without capitalism and constitutional government? If so, what is "modernity"? These questions require further thought.

4. Hasidism, in its Zaddik-principle, bears a haunting resemblance, *mutatis mutandis!* to the *Führerprinzip;* i.e., to the totalitarian mentality of the modern world. Note that many of the modern "cults" that are so popular today function along the same principle of absolute loyalty and responsibility. It would, therefore, be no surprise to find that one of the motives for the Hasidic revival among modern Jews is the security of such a system. There is something blasphemous in drawing a parallel between the Zaddik-Hasid relationship and the *Führerprinzip,* but did not both grow out of the oppression of the masses in the nineteenth century? Were not both a response to the upheavals of modernity? The latter lacked the pneumatic-rabbinic dimension, and hence it had enormous evil potential, which, as history has shown, it actually exercised. But the dynamics were hauntingly the same.

Zoharic-Lurianic thought had suffered a grave setback in the failure of its messianic salient, the Sabbatean movement. Maimonidean-Abulafian thought had suffered a grave setback with the failure of its geocentric world-view. Merkabah mysticism had long since been dead except for certain survivals in popular Jewish magic. Halakhic-rabbinic piety had become severely foreboding, morosely ascetic, and socially rigid. What then, in the eighteenth century, was to be the future of Jewish piety and mysticism? Perhaps, from some as yet unidentified stream of "modernity," perhaps from some as yet unidentified stream of mystical praxis, and/or perhaps from a simple return to Psalms and to the holy in its direct sense, Hasidism showed a new Way to God. It was a Way composed of some new ideas and of some old ones. The strangest thing is that one does not know whether to use the past tense or the present in describing Hasidism, for Hasidism also lays a claim to the present and the future of Jewish mysticism. It is to this last problem that we now turn.

11

RETROSPECT AND PROSPECT

Looking Backward: Some Conclusions

The project of presenting a selection of the basic texts of the Jewish mystical tradition is now complete. There are, to be sure, many other texts. But the selection given in the two volumes of *Understanding Jewish Mysticism* is comprehensive enough for the student-scholar who is not a specialist, and in the sections entitled, "For Further Reading and Instruction," I have noted other general and more specific sources.

What have we examined? In Volume I, we examined two currents within the broad stream of the Jewish mystical tradition. First, we studied the Merkabah tradition contained in such books as *Sefer Yetsira* and *Pirkei Heikhalot*. We noted that it was, at one and the same time, an extension of certain Biblical texts and an adaptation of certain Hellenistic modes of religion. We also noted that it contained a distinctly magical element and that it could be best characterized as "power," or "royal," mysticism. We concluded by noting that Merkabah mysticism itself disappeared but its traces could be found in the liturgy and in the later magical tradition. Second, we studied the Zoharic tradition contained in the *Zohar* and the Lurianic writings. We noted that this tradition defined the mystical element common to man and God as personal consciousness. We noted, too, that the relationship between man and God was interactive, with all the vagaries and dangers that open personal consciousness brings. God was re-mythicized and man was messianized. We concluded by noting that Zoharic mysticism, too, largely disappeared, being confined to a scholarly and spiritual elite as it became more complex. Its traces, however, could be found in Hasidism and even among modern students of Jewish mysticism.

In Volume II, we examined two more currents within the stream of the Jewish mystical tradition. First, we studied the philosophic mystical tradition contained in the *Guide of the Perplexed* and the Abulafian and Yemenite writings. We noted that in this tradition, scholastic scholarship to the contrary notwithstanding, mind was seen as a Way to the holy, philosophy a path to theology and religious experience, and intellectualization as a means to the numinous. We concluded by noting that philosophic mysticism, in its medieval form, disappeared with the loss of its intellectual structure. Its traces, however, could be found in contemplative Hasidism and in the intellectualist modes of modern Jewish religion. Finally, we studied the Hasidic tradition contained in stories, in prayer texts, and in the relationship between the Hasid and his Rebbe. We noted the appearance of a new kind of ecstasy, annihilation in the Godhead (or in the Rebbe), and a thoroughgoing spiritualization of all aspects of life and Rabbinic Judaism. We noted, too, certain traits that might be regarded as distinctly "modern," such as anti-hierarchicalism, a preoccupation with feeling and experience, a humanistic-democratic orientation, and an absolute authoritarianism. We concluded by noting that Hasidic mysticism has not at all disappeared. Rather, it is very much alive and is a claimant to the present, and the future, of Jewish mysticism.

What conclusions can we draw from this data? First, I am inclined to retain the definition of mysticism as a subset of spirituality which I proposed in Volume I: "Given these caveats, I would say that the forms and dynamics of spirituality turn 'mystical' when the reports of the experiences involved betray an abstract conceptualization of God, as opposed to a highly personalist, anthropopathic conceptualization" (p. 186). "Spirituality," then, is the broader term, and it encompasses all types of awareness of the holy. "Mysticism" is the narrower term, and it encompasses those types of awareness of the holy that betray a more abstract conceptualization of the holy. In this sense, the Hasidic annihilation tradition is the most "mystical" type of spirituality we have encountered, though each of the other traditions contains a properly "mystical" core. Thus, the Merkabah tradition, after one has penetrated the royal and magical imagery, betrays an abstract conceptualization of the holy as power. Thus, too, the Zoharic tradition, after one has penetrated the psychological and dynamically interactive imagery, betrays an abstract conceptualization of the holy as consciousness beyond the bounds of knowing. Thus, too, the philosophic tradition, after one has penetrated the cosmological and epistemological hierarchies, betrays an abstract consciousness of the holy as (contentless) mind. The Hasidic intimate-Presence tradition, with its very personal address to God, on the other hand, is surely deeply spiritual. It is surely deeply Jewish, drawing its imagery and dynamics from the prophets, the Psalms, and the liturgy and midrash. But it betrays a personalist, anthropopathic, relational conception of the holy, not an abstract conception thereof. Hence, it is "spiritual" but not "mystical," as I use these terms.

Second, I am inclined to retain the five-fold characterization of Jewish mysticism which I proposed in Volume I: its learnedness, its covenantal character (i.e., its remaining within the parameters of Torah and Halakha), its hierarchical character, its assumption that man can indeed approach God, and its diversity (pp. 187–189). The Jewish mystical tradition is learned. It is covenantal, i.e., it remains within the parameters of Rabbinic Judaism. It is hierarchical, Hasidism as a partial exception. It does assume that man can, by an act of will, reach out and touch God. And it is very diverse, not at all monolithic, in the experiences it bespeaks as well as in its intellectual structures.

Third, the conclusions concerning the "rabbinization" of Jewish mysticism and the "mysticization" of Rabbinic Judaism (Vol. I, pp. 189–191) stand unchanged. To these three conclusions reached in Volume I, I would like to add two more.

First, the Jewish mystical tradition is not only diverse; it varies according to a rather clear principle: As the experiential mystical goal changed, so did the mystical teaching. Thus, as the religious experience(s) which stood behind the Merkabah tradition gained currency, the texts multiplied and the intellectual and symbolic structures developed. The same holds true for the Zoharic, the philosophic, and the Hasidic traditions. As the experience(s) these texts bespeak gained acceptance, the literary traditions grew. We do not know where the new experiences came from or how they penetrated into Jewish circles. But each set of experiences was different from that which preceded it, and each brought with it intellectual and symbolic structures. The process was not, to be sure, so linear. In reality, one reads or talks, one experiences, and one reads or talks some more. The movement is much more like a backstitch, which circles backward yet moves forward. I am of the opinion, though, that mystical literature does not develop without mystical experience, and hence I argue that it was the new experiences which generated the new literary traditions.

Second, the Jewish mystical tradition is not only a cumulative tradition; it is also a living religious reality. It has always had a vital experiential base and was not simply an exercise in mystical casuistry. The living religious reality which stood behind the entire tradition was, and is, the holy. It is the realm of the numinous, in all its mystery, beauty, and power, that has formed the "common denominator" of the Jewish mystical tradition. (It is, indeed, the heartbeat of all genuine spiritual traditions.) This may seem self-evident, but when one considers what the guardians of manuscripts and the describers of social and cultural structures use as their definition of a religious tradition, one comes to realize that the holy, as a legitimate tool of analysis, needs some friends in the councils of the student-scholars.

Looking Forward: The Future of Jewish Spirituality

In order to speculate about Jewish spirituality toward the close of the twentieth century, it is necessary to know three things: the history of the spiritual tradition up to the present, the types of spirituality currently being practiced, and something about the nature of modern society and its values, for within it contemporary spirituality must exist. The texts, history, and types of Jewish mystical spirituality have already been presented and analyzed. The remaining two factors must still be briefly presented.

The characterization of modern society is a very difficult task, and it cannot be undertaken here. I can only share with the reader some insights that have begun to crystalize after years of reflection, reading, living, and study. The first insight is that what we believe (and, hence, what we preach and teach to one another) has very little to do with what the great analysts of modernity tell us about modernity. Thus, for example, Marx and Weber (and whole schools of social analysts) have noted that modern society is an exceedingly complex industrialized phenomenon, characterized by the centralization of power and the increasing incursion of the central power into the lives of individuals. Modernity, then, is the sum of these complex processes, and life in modern society, according to these analysts, is learning to live within, and perhaps assume control of, the central bureaucracy which regulates production, consumption, movement, etc. While it is, then, commendable for modern thinkers to talk about humanism, the holy, the meaningful, and so on, they must also recognize that such values are, at best, irrelevant to modernity and, at worst, cut directly across its grain.

Similarly, Freud on the one hand and the behaviorists on the other (and whole schools of psychosocial analysts) have noted that modern man is strongly under the influence of very powerful forces that he does not control: the unconscious, environmental reinforcement, etc. Modernity, or life in the modern world, according to these analysts, is learning how to liberate oneself to a limited degree from one's maladjustments and neuroses, and then learning how to live with the remnants thereof while gathering whatever joy, happiness, and pleasure one can. Here, too, while it is commendable for modern thinkers to talk about free-will religiosity and humanistic rights, they must also recognize that their message is irrelevant, or opposed, to the fabric of modernity. Social pluralism and the consequent relativization of belief systems, the economic and, hence the political rationalization of society, the privatization of religious practice and values, the consumer/pleasure ethic within a social and personal life largely beyond our control—these are the value trends of modernity. Humanism, egalitarianism, individualism, holiness, existential meaning, personal creativity, community—these values, though we may hold them deeply, run counter to the values of modern society. Perhaps we should preach, teach, and practice these values anyway; but we must also recognize that they do run against the current of socio-economic and psychological determinism which is the essence of modernity as seen by the great analysts of the past hundred years.

The second insight is that, any positive belief-system must be a counter-culture to these definitions of modernity. This is true of secular as well as religious belief-systems. Thus, any belief in humanism, personal creativity, spirituality, etc. is counter-cultural. Given, then, the truly counter-culture nature of any positive belief system within modern society, a *spiritual* belief system should have, in my opinion, the following three components:

1. At its core, there must be an awareness of the holy, a sense of the numinous. As Leclercq has written: "There is no spiritual literature without spiritual experience." Or as Heschel has said, "Existence is interspersed with suggestions of transcendence, and openness to transcendence is a constitutive element of being human." Or as I have written, "Man stands not only in the sunlight of this world but in the shadow of God." The holy is not to be confused with the intellectual, or the moral, or the beautiful. Each is a realm of its own. The holy—irreducible, *sui generis*—must stand at the center of any spiritual system.

2. At the core of any spiritual Way (like the two trees in the center of the Garden of Eden), there must be a sense of meaning. The meaning may derive from loyalty to one's own experience. It may derive from adhering to a revelation. It is surely connected with realistic goal-setting and achievement. But whatever its source, there must be an axiological dimension to spirituality. I think, too, that this axiological dimension must be intimately bound up with moral awareness and practice. The holy and the just are deeply intertwined. According to Biblical and rabbinic tradition, they are inseparable. (I, therefore, disagree that any single "ultimate concern," even if it be holiness itself, is sufficient for spiritual living.)

3. Any spiritual Way must have a very strong humanistic component; that is, any spiritual Way must have a deep and abiding respect for the value of the individual and of the self- and other-knowledge that this respect generates. This can manifest itself in a devotion to democracy, human rights, psychotherapy, ecology, etc. But a spiritual Way which denies the humanistic component is not spiritual and not modern. (One could advocate such values without adhering to any spiritual Way; that would be secular humanism.)

In the Jewish context, a modern spiritual Way must respond to an additional factor. It must be Jewish; that is, any modern Jewish spirituality must be continuous with the Jewish past and, hence, must provide its adherents with an ethnically distinct identity. This very factor, however, complicates the problem for the advocates of a Jewish spiritual Way, for contemporary Jews have a very effective "civil religion." This civil religion, as Woocher and others have shown, offers the contemporary Jew *full* Jewish identity without spirituality. It offers him meaning, purpose, humanistic values, national identity, and a background presence of religion. It incorporates Zionism, the Holocaust, the State of Israel, politics, social status, ritual freedom, and a sense of history, together with the rhetoric of transcendence, without specifically being atheistic or anti-religious. The contemporary Jew, thus, has open to him a Way which his forebears did not have. This Way, which is non-spiritual, is closer to the nature of social identity in the modern world than the spiritual Way. This Way, by its very existence, thus compromises the "success" of all Jewish spiritual Ways, for it is undoubtedly the Way of the majority of contemporary Jews, and it will continue to be so.

Given these reflections on the nature of modern society and counter-modern spirituality, what is the state of Jewish spirituality today? There are four contemporary types of Jewish spirituality. Each will be described and evaluated. First, Hasidism is very much alive and vital. It is strongest among its own adherents, the overwhelming percentage of whom do not practice birth control. Hasidic communities are also socially coherent, religiously militant, and politically aware. Hence, it is likely that this type of community—and, therefore, the types of mysticism and spirituality present in it—will grow in numbers and in strength. Hasidism has also devoted itself to a rather successful outreach effort, particularly the Habad movement. This success is due to the fact that Hasidism offers the modern Jew several things: (1) an authentically rabbinic and socially cohesive form of Jewish existence; (2) an authoritarian structure with which to face the modern bureaucratic way of life; (3) a sense of the holy as present and attainable; and (4) a sense of meaning, purpose, and dedication. Hasidism, thus, responds to modernity and meets the three criteria for a counter-modern spiritual Way. It is also a mystic Way. Nonetheless, I am not optimistic about the future of Hasidism in non-Hasidic circles. The ritualism, the intensity of the social cohesion, even the ecstasies are out of step with the consumer/pleasure ethic of modern society. The price of Hasidic spirituality will be too high for most Jews to pay.

Second, neo-orthodoxy of the non-Hasidic variety (a kind of born-again orthodoxy) is very much alive and vital, not only among those born to it but also among young Jews in search of a religiously traditional Jewish identity. The appeal of this Way is largely ethnic-social. Orthodoxy is triumphant (as other movements were before it), and nothing breeds confidence as much as success. It is also socially cohesive and politically militant. It is not, however, noticeably mystical, spiritual, or even intellectual. I think this movement will continue to grow because it is militantly ethnic, and because it is succeeding. But I doubt that it will ever have very large numbers (unless more of its adherents refuse birth control), and in any case, I doubt that it will produce any major spiritual insight or literature.

Third, philosophic mysticism is alive, in books. Mordecai Kaplan resurrected it in his definitions of God and salvation. Kaplan's formulation of the experience of God as the Power in the universe that makes for salvation has been repeated in various guises, and this has been accompanied, or preceded, by various liturgical reforms (Reform, Conservative, and Reconstructionist). It is a genuinely spiritual Way; perhaps also mystical. I think that insofar as the "average Jew" believes (and experiences) anything, it is probably the religious awareness of God as articulated by Kaplan. But I am not optimistic about this type of spirituality because it has not developed the intensity of religious awareness that a true mystical or spiritual Way requires.

Fourth, personal spirituality is alive, though it is rare. There is a traditional personal piety which is an attempt to live the tradition *with* spiritual awareness. If one prays, it is also to God. If one writes, it is also with consciousness of Him in mind. Personal traditional piety is Jewish religious and social living with as much Kavvana as one can master. In some circles, this traditionalist piety is also creative in a modern way. Thus, one finds a small but persistent Havurah movement, the *Jewish Catalog* (3 vols.), new periodicals, etc. There is also a non-traditional personal piety which strives to respond to the holy, the meaningful, the humanistic, and the Jewish in new ways, with new literature, with new ritual. These forms of piety are spiritual but not always mystical.

What, then, is the future of Jewish spirituality? Given the general, and specifically Jewish, problematic involved in articulating any kind of spiritual Way at the close of the twentieth century, I think I can predict the following:

1. Mass movements will continue to exist and to grow in the realm of Jewish "civil religion" and in those religious movements (which refuse birth control and) which practice ethno-politico-religious militancy. Personal spirituality, which gives lighter weight to this axis of Jewish existence, will never develop into a mass phenomenon.
2. Because personal spirituality is primarily a deeply personal matter, because it is a function of gift and training, and because, in the final

analysis, personal spirituality is a matter of loyalty to one's own experience and insight, a matter of personal living with God, it will continue to have a definite appeal to the non-Hasidic, yet spiritually sensitive, serious modern Jew.

3. I think, then, that it is in the internal commitment of the individual to the holy, the meaningful, the humanistic, and the Jewish that the future of the Jewish spirituality lies. I think it is in personal spirituality, of the traditional and non-traditional types, that the future of the Jewish spiritual Way will be found. Whether this will produce a distinctly mystical Way, whether either mass movements or personal piety will create a new current in the great stream of the Jewish mystical tradition, is, and must remain, an open question.

FOR FURTHER READING AND INSTRUCTION

Since the publication of Volume I of *Understanding Jewish Mysticism,* the following items of general interest have appeared: L. Jacobs, *Jewish Mystical Testimonies,* and B. Bokser, *The Jewish Mystical Tradition.* Both are anthologies of actual texts. There is also my survey-of-the-field article, "Some Methodological Reflections on the Study of Jewish Mysticism," *Religion* 8:1 (1978) 101–114. These works, however, must be read together with those of Scholem, Vajda, and others listed in Volume I.

The concept of "philosophic mysticism" is new to the English-reading public. For the Maimonidean and Yemenite literature, one should consult A. J. Heschel, *Maimonides: A Biography,* available only in French and German; D. Blumenthal, "Maimonides' Intellectualist Mysticism and the Superiority of the Prophecy of Moses," *Studies in Medieval Culture,* 10 (1977):51–68; and idem, *The Philosophic Questions and Answers of Hoter ben Shelomo.* For the Abulafian literature, one should consult the selection quoted in Scholem's *Major Trends in Jewish Mysticism,* as well as the Hebrew texts of the selections given here in English. S. Idel has submitted a thesis on Abulafia at the Hebrew University (in Hebrew). Abulafia's *Path of Names,* his messianic ravings, is now available in print. And A. Anawati, *Mystique musulman,* together with texts from the *Philokalia* tradition of Eastern Christian mysticism, forms a very nice cross-traditional axis of research.

In the area of the Hasidic story, the basic text is J. Dan, *The Hasidic Story: Its History and Development,* available only in Hebrew. The stories themselves can be found in the works of M. Buber (though be sure to read G. Scholem's caveat on Buber's interpretation in *The Messianic Idea*) and in the works of E. Wiesel. Interestingly there are now four or five translations and interpretations of the involved stories of Rabbi Nahman of Bratslav. For the record, the following stories printed above in Chapter 7 were written by us: "The Rebbe and the Football Game," D. Blumenthal; "The Hasid and the Computer," R. Kramarow; "The Rebbe and the Gambler," W. Belcher; and "Choose the Man" was told to me.

In the area of Kavvana, there are the works of A. J. Heschel, particularly the section in *God in Search of Man,* and E. Berkovits, "Prayer," in L. Stitskin, *Studies in Torah Judaism.* For material on Hasidic prayer, the basic text is L. Jacobs, *Hasidic Prayer,* and now, A. Green and B. Holtz, *Your Word Is Fire.* The following are also helpful: S. Dresner, *Levi-Yitzhak of Berditchev,* and R. Schatz-Uffenheimer, *Quietistic Elements in 18th Century Hasidic Thought* (Hebrew), a part of which has been translated and appears as "Contemplative Prayer in Hasidism," in *Studies in Mysticism and Religion Presented to G. Scholem,* pp. 209–226.

On the various Zaddikim, E. Wiesel, *Souls on Fire,* is the basic work for the interested reader. There are others too: L. Jacobs, *Seeker of Unity*; S. Dresner, *The Zaddik*; A. J. Heschel, *A Passion for Truth*; A. Green, "The Zaddik as Axis Mundi," *Journal of the American Academy of Religion*; and J. Katz, *Tradition and Crisis,* which deals with the social aspect. The literature on Hasidism is, however, vast, and the bibliographies in Scholem and the *Encyclopaedia Judaica* will be helpful.

For the contemporary forms of Jewish spirituality, the following will be helpful. On the Havurah movement: J. Neusner, *Contemporary Jewish Fellowship*; M. Goldberg, "Havurah, Synagogue, Federation," *National Jewish Conference Center Policy Studies '79*; and the issue of *Sh'ma,* 9/176, September 1979. The three-volume *Jewish Catalog,* edited by Strassfeld and Strassfeld, is a very valuable source of information. On the Jewish civil religion, cf. J. Woocher, "Civil Judaism," *National Jewish Conference Center Policy Studies '79,* and J. Neusner, *American Judaism.* As an ongoing source of material, the following journals should be consulted: *Shefa, The Tree Journal, Response* (the one published in Boston), *Psychology and Judaism, Moment,* and *Sh'ma.*

I would like to record the following serious corrections to Volume I: Beginning on page 15, the pericopae *above* the line should be labeled "Mishna" while the comments *below* the line should be labeled "To Mishna . . . " And beginning on page 187, the heading at the top of the page should read "Afterword." The other errors I have detected are not as serious.

The following examination questions, always given as take-home and short essay, have proven popular and effective:

1. Review a book on Jewish mysticism (other than one by Scholem) and tell why it is brilliant or terrible from a scholarly, as well as from a pedagogical, point of view.
2. Find a definition of mysticism and show how it fits, or does not fit, the texts we have studied.
3. How does the nature of the conception of God differ in the traditions we have studied?

4. Compare the role of man in the traditions we have studied.
5. Write a Hasidic story.
6. Consult *The Tree Journal, Shefa,* and one or two books on contemporary Jewish mysticism and speculate on the future of Jewish mysticism.

In addition, I have always asked students to indicate in which tradition of the stream of Jewish mysticism they would/would not do continued reading, and why.

The two volumes of *Understanding Jewish Mysticism* are intended for the teacher and student of religion, the teacher and student of medieval Judaism, and the informed layperson. I recognize that my approach, my definitions, and my conclusions (and, *a fortiori,* my personal speculations) are bold and subject to discussion. Therefore, I welcome correspondence and suggestions addressed to me at the Department of Religion, Emory University, Atlanta, Georgia 30322.

THEMATIC INDEX*

*This index is intended as a guide. It is not a concordance of the terms listed.